DUGAN LAIRD
Training Consultant

WRITING FOR RESULTS:

PRINCIPLES AND PRACTICE

A REVISION OF
**BUSINESS WRITING SKILLS:
A WORKBOOK, 1970**

**ADDISON-WESLEY
PUBLISHING COMPANY**

Reading, Massachusetts
Menlo Park, California
London • Amsterdam
Don Mills, Ontario • Sydney

FOREWORD

This book is really an extensive revision of *Business Writing Skills: A Workbook,* published in 1970. The intervening years have shown the need for major changes:

- To introduce new developments in business writing practice,
- To add more comments about the processes by which written communications are actually completed within an organization,
- To get rid of the truly embarrassing male chauvinism of the original product,
- To provide exercises which are oriented more directly to the business world, and
- To simplify the structure.

Only the last change needs comment. The student exercises are now grouped together at the end of each chapter. However, they are announced at that point in the prose where they would be an appropriate activity for learners. Of course, learners will predictably protest the exercises. They will say things like, "I have the idea. I don't need to practice!"

Or they will say, "These are school kid exercises." Don't let them fool you with such protests! There are three steps in building new writing behaviors:

1. Acquiring new knowledge.
2. Discriminating between good and bad examples of that knowledge when it's put to use in actual writing.
3. *Forming habits by repeatedly applying the new techniques.*

The exercises provide two of those three important steps. Chapter 6, The Chris Dawson In-Basket, lets learners apply all the techniques acquired in earlier chapters.

The first part of each chapter is called "In a Nutshell." This parallels, but updates, the content of the filmstrips, *Business Writing Skills.* These are published and marketed by Resources for Education and Management of Decatur, Georgia. The book and the filmstrips work together to form an integrated learning/teaching system for organizational programs. Of course the workshop can be used without the films, and vice-versa.

The workbook can also be used in totally independent study—a self-administered program. There are feedback mechanisms for most of the activities as well as a prose presentation of the principles and techniques.

The cartoons in the book are from the filmstrips, and merit a special word of thanks to John Sajem. Other special appreciation goes to Art Horrox of Manitoba Bell Telephone and Edward J. Kelly of Educational Testing Service. They both contributed particularly useful and timely suggestions.

Remember, this is a workbook. It is therefore meant to be written in, marked up, torn apart—and undoubtedly cussed at.

Now that you understand that, you are ready to go to work!

Dugan Laird
Decatur, Georgia
January 1978

CONTENTS

Chapter 1   General Concepts of Business Writing
In a Nutshell   1
In Greater Detail   7
  Purposes for writing   10 / Criteria for business
  writing   11 / Formats   13 / Levels of usage   24
Putting the Principles into Practice (Activities 1-5)   30

Chapter 2   Organizing Business Writing
In a Nutshell   37
In Greater Detail   45
  Purposes   47 / Principle of unity   50 /
  Sequences   51 / Sharing your structure   52
Putting the Principles into Practice (Activities 6-15)   62

Chapter 3   Clear Business Writing
In a Nutshell   76
In Greater Detail   84
  Sentences   84 / Words   95 / Punctuation   104

Putting the Principles into Practice (Activities 16-37)   112

Chapter 4   Friendly Business Writing
In a Nutshell   140
In Greater Detail   148
  Why friendliness is so important   149 / Friendly organization   151 / Friendly sentences   152 / Friendly words   161 / Friendly punctuation   169
Putting the Principles into Practice (Activities 38-49)   176

Chapter 5   Effective Business Reports
In a Nutshell   194
In Greater Detail   202
  How reports differ from other forms of business writing   202 / The review process   205 / Organizing techniques   213 / Style   224 / Graphic presentations   224
Putting the Principles into Practice (Activities 50-60)   226

Bibliography   240

Chapter 6   The Chris Dawson "In-Basket": A Simulation   241
A Checklist for Reviewing the Chris Dawson In-Basket   261
  Disciplinary letter to Lynn Mason   261 / Letter from Elvin Suthers   262 / Ernie Hanson's request for help   263 / D. L. Kirk's letter of application 263 / Lee Nelsen's request for review of a letter   263 / Al Barnes's request for an opinion 264 / Glen and Kim's request for an opening statement   264 / Dennis Kraemer's request for you as a speaker   264 / Al Barnes's request for your draft of a letter   265 / General comments   265

GENERAL CONCEPTS OF BUSINESS WRITING

IN A NUTSHELL

How much do we spend on business writing? What does the typical business letter cost? With recent inflation, it's impossible to say. But here is a trend showing the price in the first 20 years of this half-century.

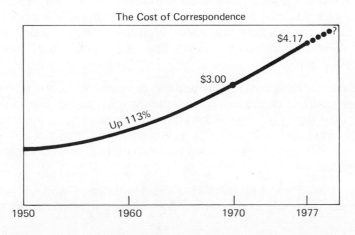

The Cost of Correspondence

If the cost increased by 113% between 1950 and 1970, just imagine what the typical letter must cost nowadays! So if letters are so expensive, why do we write them? Do we get our money's worth? Do we get more than $4.17 value from every letter?

We write for as many reasons as we have messages to send. Whether we use an informal memo, a company manual, or a lengthy report, we find the written word a necessary tool in doing our work.

Yes, we write for as many reasons as there are messages; every communication has its own individual reason for existing. Yet we can also identify a few general reasons for writing.

First of all, we write to inform . . . to transmit information. We want our readers to know something they wouldn't know if we didn't write. The minutes of meetings often serve this purpose; company manuals, with their policy statements and procedural specifications, are perfect examples of "writing to inform."

No, they're not! Too often they are "imperfect examples" of business writing. They lack clarity. Like this example:

"Any employee whose current salary rate exceeds the new top of the salary range for his or her classification will not be eligible for the general increase unless the new top of the salary range for his or her classification exceeds the employee's current salary rate."

The person who wrote that could probably prove, with lengthy analysis, that the quotation is perfectly logical. But what reader wants to do all that analysis to find whatever sense is hidden behind those words. When we write to inform, we are just as successful as we are *clear!*

Secondly, we write to request. We want our readers to do something, or to think something; we want someone to feel a certain way about something. So why don't we just call them on the telephone? Or why don't we just call out to them across the office? Well, sometimes we do. But even after we've spoken to our associates, they may say, "Fine. Would you put that in writing?"

And there's our third motive: we write to document. As a matter of fact, American business organizations reportedly spend over five billion dollars each year doing just that. When minutes of meetings are addressed to those who attended, the motive is a document: at other times letters are documents of transactions between two individuals, as in discipline hearings or decisions.

We have these three pervasive motives for writing—and yet very few business people really like to write. Too often our words come back to haunt us. We omitted messages we thought important, or we somehow sent messages we didn't think we sent at all. Such ambiguity is probably inevitable. After all, words are flexible—and thus fickle! For example, we might say that our boat is fast when we mean that it is securely tied to the dock. But the people to whom we say that may think that we're telling them how "fast" the boat will travel through the water.

No matter which motive we have for writing—whether we want to inform, to request, or to document—the words we send on the printed page really convey two messages: the words themselves, and an image of our own personality.

All of us surely want to create a good image of ourselves. If we analyze that image, we'll uncover the criteria for effective business writing.

First, we want our writing to create the feeling that we're *well-organized*.

Secondly, we want to be clearly understood. As you read the following letter, do you find a good example of the second criterion, *clarity?*

July 6, 19XX

Union Merchant Company
123 Medinah Court
Itasca, Iowa 50579

Gentlemen:

Reference is made to a telephone conversation of recent date between your Mr. Black and the undersigned, resulting from which you will please find enclosed herewith a copy of our computation dated June 3, 19XX wherein we have listed re-wiring prices along with labor charges of our S-1270 Hoist Pulley.

If we in this office can be of any further assistance, please do not hesitate to contact us.

Respectfully,

D. E. Devlin

D.E. Devlin
Sales Manager

DED:pl

Get the message? Of course not. Business writing needs to be clear—and it needs to be clear to the reader on the first reading. This wordy letter, full of old fashioned phrases, lacks clarity.

Business writing also needs another quality. What kind of image do you as reader get of Mr. Devlin, the writer? Can't you just picture the person who'd say "Reference is made" and "the undersigned" and "herewith" and "contact" instead of "get in touch" or "give us a call"? You probably got the same image most people would get: a stodgy, old-fashioned windbag with a stiff starched collar, high-button shoes and a stale cigar. Words like "of recent date" and "you will please find enclosed" just add to the "ancient" image. They put this writer right in the middle of the last century. So we see that there's a third criterion for our business writing. We not only want it to be well-organized and clear; we want it to be *friendly.*

Business writing which achieves these three qualities is not only more effective, it is also more economical. The cost of business communication shrinks considerably when our readers get our meaning the first time. Now, let's learn to recognize writing which meets those three very basic criteria.

Here is a revision of that letter we just saw. Is it organized? clear? friendly?

"Here is a copy of our cost estimate for the S-1297S Hoist Pulley. Thanks so much for phoning and giving us a chance to re-submit our bid. (Where do you suppose that missing letter of June 3 is hiding?)"

Well . . . that's certainly clear and organized—and it is also a great deal friendlier than the first version.

Now let's talk about format.

For business letters, two standard formats are common. (By the way, we use the word "format" to define the position of the elements and words on the page.)

The Block format types the date at the top center, but the address and body of the letter all start on the left-hand margin. In the Block format the paragraphs are not indented; rather, there is double spacing between them. The complimentary close, and the name and title of the writer (if used) are aligned under the date at the end of the body of the letter. There may be initials of the writer and the typist at the left margin, a line or two lower than the signature.

The second common format is known as the Simplified format. All the elements start at the left margin, and the inside address (or salutation) and complimentary close are omitted altogether. A subject line sometimes appears in place of the salutation. Reference lines, citing previous correspondence, may appear in both formats.

Which format is the more economical? Well, quite obviously the Simplified format is easier to type. The secretary spends far less time positioning the carriage—and omits altogether the time, the effort and the cost of the salutation and the complimentary close. Many business people feel that nobody ever reads these elements anyway.

Which format is more correct? Both formats are completely acceptable. After all, format is purely a matter of style. Some people feel the Simplified format is a bit cold, even less polite because there is no salutation and no complimentary close. Does the presence of a formal detail make a real difference in the warmth of the message?

Probably not. If you have a clear, well-organized message, then there are better ways to make it friendly and warm than the format. For example, using the reader's name in the body of the letter is a friendly gesture.

The Simplified format will save some typing costs. Another way organizations save money is by using memos instead of letters. Many memos are simple, one-way forms which use just one sheet of paper on which to share information that demands no reply. Such memos encourage longhand to avoid typing costs—especially if the pre-printing appears in script rather than in capital block letters. When memos require a response, carbon copies are included, or carbonized paper is used. The originator writes on the top sheet, and keeps one carbon as a follow-up. The receiver can reply on the same top sheet. Thus both the receiver and the originator hold a complete file. Of course, any memo forms which you develop for your organization should serve your specific needs, and should reflect a style suitable to your organization.

What about the language you use in your business writing? It is also a matter of style. Remember the stodgy letter we read a few minutes ago . . . the one with the words like "the undersigned" and "enclosed herewith?" That language is perfectly proper, but it is pompous and outdated. We discovered that that same message could be expressed more informally—and that informality is also quite correct. It also reflects a much better image of us as writers. And it makes life so much easier on our readers!

Now let's talk about three different styles of grammar.

One style is called "slang." Slang consists of many things. One element of slang is forced meanings, like the phrase "turns me on." Another element consists of technical jargon, as the word "astronaut." Some slang vanishes from the language quickly because it goes out of style; other slang words and forms become a permanent part of the language. Of course, we use slang whenever we employ any technical jargon in business writing. However, we seldom use the forced-meaning type of slang.

Another style is called "vulgate." This merely means "popularly used." Vulgate is by no means formal, but it is the style we commonly use when we are writing. Thus vulgate usage tends toward the complete sentence (normally shorter than spoken sentences) and more direct structure.

The third style is called "colloquial." This denotes the style we commonly use in spoken communication. "Colloquial" merely means spoken English. It's full of interruptions of ideas—and quite often it's full of the forced-meaning kind of slang.

There isn't any specified style for business writing. People who don't write very much get the mistaken notion that there are special words and phrases one must use in business writing. If you bite on that mistaken notion, then your writing may have all the clichés like those we say in the letter from Mr. Devlin. There is a word for those clichés: the word is "gobbledygook."

In any single piece of writing you may include some elements of all three levels of usage. In fact you are probably going to use slang if you use the proper, precise technical jargon needed to be clear. You will be colloquial if you try to be friendly and conversational. In achieving the taste that goes with those accomplishments, you'll reflect good vulgate usage and grammar.

Some people use grammar as a barrier to communication. They think of grammar as a set of rules. But grammar is the way we use our language. To think of grammar as a set of rules is to fail to understand how language works. Common practices, or grammar, are established because people do those things and understand those practices. There is no way to legislate grammar!

Grammar involves taste. We would be uncomfortable using the word "ain't" in our business writing because other people would not use it in their business writing. The word is not wrong; it just isn't stylish in writing.

Here's a question for you: Is it ever correct to split an infinitive?

That word "correct" should be a giveaway. Of course it's correct. Remember, grammar is concerned with style—not with correctness. As a matter of fact, Shakespeare was addicted to splitting infinitives. Fowler, the greatest authority on grammar says, "Those who neither know nor care what a split infinitive is are the vast majority—and a happy folk to be envied by most of the minority classes."

Ending a sentence with a preposition is another thing we hear a lot about. (Yes, we know! That last sentence did it!) You can understand why Winston Churchill reportedly sent a cryptic note back to the editor who had relocated the prepositions in the manuscript for Churchill's memoirs: "%¢&!@ ☆ . Put these back where I had them to begin with. This is an imposition up with which I will not put!"

As the authorities suggest, a great many who are quick to correct other people's English don't really know much about usage themselves. Usage means style, and grammar texts reflect the style with which language is being used when those texts are published. They are no more rule books than are magazines which report trends in ladies' fashions.

The limitations on our style exist (if they exist at all) in statements by our employers about the usages they approve and disapprove. But insist on *written* statements of writing standards. Too many organizations are haunted by legends. They actually are myths growing out of hand-me-down gossip about what a forceful manager did years ago. Maybe the "previous Director" once changed "never" to "seldom." The myth lingers: "You must never say 'never' around here. Never ever!" Apart from published style manuals, there are no rules. Thus our concern is not to learn what is right and what is wrong. Rather, it is to develop a personal, individualized style with which we are comfortable . . . a style that's well-organized, clear, and friendly.

We exercise considerable choice in style. Indeed we can select details of style which best express our ideas and our own self-image. These decisions involve our own comfort levels, the message we are sending—and above all, the reader to whom we are writing. If we make appropriate choices, we are governed by the probability that those choices will cause the reader to understand when we want to inform or document, and to take action when we are making a request.

IN GREATER DETAIL

How much do we spend on business letters? All the studies indicate that the average letter costs more than four dollars—and that's conservative!

In 1977 the Dartnell Corporation analyzed these costs. The components of the price tag looked like this:

Dictator's time	$ .95	(22.8%)
Fixed charges	1.07	(25.7%)
Secretarial time	1.19	(28.5%)
Waiting time (nonproductive labor)	.32	(7.7%)
Filing	.21	(5.0%)
Material	.15	(3.6%)
Mailing	.28	(6.7%)
	$4.17	100.0%

An earlier study showed that dictator's time cost 72¢, while "final changes" cost 76¢. Those data deserve closer scrutiny. Apparently we don't find it easy to say what we want to say. And so we do it again, or give it to someone else to review and change.

A later United States Government bureau study estimated the annual cost of paperwork in the nation's capitol at $14,200,000,000.00. That's right! Fourteen *billion*, two hundred million dollars. In just a year! The study further speculated that over $2,700,000,000 was invested in filing—and that if one document could be destroyed every second, it would take 2000 years just to get rid of all that government paper.

And still we write. Why? Because we have messages to send to people who aren't right there beside us. Whether we use an informal memo, a letter, a report, or a regulations manual, we find the written word a necessary tool in doing our work.

It's rather a pity, too. When we write, we use a third-rate communications medium. We might even distort a comment from the comedy writer, Goodman Ace: "It's called a medium only because the things on it are rarely well-done!"

But writing is truly a limited medium. When we decide to write, we deprive people of our vocal inflection and body language. Above all, we deprive them of that invaluable resource: immediate two-way feedback. Telephones can give us that two-way feedback, and yet we still rely on the business letter. After a successful telephone conversation, one party asks, "Will you put all this in writing?" Few of us have the courage to protest—or even to ask, "Why?" Even now, when rich audiotape and videotape resources are available, we seldom document or negotiate via these richer media. Pity!

Our pathetic reliance on writing is a pity in yet another sense: So few business people really like to write. They didn't choose their present profession because it would permit them to write letters or reports; they didn't accept their present position because it would offer lots of chance to practice writing skills.

Well, true, a few people really enjoy writing. These persons are generally either "born writers" or those who acquired unusual skill through special training. A second group strongly and openly hates to write. Then there is a third group, probably the vast majority, who put up with writing as an unavoidable evil. They probably feel about writing much as the new widower felt in a favorite Harry S. Truman anecdote. Asked to ride to his wife's funeral in the same car as his mother-in-law, the man replied: "Well, alright. But it's going to spoil my whole day!"

This distaste for writing really shouldn't surprise us. All too often our words come back to haunt us—even after we've revised our first draft until it had (we thought!) a splendid polish. Then readers ask what we really meant, or they take exception to viewpoints we never meant to express. We think we've used just the right word . . . that we've removed all ambiguity. We're sure we've expressed ourselves clearly, yet we get punishing feedback indicating that we actually muddied an important idea . . . or that we somehow implied something we never meant to imply at all!

Now that raises a very significant point: *No technique can replace thinking!*

Look at it this way: If you're really using your head, you can find a way to express yourself. But only non-thought can explain this next question: "Why name your son John? Every Tom, Dick and Harry is named John!" Only failure to think can explain "We have had good success" or the college course entitled "Elementary Advanced Psychology." Edwin Newman has written *Strictly Speaking* and *A Civil Tongue* to share actual examples of non-thought: "a tripod of *four* wooden poles" or "vinyl recliners 'slightly as is.' " In Bernstein's *The Careful Writer*, we find these gems: "It's a shut and dried case" and "Women have been left out in the lurch." A recent TV soap opera script carried the puzzling line, "If your father were alive today, he'd be turning over in his grave!"

This workbook can cut down on the distaste and the misunderstanding; but its techniques won't help you one bit if you don't take time to think! Skill as a business writer may or may not make you enthusiastic about writing, but hopefully it can remove the curse from your writing assignments. By acquiring just a few general concepts, plus a reasonable number of specific techniques, you can develop skills. Those skills will, in turn, cut down on the number and the intensity of the phobias and traumas. You can at least get to the point where you "can handle" writing tasks. That's the point of this book.

In this first chapter we will examine those general concepts which govern most business writing. We have already looked at the cost of written communication. Next we will examine the general purposes of business writing. After that we will look at standard formats for business letters. Finally, we will discuss the issue of English usage, commonly called "grammar." After this discussion, there will be a few exercises. These are designed to help you *apply* the concepts. And of equal importance, they help you do some self-diagnosis and goal setting.

On pages 30 and 32, Activities 1 and 2 will help you get started in that self-diagnosis and goal setting.

Purposes for writing

Why do we write? Because we have a reader.

That sounds like an oversimplification, but it is no understatement to say that the one real reason for business writing is the person who reads it. Good writers keep the reader in mind all the time they are writing. Concepts of the reader govern the writer's decision about what to include . . . what to exclude . . . the sequence in which to present the ideas . . . the words to choose and the words to avoid.

Another way of looking at it is to say that every message has its own purpose—the precise response we want of our reader.

As people involved in doing business with others, we write for as many reasons as there are transactions. Every communication has its own individual reason for existence. Yet we can also identify a few general motives for writing—categories of purposes.

First, we write to *inform*. We want to transmit *inform*ation. We desire to share some opinions or some facts. And so we write a document to let our readers in on those facts or opinions.

We also write to *request*. The written document then becomes a way to get action from our readers. We want then to do something, or to think something, or to believe something . . . to feel a certain way.

When we wish to inform or request, why don't we just call our readers on the telephone? . . . or walk over to their desks and have a conversation? Well, we often do communicate that way. But sometimes the people aren't there at the moment; they live in different cities or different time zones. And sometimes (probably too often!) even when they are near us and even after we have communicated directly, they will say, "Fine! Will you put that in writing?"

That's our third motive for writing: to *document*. Either the receiver or the organization feels a need to capture the message in print. It wants a paper "record" so the message will be there for possible future reference. Remember the $2,700,000,000 invested in maintaining those documents requested by the government in Washington, D.C.?

There are our three purposes: to inform, to request and to document.

No matter which motive we feel, the words we send on the paper really convey two messages: the literal meaning of the words themselves and an image of our own personality. A major reason for being an effective business writer is to create a favorable image. If we can establish the qualities we want to create in the image our reader's form of us, then we have also discovered some criteria for good business writing.

Criteria for business writing

We think first of *organization*. We want our readers to believe that we are well-prepared, that we can think logically, and that we cared enough about them to take time to plan our message. We don't want to appear like the proverbial puppy, chasing its tail around in circles. But that is exactly how we do appear when we just talk about a succession of ideas with no apparent relationship and with no sensible sequence or plan—in short, with no organization.

Of course if we do have a plan, we benefit too. We waste less time and we spend fewer words when we establish a plan and follow it. That's what good organization is all about.

Second, we want our writing to be *clear*. We want our readers to understand, to "get the message." What's more, we want them to get the message the first time they read it.

How many times must you read this next paragraph before you make sense of it?

"Such precautions will be made as will completely obscure all federal buildings occupied by the federal government during an air raid for any period of time from visibility by reason of internal or external illumination. Such obscuration may be obtained either by a blackout construction or by termination of illumination. This will, of course, require that in building areas in which production must continue during the blackout, construction must be provided that internal illumination may continue. Other areas may be obscured by termination of illumination."

That was supposedly written by an aide to Franklin D. Roosevelt when the President thought we might see enemy air raids on Washington D.C. during World War II. The legend goes that when Roosevelt saw the wording, he found it less than clear—and changed it to read, "In areas where you have to keep the work going, put something across the window. In buildings where you can afford to let the work stop for awhile, turn out the lights."

Finally, we want our letters to be *friendly*. If we create an image of well-organized clarity, we are businesslike. But we want more. Even when the information or the request isn't very popular, we can appear to be nice human beings. Thus our third criterion for business writing: friendliness.

Let's look at an example—a real one. In this case, the customer had ordered by mail, but had not enclosed payment. The manufacturer sent back this letter:

TO: BUSINESS OFFICE

Thank you for your order. All orders under $10.00 are payable in advance only. Please return the attached with your payment and the order will be filled promptly.
Thank you,
Circulation Department
Engineering Technology, Incorporated
140 Woodside Lane
Dunover, New Jersey

It will be no surprise that the customer made the purchase somewhere else! That letter is businesslike—at the cost of being friendly. Some would call it a rude letter. And yet the traditional courteous words are there: "Thank you" starts and closes the letter. But the first one sounds merely traditional and the second only curt. We would certainly want our own writing to be warmer than that!

Thus we have three criteria for our writing, and for the image we create in our readers. We want to be well-organized, clear and friendly. When we have achieved all three goals, we are sending messages which will get the results we want. That's what business writing is all about: results from readers. But at the same time, our writing tasks are far more bearable, maybe even just a little bit pleasant, when we are organized and can say things clearly and warmly.

Business writing which achieves these three criteria is not only more effective; it is more economical. The cost of business writing shrinks significantly when we express ourselves quickly, and when our readers get our meanings the first time they read the words. The savings are even more astounding when, after just one reading, our readers agree with us or do what we request. And from our own viewpoint, the nice part is that we get these desirable results with less blood, sweat, tears, and curses!

Formats

Now that we have considered the costs, purposes and criteria of business writing, let's take a look at formats.

When we speak of formats, we refer to the position of the words on the page. In current business writing, two standard formats are common: the Block format and the Simplified format. Both represent simplifications of earlier formats which used more centering, indentation, and flourishes. They even included some elements which, like the tail on the tadpole, have vanished altogether.

Examples and explanations of both formats appear on pages 14 through 17.

The Block format is by far the most common in business letters. It really consists of two "blocks" of print, one at the left margin and another at the center (or slightly right of center.) As the sample on the opposite page indicates, the elements of the Block format are:

- THE DATE—Typed at the top center, or just to the right of center.
- THE ADDRESS—At the left margin, three or four lines lower than the date, including the address and firm—and a Zip Code.
- A REFERENCE LINE—This is an *optional* item. (None is needed in this example.) If used, references lines give the initials of earlier writers on the same subject as this letter, the initials of the receiver, and the date of the correspondence. In most formats, the Reference Line appears directly below the date, two lines lower. It may thus be higher than, or at the same level as, the address.
- A SALUTATION—Sometimes called the Inside Address, this appears at the left margin, usually two lines beneath the last line of the Address.
- A SUBJECT LINE—This is also an *optional* item, and rather rare. Most writers prefer to handle this by mentioning the subject in the first sentence.
- THE BODY OF THE LETTER—This starts two lines below the Salutation (or Subject Line if one is used.) Paragraphs are not normally indented nowadays, but there is a double space between paragraphs. This tells the readers that there is a transition in thought, letting them know that they are leaving one supporting idea and going on to another. Note that although the first line of the new paragraph is not indented (That would violate the "block" motif!), it's permissible to indent lists within any paragraph.
- A COMPLIMENTARY CLOSE—This appears two lines below the last line of the Body, and directly below the date. It's thus at the center, or slightly right-of-center.
- A SIGNATURE—In longhand, this signature requires from two to four lines.
- A TITLE—Usually appears directly below the signature.
- A TYPED VERSION OF THE WRITER'S NAME—Though optional, this is almost always there.
- INITIALS—These often appear at the left margin, usually one or two lines lower than the end of the signature. The first initials appear in capital letters and represent the writer; they are separated by a colon from the initials of the typist. These appear in lower case.

Example of Block Format

January 21, 19XX
(Reference line: omitted this time)

Ms. Sheryl Crane, Director
Computer Application Planning
Collager Corporation
40 Pearson Place
Lithonia, Illinois 60699

Dear Ms. Crane,

Congratulations, Sheryl! Your enthusiastic participation on last year's National Conference Design Committee has been a source of great satisfaction to all of us here at CCCA. We are delighted to tell you that you are the winner of this year's MACRO Award for exceptional service.

Formal presentation will occur at next summer's national conference in Dallas during the Recognition Luncheon on Wednesday. We want the program to be 100% accurate, so will you send us:

- Your full legal name,
- Your exact current job title,
- Your complete business address, and
- A recent glossy photograph?

We certainly look forward to seeing you at the Recognition Luncheon, and to many future years of pleasant work for CCCA.

Sincere Congratulations,

Dorise DeSault

Dorise DeSault, Chairman
Awards Committee

DDS:dl

The Simplified format rearranges certain elements to the left margin, and eliminates other elements.

- THE DATE—Appears at the left margin.
- THE ADDRESS—Appears in its usual position at the left margin.
- A SUBJECT LINE—This is an *optional* item, and when used appears two lines directly beneath the address. (Not used in the example, opposite.)
- A REFERENCE LINE—This is also an *optional* element, used rather rarely in the Simplified format. When it is used, it appears below the Address or below the Subject Line (if there is a Subject Line.) Note that these optional elements appear at the left margin, beneath the *Address;* there is no Salutation in the Simplified format.
- THE BODY—Used in the same way as in other formats. Note again that there is no indentation at the first line of paragraphs. That would be quite inconsistent with other stylistic features of the Simplified format. Note too the appropriate use of indented lists.
- THE SIGNATURE—Follows the Body, and is positioned at the left margin. There is no Complimentary Close in the Simplified format.
- THE NAME AND TYPED NAME (if any)—Appear beneath the signature.
- INITIALS—If used, appear two lines below the completion of the signature.

Example of Simplified Format

January 21, 19XX

Ms. Sheryl Crane, Director
Computer Applications Planning
Collager Corporation
40 Pearson Place
Lithonia, Illinois 60699

Congratulations, Sheryl! Your enthusiastic participation on last year's National Conference Design Committee has been a source of great satisfaction to all of us here at CCCA. We are delighted to tell you that you are the winner of this year's MACRO Award for exceptional service.

Formal presentation will occur at next summer's national conference in Dallas during the Recognition Luncheon on Wednesday. We want the program to be 100% accurate, so will you send us:

- Your full legal name,
- Your exact current job title,
- Your complete business address, and
- A recent glossy photograph?

We certainly look forward to seeing you at the Recognition Luncheon, and to many future years of pleasant work for CCCA.

Dorise DeSault

Dorise DeSault, Chairman
Awards Committee
DDS:dl

You'll note that this letter doesn't call for a Subject Line or for a Reference Line. Had they been needed, they would have appeared beneath the address at the left margin, above the words "Congratulations, Sheryl!"

The Simplified format was introduced nearly 50 years ago by an association then called the National Office Managers Association. (It was once called the NOMA format.) Since then NOMA has become the Administrative Management Society, so some people now call the Simplified format the AMS format. By any name, the format represents certain streamlining and certain efficiencies. Its proponents like those efficiencies. They mention an even greater advantage, too: the reader's attention is focused on the message rather than on the format.

Nevertheless, the Simplified/NOMA/AMS format has not really been widely adopted in North America. Those who oppose it feel that the absence of a Salutation and a Complimentary Close make the format less polite. They sense a coldness.

A few informal studies show that readers scarcely notice the format of a letter. They may be aware of typographical errors and smudges, but they can rarely tell you the wording of the complimentary close after they finish reading—or even if there *was* a complimentary close, for that matter. When readers are asked to rate letters for their relative warmth, their evaluations show no correlation between format and friendliness. What becomes clear is this: if the message is friendly, the readers will rate the letter as friendly despite the format. If the message and style are cold, no format can give it warmth. You could word your complimentary close "Affectionately" or "With love," and a cold letter would still seem cold. When unhappy messages are perceived as warm and friendly, writers have tried to be empathic with their reader's needs and viewpoints. It's that empathy, not the format, that brings warmth to the business letter.

If you have a well-organized letter, clearly expressed, then there are better ways to secure friendliness than through format. For example, using the reader's name in the body of the letter is a friendly thing to do. It should happen only once (or at most, twice) in any letter, and it should appear at a useful point in the sequence. We've all seen the frighteningly unfriendly computer-generated letters which interrupt the flow every few sentences to inject "your name" or "your town," the data loaded into the computer's memory. But if you use a reader's name judiciously, in the first sentence, in a summary, or in making a major transition, you can add warmth to your writing.

Since the Simplified format does not necessarily produce "colder" correspondence, it does represent an effective way to save a little bit on the production costs of business writing. Activity 3, on page 34, will help you fix the elements of the formats in your own mind. Activity 4, on page 35, will help you plan the installation of any format change you might want to suggest for your own organization.

Most organizations save time and money by using memos instead of letters for a great deal of their writing. The memo format eliminates all the cost and effort of typing, and cuts out formal details like addresses, salutations, complimentary closes, and titles. It uses a simple FROM and TO specification at the top, usually with a place for the DATE and the SUBJECT.

AN EXAMPLE OF A TYPICAL MEMO

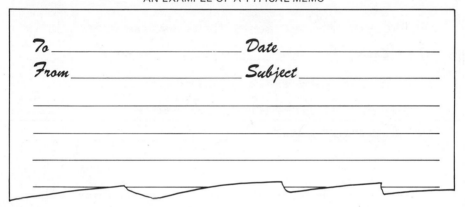

Many organizations have found that printing these memo forms on half pages (5½" x 8½") further cuts costs; people write shorter memos! To further encourage speed and informality and economy, other organizations use only script lettering when they preprint the forms. They discover that if the printing looks like handwriting, people tend to write out the memos rather than take the time to type them formally! (When writers do use the typewriter for memos, company regulations usually encourage strikeovers. The memo is an informal format; perfection and aesthetics are not criteria.)

Another advantage of the memo is that it can cover several subjects—a sort of "current things" diary between two people. It's thus an ideal way to bring people up to date on recent activities, an excellent medium for informal short-interval reports.

The memo can also produce a satisfactory document of a total two-way transaction. Carbonized papers permit the originator to inscribe the address and the original message on the top sheet. The bottom copy is removed as a "tickler" file. If there is no reply by a specified date, the originator can follow up by a second memo or a telephone call. The

Memo and Reply

To _Muriel Soney – GO_   Date _4/21_
From _Dave Wright – SP_   Subject _Meeting Room_

could you tell me the exact dimensions of
the "council" and "Creighton" rooms so
we can plan activities for break-out
groups at the Annual Labo Planning
Meeting next month?   DW

Here are dimensions for all the 5th floor Rooms:
Council – 42' x 36'6"
Creighton – 36'6" x 27'6"
Downey – 36'6" x 27'6"
Eaton – 30' x 20'6"
Fresno – 20'6" x 14'

                              M.S. for D.W.

receiver gets two copies, and puts the reply on the top sheet. As shown
in the illustration, Ms. Soney now has a copy of the entire transaction.
So does Mr. Wright; he gets back the second copy. This copy gives him a
document of the entire transaction. He can now remove the third copy
from his "tickler file" and destroy it.

That destroying the "tickler" copy is an important point. Remember how expensive filing is? The memo form permits a single piece of paper in both files. Yet countless business offices can uncover carefully stapled first and third copies—with the intervening carbon paper! Up to four sheets are filed, when two would be more than enough.

Why "more than enough"? Because the very nature of the content of the memo is often a clue to the temporary importance of the content. Take a hard look at the filing practices for your memos. Are they really needed for posterity? . . . or even for tomorrow's reference?

The three-page memo expedites a two-way communication. When the sender needs only simple information, the one-page memo can work just as well. As shown here, the receiver can return the original memo to the sender. If a file copy is mandatory—It seldom is!—a copying machine will do the work quickly and inexpensively.

INTRACOMPANY MEMO

To *Fred Collins -RG*   Date *March 14*

From *Avis Brewer -SA*   Subject *PRP Manuals*

Fred, what's your best estimate about these manuals? off-the-press date? shipment?

MARCH 21

MARCH 25-28

Many organizations have further reduced the cost of business correspondence by using the window envelope. The envelope itself will cost a couple of pennies more, but there is no need to type the address a second time: the address on the letter itself shows through the window.

This procedure will save anywhere from a nickel to a dime per letter. It is becoming increasingly common. Even the United States Government uses it for all paychecks and for a great deal of correspondence to their tremendously long mailing list.

Sometimes the reply can be quite short. To write a full, individually typed letter would be cumbersome and expensive. Some organizations merely write or type their answers on the inbound letter. When they do this they usually stamp or staple an explanation. Here are some samples of those explanations:

In order to get your answer to you as soon as possible, we're using your own letter.

We felt sure you'd rather hear from us today than wait for a formal reply.

This informal reply is designed to speed our answer to you.

We felt you would prefer a prompt reply to a formal letter. That's why we are jotting our reply on the letter you sent to us.

So that we may answer you immediately . . .

. . . We are taking the liberty of making a marginal notation on the letter itself.

We hope you will agree that a prompt response is more important than formality.

Such devices as simplified formats, memo-and-reply forms, window envelopes and "jiffy answers" can reduce the total cost of business writing. So can eliminating reviews by successive levels of management. Remember those costs of writing—and the components? The estimate was 72¢ for writing and 76¢ for rewriting. A great deal of that revising is done not by the writer, but by the writer's boss. Such reviews can do one of two things. First, they can improve the writing and train the writer. But secondly, they can merely shift the prose into the reviewer's style and teach writers that it doesn't matter how they write—it's going to get changed anyway!

Editorial review by the writer's superior is a useful management activity when:

1. Each review is used as a way to train new members of an organization about policy and writing standards,

2. The reviewer can give a technical explanation of the change. That is to say, the reviewer can point out that the original version did not correctly reflect policy, or that it was inappropriately expressed.

An example of a proper editorial change might go like this. Let's assume that the original version said, "It is recommended that the sales slips be forwarded first to the QCS and then to the Manager of Accounting." Let's further assume that the boss/editor changes this to read: "We recommend that the Quality Control Specialist (QCS) check the sales slip before the slips go to the Manager of Accounting. The QCS can thus review errors with the sales clerks so they get immediate feedback—rather than delayed review of their performance." In explaining the changes, the boss/editor can give technical reasons: (1) using the active voice for a key recommendation; (2) defining the technical jargon, in this case QCS; and (3) giving the reason for the recommendation. The first two are writing techniques; the third is both a management policy and good writing practice.

When boss/editors make such explanations, they share standards and train their subordinates; they aren't merely imposing their style on others. Organizations which are populated with bosses who make changes just because "it sounds better this way" squander lots of time and feelings. They also breed poor writing! Why? Because there is no possible way subordinates can guess what the boss/editor will think "sounds better" at the precise moment of the review. Besides, it changes from letter to letter, from day to day. Smart employees therefore just dash off anything any old way: it's going to be changed anyway! (The chapter on reports discusses this problem more deeply.)

That takes us to the issue of style. To a small degree, style is reflected in format. To a much greater degree it is reflected in the writer's use of language.

Levels of usage

Technically, style in the use of language is called grammar. There are really three common levels of usage in American grammar. The first level is called "slang." There are actually several types of slang. The one we most often think of is forced meanings . . . phrases like "turns me on" and "far out" and "the old lady" or "So's your old man!" (If you remember that one, you've been around for awhile!)

Some slang vanishes rather quickly, because it doesn't remain useful. For example, "snafu" was a polite acronym for a war time crudity. However, the term is rarely used nowadays. The same applies to a much older slang word: "doughface." We no longer need a word to describe northern congressmen who aren't opposed to slavery; the word has only historic value. Or take the word "pad." It now has two meanings: It's something to write in, or else spend the night in!

But there is a second form of slang which has greater longevity. It is technical jargon. We don't usually think of technical jargon as slang, but it really is. Words like "astronaut" and "cryogenics," "fuselage" and "hypochondria" entered the language because they specified a new discovery. They lingered because the thing they specified continued to be part of our lives. Another example is "gobbledygook." Legend has it that this word was the explosive, contemptuous word one manager invented to describe the longwinded abstractions written by subordinates. It's a perfect example of slang: it has no technical origins but it describes a technical phenomenon technically. The word even sounds like the thing is describes. It has lingered. It appeared in dictionaries within a few years after its genesis. It represents both a technical term and forced meanings. The word is now defined (*Webster's New Collegiate Dictionary*, 1974) as "wordy and generally unintelligible jargon."

Effective business writers try to avoid gobbledygook, but they will inevitably use some slang. The effort to be precise involves slang in the form of technical jargon. Most business writing also involves the forced meaning type of slang on a few occasions. Those occasions come up when the writer and the reader are very well acquainted, when the subject is generally amusing, or when the writer wants to show a special joviality. In many of these occasions, the writer will put the "forced" word within quotation marks.

When words and forms enter the language as slang, there is a tendency for them to endure and to become common speech. We call that spoken level of usage the "colloquial" level. That's a big word to describe a concept as simple as "spoken English." Yet colloquial English is just that: the style we use when speaking. (As a matter of fact, the word "colloquial" is a perfect example of technical jargon.)

Because colloquial English is spoken, it is subject to all those things people characteristically do in conversation. It is full of interruptions and contractions; it gets slurred; it is often full of expressions we don't put down on paper! For example, in business writing we typically avoid slang which is vulgar or obscene. True! Vulgarity and obscenity have begun to appear in newspapers and magazines which would never have printed them ten years ago! But very few such terms have invaded business letters or reports.

However, certain colloquial usages *do* appear in business writing. One good example is contractions. Ever since the turn of the century (from the 1800's to the 1900's) good business writers have been saying things like "doesn't" and "don't" and "won't" in their letters and reports.

What does this tell us? That the natural style of business writing dips now and then into slang and colloquial levels of usage for its forms and vocabulary. *There isn't any special style for business writing!* Now and then people who haven't written very much get the mistaken notion that they should use special words and phrases when they write a letter or report. Unfortunately this just leads them to gobbledygook and to misunderstanding; they end up expressing themselves badly and confusing their readers. Their writing creates a bad image because they have thought vaguely—and expressed that vague thought in an inappropriate style.

Still others think they should write the way they talk. That's also a delusion. In fact, it's really impossible. Speaking and writing are distinctly different media. Speech permits two-way feedback. It offers facial expression, vocal inflections, tone coloring and emphasis. These facial and vocal inflections add immeasurable richness to the message. Take this example: Assume you lead an important task force in your organization. So far, things have gone badly. Group meetings have been sluggish, unproductive. You want to change that with next week's session. If you were face-to-face with members, speaking to them, you might say, "I hope our next meeting will turn what hasn't been a very dynamic program into something we can all be proud of." But suppose they first met that same sentence in writing! How many of your readers would make sense of it?

Although there is no special style demanded in good business writing—no "gear" into which we can shift—there is a word for the level we use in writing our language. That word is "vulgate." It comes from the Roman Christians who wanted a popular bible. They translated the original language into their own; the result was the "vulgate" or popular bible. Today the word denotes commonly accepted text or reading.

Vulgate English is by no means formal. With our modern trend toward informality, colloquial words and forms have a strong tendency to become common in vulgate usage too. Our dictionaries used to distinguish between levels by indicating "*col.*" for words, spellings or forms heard only in spoken English. But the upward movement into vulgate usage is so rapid that most dictionaries no longer note the distinction. (They do indicate if a word or usage is still "slang.")

In business writing we are following good vulgate levels of usage when we express ourselves in complete sentences—at least most of the time. (There are occasions for non-sentences in letters and reports.) Written sentences are normally shorter than those we speak aloud—despite the tendency of too many writers to go on *ad infinitum* before a period or a question mark. The structure of written sentences tends to be more direct than that of spoken sentences. Why? Because of those inflections we can share when we speak. As a matter of fact, when we speak to another person, those facial and vocal inflections can add meaning and continuity to our message in ways which are not ordinarily available to either the writer or the reader of the printed sentence—if you follow what we mean, and we doubt that you do because this extremely long sentence was deliberately made extremely long just to illustrate the point we are trying to make about the tendency of written, vulgate prose to be shorter and more direct than the spoken sentence!

In any piece of writing, you may include elements of all three style levels. In fact, as we have noted, you will just about have to use some slang or jargon to express yourself clearly. You just about have to use some informal structures (as parenthetical expressions) if you want to appear warm, friendly . . . human.

Grammar is really the study of what is to be preferred and what is to be avoided in the use of language. That raises the issue of who determines what to prefer and what to avoid. Popular usage is the ultimate determiner. Textbooks and dictionaries can only reflect what the masses of users do with a language. As E. B. White says in his introduction to Strunk's classic *The Elements of Style,* "Style rules . . . are, of course, somewhat a matter of individual preference, and even the established rules of grammar are open to challenge." (From page xi of the second edition, published in 1972.)

In 1966 a spokesman for Random House publishers commented: "We found that the language was changing so fast we had to turn to computers and data processing to keep up with it." (*TV Guide*, December 24, 1966, p. 22)

One common type change is the loss of close distinctions. For example, the word "none" really means "not one" and would take a singular verb, such as "is" or "was." But how many people still make that distinction? We were probably all taught that the past tense of the verb "dive" is "dived." The word "dove" defined a bird, and there was no such word as "d-oh-ve." But with idolized sportscasters telling millions of Americans that the middle linebacker "dove" into the line, you can bet that next generation will hear of no such distinction. Americans have acquired a new past tense of the word "dive" whether they like it or not!

Nor is English usage one bit logical. As an anonymous ditty says:

"If the singular's 'this' and the plural is 'these,'
Why isn't the plural of 'kiss' called 'keese'?
Now the masculine pronouns are 'he' 'his' and 'him,'
But imagine the feminine 'she' 'shis' and 'shim'!"

In a very real sense, our language and its grammar are servants of the people—not vice versa. Yet a few dyed-in-the-wool conservatives and stern secretaries use grammar as a barrier to communication. How? They insist that rules dictate what users can do with language. They ignore or reject the more correct viewpoint that writers establish the rules because those rules get results in readers and listeners. Rules exist because writers and readers and listeners and speakers are comfortable with the usages. Grammar is more properly viewed as style. Styles are set because people are comfortable with them. They thus become ordained by habit.

Grammar is the way we use language. To think of good grammar as good taste is to use the language intelligently. For example: we would be uncomfortable using vulgarities or obscenities in our letters; we would feel unstylish saying "ain't" or using double negatives in our report. But we might very comfortably (even unknowingly!) split an infinitive or use a preposition to end a sentence with.

What about those very two issues? Let's look at a real authority, H. W. Fowler's *Modern English Usage*. (Its American counterpart, Nicholson's *A Dictionary of American English Usage* hasn't been revised in a long time.) Fowler says, on page 579 of the Second Edition: "The English speaking world may be divided into (1) those who neither know nor care what a split infinitive is; (2) those who do not know but care very much; (3) those who know and condemn; (4) those who know and approve; and (5) those who know and distinguish. . . . Those who neither know nor care are the vast majority, and are a happy folk to be envied by most of the minority classes."

On pages 473–475 Fowler deals with the preposition at the end of the sentence. "It was once a cherished superstition that prepositions must be kept true to their name and placed before the word they govern in spite of the incurable English instinct for putting them late . . . Those who lay down the universal principle that final prepositions are 'inelegant' are unconsciously trying to deprive the English language of a valuable idiomatic resource, which has been used freely by all our greatest writers except those whose instinct for English idiom has been overpowered by notions of correctness derived from Latin standards . . . If the final preposition . . . sounds comfortable, keep it; if it does not sound comfortable, still keep it if it has compensating vigour, or when among awkward possibilities, it is the least awkward." (There at the end, Fowler may have been forecasting Winston Churchill's reported comment after an editor rearranged Churchill's prepositions to an "internal location.")

In *Modern English Usage*, Fowler notes that there is "not much sense in trying to apply the rules of a dead synthetic language [Latin] to a living analytical one." He adds that it took us a long time to realize this, and that "despite the grammarians, not thanks to them, our language has won ease and grace." (p. 231)

The important thing is not which style we choose, but believing that a style is useful if it causes readers to understand when we are trying to inform, or to agree and to act when we are requesting. Our concern is not to learn which style is right and which is wrong; our most important concern is to develop a style with which we are comfortable . . . a style which is well-organized, clear, and friendly.

It must also be apparent that when we choose a style, we consider such things as:

- The message we send,
- The reader to whom we send it,
- The standards recommended by the organization for which we work, and
- Our own personal comfort levels with the way we express ourselves.

If we make intelligent choices, we will be able to inform, request or document effectively and efficiently. That is what matters—not a non-existent rulebook.

In a sense, there is really just one basic principle: to keep our readers as the focus of all our decisions. Only the policy of our own organization need limit our choices. The reader does indeed sit squarely in the center of our writing target. All our decisions about what to include, how to sequence it, or how to express it, depend upon our estimate of what will and what will not cause our reader to make the desired response.

Effective reader-centering means that we select, sequence and express all our ideas with the reader in mind. If we give some attention to being clear and friendly, the reader will like being the center of our attention. The reader will be as comfortable with the desired response as we are with our business writing.

PUTTING THE PRINCIPLES INTO PRACTICE

To know how to do something represents one level of accomplishment; to *do* it is another, more difficult level. In each chapter of this workbook a section called "Putting the Principles Into Practice" gives you the chance to apply the principles examined in that chapter. There are activities which *let you put to work* the things you have just learned.

In this chapter, those activities involve some self-diagnosis and goal setting, as well as some direct applications of the knowledge contained in the chapter. We think you will find these activities useful in your program to improve your business writing skills.

✳ Activity 1

Self-assessment is always worthwhile. In improving our business writing, such self-appraisal is imperative. When you complete this training you will want to compare your new skill level with your present ability.

Here is a chance to get a sample of your present skill level. Think for a moment of a business letter you must write within the next few days. It's probably a reply to a letter now resting in your "IN" basket. Of course it might also be a letter you must initiate in order to start something going. Whatever letter you choose, write the body of that letter in the space provided on the next page.

In order to get a useful sample, try to write on a topic which will produce a minimum of 150 to 200 words. At the end of the training you will have a chance to revisit this initial letter and appraise your progress.

✱ Activity 2

Growth and development depend upon two honest appraisals: your estimate of your present skill, and your goal for the future. Use an "X" to show where you rate yourself on each of the questions below; let an "O" show where you want to be at the end of this training.

A. ORGANIZING MY IDEAS: Do my messages have a solid structure?

I'm very   I'm about   I'm very
disorganized   average   well-organized

B. CLARITY: Do people ever follow-up to ask, "What did you mean by that?"

I'm very   I'm sometimes   I'm   They get me on   I'm
foggy   hard to follow   "so-so"   second readings   clear

C. FRIENDLINESS: Do you create a friendly image—or are you a "cool cucumber"?

Cold and   Sometimes warm—   Warm and
impersonal   sometimes cold   friendly

D. EFFICIENCY: Is the time you spend in writing a reasonable investment for the results you get?

I spend too   I'd like   I can live   It's not   I'm quite
much time   to spend   with it   too bad   efficient
                   less time

E. COMFORT WITH WRITING: Do you hate the writing tasks—or love them?

I hate it!	I try to avoid writing	I can live with it	I sometimes volunteer to write	I really like to write!

F. THE BOSS'S OPINION: What does your boss say about your writing skills?

"It's bad!"	Often asks me to do rewrites	Makes a few changes	Grins and bears it	Rarely asks for rewrites	"It's very good!"

Did you check many of them on the "high" side. We hope you did. But if the boss likes your writing, or rarely asks for rewrites, and if you are relatively well satisfied with your writing, there is a question.

Why do you need this training? We happen to think that training should have direct on-the-job application. If both you and your boss appraise your writing favorably, shouldn't you and the boss have a heart-to-heart talk about why you are enrolled in this training?

✱ Activity 3

Many organizations use a single format for all business letters. This activity assumes that your organization might make such a decision, or reconsider a previous decision about format.

To make a decision about which format, Block or Simplified, is most appropriate you might want to take a typical letter and prepare it in both formats. We suggest a letter which you regard as important—one in which the reader's affirmative response was of critical importance to you.

After you have looked at each version, make a determination about which you prefer. The matrix printed here may help you, serving as a notepad for your value analysis.

	THE BLOCK FORMAT	THE SIMPLIFIED FORMAT
ADVANTAGES		
DISADVANTAGES		

✱ Activity 4

Does the format you are now using need improvement?

That question might apply to your letters, memos—even to the envelopes or traditional formats used in regular reports.

If any of the existing formats contain needless elements or decor, you may want to design an improved format. If so, detail it and then plan the strategy by which you will get it adopted and implemented. Consider such things as:

1. People whose involvement would enhance the quality of the format or the probability of approval.

2. People whose approvals would be necessary. If you don't get their energy enlisted in your campaign by involving them in the design, what evidence or arguments can you use on each one? Be specific. Remember that not all people will respond the same way to a single argument.

3. What existing systems might you use to institute a new format? Consider things like a suggestion program, an economy campaign, a training program.

4. The specifications and examples which would need to appear in the manuals or bulletins. The more you have these "perfect," the greater the possibility that others will see the value in your proposal.

✱ Activity 5

Including slang in your own business writing is a personal matter—well, it's a personal matter unless you work for an organization which says that you should or that you shouldn't. In either case, you need to know slang when you see it. Failing that, you need to look up each construction in the dictionary to check each item. (Yes, they still indicate slang forms in most dictionaries; they don't, however, indicate colloquial usages any more.)

Which of the following are indicated as "slang" in current dictionaries?

A. I think we may safely regard the Sanderson account as in the bag for next year.

B. While the rest of us were sitting there gassing, Joe Forbes suggested a very novel approach to solving our turnover problem

C. Unless we take quick action, we may end up in a real fix.

D. To make our seagoing employees safe at all times, we should issue a Mae West to each worker, and then train all of them in the proper use of this equipment.

E. Someone must have done a snow job on the Personnel Managers; they have altered their position completely.

F. Robert DeMet is no blockhead; he uses his nut to come up with some extremely creative ideas.

G. It may be significant that this employee once resigned from the firm to become a flatfoot. He returned to us a year and a half later.

H. He will undoubtedly spend at least five years in stir for this misappropriation of funds.

Review

Webster's New Collegiate Dictionary (1974) indicates two cases of slang in those sentences: the word "nut" used to describe a person's head, and "in stir" to denote "in prison." None of the other usages is called "slang" in that dictionary.

CHAPTER 2

ORGANIZING BUSINESS WRITING

IN A NUTSHELL

Well-organized writing can create a favorable impression of ourselves as individuals—and of the organization we represent. Good organization is every bit as important as format and English style.

Organization is like architecture: no matter how pleasing the decor and ornamentation, the impact is limited to the quality of the structure on which it is displayed.

Good organization is an investment—an investment in time-saving for you the writer, and for the people who read what you write. The writer who doesn't invest at least a moment or two in deciding how to organize ideas is very apt to waste time while writing and dictating the message. Perhaps even more important, such writers waste the time of their readers. The poor readers must wander through the maze of the writer's hasty thinking . . . and wander . . . and wander . . . or just give up in disgust!

The first step in organizing business writing is *planning*: the second step is *sharing* that plan with your reader.

To help your reader get the message you send, and to help the reader get it on the first reading, tell your reader immediately your purpose in writing. Is it to inform? . . . to request? . . . to document?

Which of those purposes prompted the letter you are about to read?

---

156 East Laurel Lane
Poughkawsett, Washington
December 15, 19XX

Mr. Ralph Loy
234 Delphi St.
Decatur, Arizona 85099

Dear Sir:

We have contacted the Heller Publishing Company of 66 East 30th Street, Mohawk, Ohio, who prints a publication known as *Engineering in Business and Government.*

In their February, 19XX issue, we were impressed with articles on "Designing Engineering Curricula," of which we were told you were the author.

When we inquired where we might obtain the book, we were referred to you.

Could you possibly direct us to the publishers of "Designing Engineering Curricula," or a bookstore in the Seattle area where this book can be obtained?

Thanks for your kind attention to this matter.

Sincerely,

Sterling Moslov

Sterling Moslov

P.S. We checked with Porter-Holt and they did not have the book in their store.

SM:dl

You really have to work to discover the purpose, don't you? There is so much data there that it looks as if the letter were intended to inform or to document. But put yourself in the reader's place: would you know what to do with all that history and all that background? Probably not.

But after some analysis we finally discover that phrase, "Could you direct us . . . ?" It's hidden away in a short paragraph, nearly at the end of the letter. This makes us ask, "How much of Mr. Moslov's letter was really necessary?"

Only that purpose statement is necessary. All the rest wastes the time of the reader. It is equally wasteful of Mr. Moslov's time.

The real message of that letter is all summed up in one short sentence. If you received only that, you might think the letter a bit short—even terse. But ask yourself how friendly or how considerate it is to ask anyone to read a lot of irrelevant detail! We will come back to this issue later, and we will formulate a principle about what to include and what to exclude in our business letters. For now, just remember that business people must read over 6000 pages at their desk every year. They like short letters.

Every unit of well-organized business writing has a single purpose. That applies to the paragraph, the chapter, the memo, and the letter—especially to the business letter. In fact, this principle is so important that we can formulate it as our first principle of organization:

> PRINCIPLE 1. A WELL-ORGANIZED BUSINESS LETTER
> HAS ONE PURPOSE—AND ONLY ONE.

Why is a single purpose so important?

The principle is vital for several reasons. First, the reader who gets the letter wants to get the main idea easily and quickly. That's impossible when there are several purposes, or responses expected. Secondly, the reader wants to know in what one place the letter can be filed. If the reader ever needs the document again, this single purpose is important.

If you are like most business people, you want the main idea, or purpose, stated first. This placement helps readers comprehend the entire message with greater insight—and faster. When we put the main idea first, all the other elements make a lot more sense for our reader.

So there we have our second basic principle of organization:

> PRINCIPLE 2. STATE THE PURPOSE OF YOUR LETTER IN THE FIRST PARAGRAPH—PREFERABLY IN THE FIRST SENTENCE.

(When we talk about the psychology of organizing ideas, we may find a very, very few exceptions to that rule. But that will come later—and in nearly every case, effective business writing states the purpose just as soon as possible.)

Let's apply these first two rules to an actual letter:

Dear Mrs. Hayes:

We have received the refund application completed during April while travelling from Creston to Centralia.

Since your claim reached us by other than normal means, we will need additional information in order to process any refund you may be due.

Trip 668 on April 27 cancelled and we will need to know what alternate trip and date you used and what carrier you did use.

Normally these forms are returned to the cabin attendant who attaches it to your ticket. In this way the refund is handled routinely when it reaches our office.

Will you also tell us the date and location of office your ticket was issued, and what type of refund you expect.

A copy of this letter is attached so that your reply can be readily identified. We will appreciate your prompt answer.

Thank you for your patience and cooperation.

Sincerely,

D. R. Larkin

D. R. Larkin
Refund Coordinator

DRL:ghd

What about that first paragraph? Quite clearly Mr. Larkin didn't put his purpose there. We wonder why he went to all that trouble just to tell Mrs. Hayes that he received her application! Is he congratulating the U.S.

Postal service for making the delivery? Yet in Mr. Larkin's clumsiness and obscurity, we can learn something: cut those meaningless acknowledgements that tend to clutter up the first paragraph of so much business writing.

It's great to give your reader a point of reference. But rather than bore your reader with a lot of irrelevant detail, try one of these devices:

1. A reference line, or

2. A reference to the topic in the first sentence.

3. An immediate connection between the topic and the statement of the purpose. By *purpose*, we mean the response you actually want your reader to make.

And when you name the topic, do just that: *name* it; don't write a history book about it.

By now you have probably decided that the purpose of that last letter is to request additional information. If you put that request in the first paragraph, you can avoid the trap the real writer fell into. Notice how the original bad planning caused Mr. Larkin to repeat the phrase three times: "We will need additional information," "We will need to know," and "will you also tell us . . ." This repetition probably actually forced the reader into a long search for the several units of data Mr. Larkin was seeking.

By taking just a minute to plan our message, we can quickly send a clear signal. The secret lies in putting both the purpose and the reference into the first sentence. In the letter to Mrs. Hayes, how about: "Can you give us some added information so we can quickly process your refund application for Trip 668?"

Once the writer states the purpose and the reference in that first paragraph, there is no need to repeat—and all the questions will probably appear in a list within a single paragraph. It might look like this:

"Specifically, will you tell us:

1. On what date did you buy your original ticket?
2. At what office? (The street address will be helpful.)
3. What company did you use in getting to Creston?
4. On what date did you make the trip?
5. What was the trip number?
6. Shall we credit a charge card? (If so, give name and number.) Or shall we send you a check?"

This should make life a lot easier for Mrs. Hayes. Just putting the purpose in the first paragraph, and listing expected actions in another, single paragraph would be helpful to any reader.

That letter to Mrs. Hayes also gives an excellent example of a third principle:

> PRINCIPLE 3. PUT SUPPORTING IDEAS INTO SEPARATE PARAGRAPHS.

This merely means that similar ideas shouldn't be scattered throughout the letter, and that dissimilar concepts shouldn't be crowded together inside a single paragraph.

Sequence is important too. That provides another principle:

> PRINCIPLE 4. ARRANGE THE PARAGRAPHS IN A METHODICAL ORDER.

One of the most common orders is from the "most important" to the "least important." Readers have grown accustomed to that: they expect to hear the "big guns" early. When you use this sequence, be sure to stop when you get to the point where the least important data or subtopic is no longer worth mentioning.

There are other sequential plans. You might want to consider such sequences as:

- Most acceptable to least acceptable
- Chronological
- Geographical
- Organizational units (as Sales, Accounting, Manufacturing)
- Familiar to unfamiliar
- Cause to Effect
- Effect to Cause.

No matter what sequence you choose, you can see why good paragraphing is such an important principle. And it's just as important whether you're writing a letter, a report, a procedures manual—or even a simple memo.

A paragraph structure should go from the big idea to the smallest detail worth mentioning. If it's too small to mention, then omit it. But the point is this: that everything in the paragraph helps to support the "big idea" of that paragraph as expressed in the *topic sentence*.

This is so important that we will formulate it as one of our principles:

> PRINCIPLE 5. WELL-ORGANIZED PARAGRAPHS BEGIN
>   WITH A TOPIC SENTENCE.

A topic sentence tells the reader what the paragraph is about. The rest of the paragraph then supplies supporting, explanatory ideas and data which expand, clarify, or give evidence to prove the truth of the topic sentence.

Let's revisit our revised letter to Mrs. Hayes—the one where we asked for more information. Note that we indented and listed the questions we wanted Mrs. Hayes to answer. The topic sentence ("specifically, will you tell us:") tells her what the paragraph is about; the indented list gives her the detailed development of that topic. By indenting and listing we can let our reader know the logic by which we develop our topic sentences.

We have also added numerals. To add numerals or letters is helpful for readers who may need to respond to only one element within a list of actions or topics.

Note too that the list gives Mrs. Hayes room to jot her replies right onto the letter. That makes sense out of that stuff about "a copy of this letter is attached so that your reply may be readily identified." Only let's hope that when we revise Mr. Larkin's letter we say it from the reader's viewpoint! Something like, "You can just jot your replies on the carbon copy—no need to write a new letter." Now the extra copy is a thoughtful device to help speed the process.

In many letters, the layout on the page can reflect our organization. This is important enough to qualify as our sixth principle:

> PRINCIPLE 6. LET THE LAYOUT ON THE PAGE REFLECT
>   YOUR ORGANIZATION PLAN.

This principle reveals that we organize on two bases: logical and psychological.

In fact, three rules are devoted to the *logical* organization of our letters:

> PRINCIPLE 1. A WELL-ORGANIZED BUSINESS LETTER
>   HAS ONE PURPOSE—AND ONLY ONE.
>
> PRINCIPLE 3. PUT SUPPORTING IDEAS INTO SEPARATE
>   PARAGRAPHS.
>
> PRINCIPLE 5. WELL-ORGANIZED PARAGRAPHS BEGIN
>   WITH A TOPIC SENTENCE.

All the principles are logical, but in addition these next three rules have important psychological impact on our writing—and on our readers:

> PRINCIPLE 2. STATE THE PURPOSE OF YOUR LETTER IN THE FIRST PARAGRAPH—PREFERABLY IN THE FIRST SENTENCE.
>
> PRINCIPLE 4. ARRANGE THE PARAGRAPHS IN A METHODICAL ORDER.
>
> PRINCIPLE 6. LET THE LAYOUT ON THE PAGE REFLECT YOUR ORGANIZATION PLAN.

What if the response you want from your reader is apt to be distasteful? Well, that's when there may be an exception to that rule about stating the purpose in the first paragraph. If our reader will find the purpose distasteful, we may decide to let the facts speak first, then state the purpose. This happens very, very rarely. When we do use this sequence, we want to make certain we aren't "toying" with our reader in a communicative "cat and mouse" game.

If we understand this, then we understand another basic and vital principle about purposes. *The purpose of writing is the response we want from the reader!* From *our* viewpoint, we write to inform, request, or document. But we want our readers to understand, agree, or act!

Quite often we can do a good job of arranging ideas and expressing ourselves psychologically by using the inbound letter. Here's how it works. The reader has written us first, revealing a value system and a vocabulary that are meaningful to that reader. What better sequence could we use than the very same sequence the reader gave us? What better vocabulary can we select than those words with which we know our reader to be comfortable?

Furthermore, this technique saves your time. And that's a big reason for organizing—remember? "An investment in time saving for both us and our reader!" If we can send the message the first time we write it, and if our reader can get the message at the first reading—above all, if our reader can and will take the desired action after the first reading—then our planning and sharing has paid big dividends.

Let's review the ways we can share our organization with our reader:

1. State the purpose (desired response) in the first paragraph.
2. Divide logical units into separate, distinct paragraphs.
3. Indent and list sequential actions or key supporting ideas.

Just a word of caution about that indenting: once or twice is enough. If you try to show so many levels of subordination that you're beginning to type at the center of that page, you've gone too far!

To achieve excellent organization, we need one more principle:

> PRINCIPLE 7. INCLUDE ONLY WHAT YOUR READER MUST KNOW
> IN ORDER TO UNDERSTAND OR AGREE.

Remember that lengthy letter seeking the source of the book on engineering curricula? It's the perfect example of what happens when writers ignore this rule. Consideration for our reader demands that we tell just enough—that we not burden the reader with semi-relevant or redundant detail.

When our mission is to inform and to document, let's tell our reader just enough to assure understanding. When our mission is to request, give just enough to persuade our reader. That's why we state the rule, "Include only what your reader must know in order to understand or agree." If you include only what your reader must know in order to understand or agree, if you state the purpose first, if you arrange paragraphs methodically, and if you use a "sharing" page layout, then you have a sound psychological message.

And when you have organized logically and psychologically, you are ready to write. You are organized.

IN GREATER DETAIL

One big reason for being well-organized is the time saved for ourselves and for our readers. In addition, good organization does a great deal toward creating that favorable image we seek when we write. Readers grow restless and confused if our purpose is hidden or tardily stated. If our ideas ramble all around the subject and away from the purpose, or if the messages contain details of dubious relevance—well, our readers are bound to see us as less than an effective, efficient, friendly person.

At its very best, poorly organized business writing implies careless thinking; at its worst, it implies our lack of concern for the reader.

Thus, even if your style in grammar is appropriate, and even if your formats are sound, and even if your individual ideas are stated clearly, the total impression can be bad unless your ideas are well organized.

Good organization is an investment in the final, total success of your communication. It's an investment in time saving: time saved for you, the writer who won't have to do it over again, and time saved for your readers, people who will "get the message" at first reading.

Let's examine that assertion more closely. Writers who don't invest at least a few moments in deciding what response they want from their readers run certain risks. The minimum risk is that they will repeat themselves or include things that need not be said at all. A more dangerous risk is that they will omit a key idea. The result? A reader who doesn't make the desired response. Thus the entire communication fails: the letters must be followed up with a call or another letter; the reports represent wasted effort in behalf of positions nobody "buys."

The lucky non-organizers are those who get the chance to rewrite. It's frustrating (but not fatal) to find when you read the final typed draft that you "can't live with" what you've created. It's tedious to make new plans, to pick up the pieces and to do it all over again. But that's better than to send the message and get no results! The alternative to either of these dire results is to invest a little time in organizing. Only that planning will save time in major revisions, or avoid total failure of the writing to do the job for which it was intended.

And let's remind ourselves that our readers gain as much as we do from this planning. When readers get unorganized communications, they must wander through the endless maze of hasty thinking. They must make sense out of sloppy paragraphs which don't seem to relate to one another very well—and which seem to relate to the main purpose not at all. When this happens, it can't be too surprising that our key readers may just give up in confusion—or worse, in disgust. In those cases everybody's effort, reader's and writer's alike, has been wasted. The writer's image in the reader's mind is a bad one—more like a puppy chasing its own tail than that of a friendly businessperson.

That reveals an important principle about organizing business writing. *It involves two steps: planning and sharing.* Just as important as designing a good structure for our ideas is sharing that design with our reader.

"Let your structure show!" is a good motto for the well-organized business writer. Why hide the design? Better by far to share it so your reader can use the design to get the richest possible meaning.

First, let's talk about the planning phase of the organizing process.

The basic decision we need to make if we are to be well organized is to determine the purpose of our message. It's helpful to *think of that purpose as the response we want from our reader.* After all, we write to get results, and those results are behaviors by our readers. If we write to inform or to document, then the result we want is comprehension. If our

readers say "I see!" we have succeeded. If we are writing to request, then our response (or purpose) is readers who agree or take action. "It makes sense," or "Let's do it!" are the desired responses.

Organization starts with defining that purpose precisely. That's the planning part. The sharing part comes by stating that purpose in the opening paragraph of a letter or the position statement of a report, by effective transitions, and by topic sentences in subordinate paragraphs.

Purposes

Let's talk more about central purposes . . . what they are, where they should be stated, and what they are not.

We need to know first of all that few messages make any sense at all without a central purpose. From the reader's viewpoint, messages make the greatest sense when the purpose is stated at the very beginning. With letters, for example, the purpose should appear in the first paragraph. Thus readers know at once why they got the letter. That will tell them what's expected of them. When they know what's expected of them, they also know how to interpret the supporting ideas which will follow. In effective reports, readers immediately know the position taken by the report, and the areas of discussion into which all the succeeding data will be divided. These are important messages. Readers cannot get them by osmosis, or even by implication. Effective business writers state their purposes explicitly and early.

We must be able to distinguish between a central purpose and a subject, and between a central purpose and critical data.

- A purpose is the response we want from our readers.
- A topic is the subject within which the purpose exists.
- Critical data include ideas and evidence which must be expressed in order to secure the desired reader response.

Here is an example: On the topic of "promotable people" we may want to tell our reader about five deserving employees in our department. Our purpose is to get the reader to consider these five for the next opening in a higher position than they now occupy. Critical data would include the names and qualifications of the five employees.

Here is another example: Do you remember the letter to Mrs. Hayes in the "In a Nutshell" section of this chapter? Mrs. Hayes, you will recall, had wanted a refund for an unused portion of a travel ticket. Well, "Refund Application" is the topic; "Please send us additional information" is the purpose; critical data would include at least the six questions which Mrs. Hayes must answer.

And a third example: You are requesting payment of a delinquent account. Your purpose is to get payment. Critical data would include details about the actual amount, how late the customer is, and the consequences of continued delinquency. The topic is simply "Unpaid Balance."

Activity 6, on page 62, will give you practice in distinguishing between topics and purposes.

However, before we leave this distinction (among purposes, topics and critical data) let's re-examine that letter from Mr. Moslov. He was the man who wanted the book about *Designing Engineering Curricula*. His purpose was to get information; his subject was the search for the book; the data which he actually did provide was scarcely "critical." None of it helped the reader respond with the necessary information. (Well, perhaps the fact that Porter-Holt did not stock the book could be made helpful. But Mr. Moslow put that in a footnote!)

In well-organized letters the purpose is developed with just enough detail to make the response possible and attractive to the reader. "Just enough and no more!" Mr. Moslov might much more wisely have written a one-

156 East Laurel Lane
Poughkawsett, Washington
December 15, 19XX

Mr. Ralph Loy
234 Delphi St.
Decatur, Arizona 85099

Dear Sir:

We have contacted the Heller Publishing Company of 66 East 30th Street, Mohawk, Ohio, who prints a publication known as *Engineering in Business and Government.*

In their February, 19XX issue, we were impressed with articles on "Designing Engineering Curricula," of which we were told you were the author.

When we inquired where we might obtain the book, we were referred to you.

Could you possibly direct us to the publishers of "Designing Engineering Curricula," or a bookstore in the Seattle area where this book can be obtained?

Thanks for your kind attention to this matter.

Sincerely,

Sterling Moslov

Sterling Moslov

P.S. We checked with Porter-Holt and they did not have the book in their store.

SM:dl

paragraph letter. A good letter would have said, "Would you tell us the name of a Seattle store where we can buy your interesting book, *Designing Engineering Curricula?*" Then the complimentary close could say "Thanks so much." But as it is, Mr. Moslov wasted at least four of his six paragraphs, and his reader had to wander through all that extraneous detail just to find the well-hidden purpose! (Let's count his footnote as a paragraph.)

That letter should certainly help us see why organization is such an important investment in time saving for both writers and readers.

Principle of unity

A well-organized business letter has just one purpose. This principle of unity applies to other forms of good business writing: reports cover a greater span of subject, but good ones ultimately develop a single viewpoint or position. Manuals cover all phases of an operation, but each chapter focuses on a specific set of performance practices and policies. Even when informal memos deal with more than one temporarily important topic, the considerate writer assigns each topic to a separate paragraph. But in the business letter, this principle of unity is critical. Indeed it is so important that we should regard it as our first principle.

> PRINCIPLE 1. A WELL-ORGANIZED BUSINESS LETTER
>   HAS ONE PURPOSE—AND ONLY ONE.

There are several reasons for this. First of all, a reader will inevitably be confused if the letter seems to expect several unrelated responses. ("Just what does this character expect of me?" will be the probable response—but surely not the *desired* outcome.) Then there is another compelling reason for a single-purpose business letter: the filing system. Eventually someone must decide where to file the letter. If it deals with several subjects, or if it expects several responses, what's the poor filing

clerk to do? Perhaps we should note that our filing systems are notoriously inefficient. One government study indicated that a paper, once filed, has only one chance in five of ever coming out of the cabinet again. In what other system would we tolerate a 20 percent efficiency? Maybe in batting averages for baseball pitchers, but where else in the world of commerce, industry or government? Nevertheless, we *do* have filing systems and we do need a single place in which each letter can be filed in case it becomes that one-in-five which the reader will need later on.

Sequences

Now that we have established the basic principle of unity, let's review the effective placement of our statement of purpose. First! If not first, then early! This is the Principle of Primacy. It leads to our second basic principle.

> PRINCIPLE 2. STATE THE PURPOSE OF YOUR LETTER IN THE FIRST PARAGRAPH—PREFERABLY IN THE FIRST SENTENCE.

This means that we state our purpose in the first paragraph—hopefully in the first sentence. The reason would be obvious by now. The reader who can discover your purpose right at the start of the letter can make sense out of everything that follows . . . can relate each supporting detail to the central purpose. This mental processing allows the readers to handle their reading "workload" more rapidly and more pleasantly. Just think how much faster you could handle all your inbound mail if all the writers told you in the first sentence what response they were seeking from you!

There's another advantage to training yourself to put the purpose of your letters in the first paragraph: it frees you from that annoying and expensive habit of including irrelevant background. Need an example? Just recall Mr. Moslov and his search for the book. Need other examples? Just recall the letters you've received which begin by telling you the writer had received your letter on this same subject. Well, how could they be replying if they hadn't got your letter? Why not just go ahead and respond? If they trust your memory so little, they can include a subject or a reference line. If they do a decent job of organizing, they'll tie the subject into their statement of purpose in the opening paragraph.

Thus instead of writing "We have received your letter of March 4 in which you asked for prices of our frames," you can open with "Here are the prices you requested in your welcome March 4 letter." Why say, "On September 12 we wrote you about your possible interest in speaking to our annual Management Meeting in Tampa in July, and on September 25 you wrote that you were interested but that it would depend on the actual date and the topic. Well, we are happy to tell you that we have definitely set the Awards Dinner for July 17 and decided that we want to hear about 'The Challenge of an Encroaching Government to Modern Management!' "?

Why not open with something more to the point? Like, "We hope you like the topic and timing for the speech we've discussed. Can you talk to our managers at noon of July 17 on 'The Challenge of an Encroaching Government to Modern Management'?"

When you avoid needless background and acknowledgment, both you and your reader can get down to business right away. But first paragraphs sometimes do the writer more good than they do the reader. The writer hasn't got organized yet—but dictates an opening paragraph to get "warmed up." Thus writers merely acknowledge that the mails are still getting through; thus they distract readers with background which isn't pertinent or useful to this particular letter. A simple word linking the topic to the action you desire of your reader will do the job for both you and your reader.

Sharing your structure

Let's spend a few paragraphs talking about reference lines and subject lines. Both are helpful ways to "position" your readers, to make them ready for your message. Above all, they avoid boring your reader with a lot of irrelevance.

With a subject line you just name the topic; you don't write a history book about it. Here are some examples:

- Request for Recommendation: William F. Dysart, Jr.
- Commendation: Celia Dowgaard
- Summary of NSPI Conference
- Minutes of March 5 Steering Committee Meeting
- Overdue Account: #456-789-321
- Request for Funds: Attending Chicago SME Conference, June 2-7

Such subject lines appear two lines below the salutation; in the Simplified format they replace the salutation.

A reference line serves a different function. It helps readers locate the file related to this particular correspondence. Thus a reference line cites previous letters on the same subject. It may cite texts, manuals or legal documents. Reference lines include the initials of the writer, followed by the initials of the address, followed by the date of the letter. Here are examples:

JWL/GHS/7-5-80 indicates that someone whose initials are JWL wrote someone with the initials GHS on July 5, 1980.

KRA;PNY; 7/7/81 indicates a letter from someone initialled KRA to someone whose initials are PNY on July 7, 1981. Organizational custom determines what punctuation will appear between elements of the reference line.

Reference lines need not contain only a single item. For example:

JWT/KLP/5-5-80; KLP/JWT/4-20-80; Regs. Ch. 56, Par. 89

In the Block format the reference line usually appears in the upper right aligned directly beneath the date, an inch to an inch-and-a-half lower. In the Simplified format the reference line appears below (or in place of) the Subject Line. Thus they appear at the left margin.

When replying to a single letter (where there is no other correspondence on this transaction in the file), reference lines are a bit "heavy." The opening sentence can handle the referencing and state the purpose. For example:

- "We agree with the position you outlined in your May 3 letter."
- "Here are our answers to the questions you asked when you wrote us on March 2."
- "We are happy to share our views on tuition refunds, as requested in your May 21 letter."

Let's remind ourselves that stating the purpose first is always a friendly thing to do. Well—nearly always.

There may be a very few occasions when you will decide to postpone your statement of purpose. For instance: if the response you desire will be very distasteful to your reader. In just a few such messages you may decide to present the facts first, letting them lead your reader to the logic of the desired response. In a way, this is using logic for psychological purposes. When you do this, be very certain that you aren't merely manipulating—"toying" with your reader in a cat-and-mouse game which will eventually prove to be at least as distressing as the bad news itself.

What if your purpose is to apologize? Or what if you must apologize as part of the development of your purpose?

Do it first. Do it in the fewest possible words. But apologize for something specific. Better say "We regret our tardiness," or "We are sorry we shipped the wrong color," than just "Please accept our apologies" or "We goofed." That jocular phrasing isn't very appropriate to an apology unless you are very well acquainted with your reader. ('This doesn't mean that you must never use a "slangy" approach in business writing—only that you do so very rarely—and not when apologizing!)

Activities 7, 8, and 9, on pages 63, 64, and 65, will help you analyze unpopular purposes and proper placement of purpose statements.

Another basic organizing technique is to put similar things together—in separate sections, and above all in separate paragraphs. In fact, this is a great deal more than a mere technique; it is a basic principle.

> PRINCIPLE 3. PUT SUPPORTING IDEAS INTO SEPARATE
> PARAGRAPHS.

Paragraph unity is critically important. What does that mean? It means that any single paragraph discusses just one topic, or one subtopic, or one sub-subtopic, or just one sub-sub-subtopic. Why is it so important? Because readers do not follow our total plan unless they perceive each paragraph as a unit, developing *one* discrete unit.

Readers depend upon paragraph separation as a way to get meaning. How? When readers see the white space between paragraphs, they know that we are moving from one subtopic to another subtopic, that we are beginning to examine a new facet of a larger topic, or that we are starting to develop the central purpose from another viewpoint.

Does this next paragraph pass the "unity test?"

"There are three reasons why this unit cannot meet our needs. The total weight exceeds our maximum allowance by almost a full pound. It weights 80 ounces instead of the 66 ounces allowed in our specifications. The warranty extends for just 12 months, just half what we have always insisted upon for such units. Finally, the wiring violates several practices recommended by the Fire Underwriters Association. The dimensions are within tolerance, and the housing is exactly what we require."

Well, the first sentence tells the reader that the paragraph will develop reasons why the item is *not* acceptable. The evidence continues to do that until the very last sentence—and then the unity vanishes. Comments about requirements the unit *does* meet belong in a separate paragraph—if they belong in the message at all. (They might belong in the message if the readers are expected to be upset at rejecting this unit.

In that case, the approach would probably be to use a Pro/Con analysis, showing first the few acceptable things, then the overwhelming list of shortcomings, and finally drawing the conclusion that the "unit does not meet our needs." But the point is this: had that been the approach, the writer would have used three distinct phases, one for each step in reaching the conclusion.)

By and large, letters will have as many paragraphs as there are necessary ideas to develop the single central purpose. The opening paragraph will not list supporting ideas unless the letter is long, or the purpose distasteful.

By and large, a report will have as many areas of discussion as it takes to develop the position. Each area of discussion will be supported by as many paragraphs as it takes to develop that area.

Let's look at a few examples. Suppose the first paragraph of the letter says, "We are interested in the suggestion you made in your May 4 letter; however the proposal raises three interesting questions." The reader now knows that there will probably be three paragraphs in the rest of that letter. (If each question requires lengthy explanation and analysis, there will be three sections and a good many more paragraphs.) The reader doesn't yet know what the three questions are—only that the letter will raise and develop three issues. Most readers assume that the statement of the question will start each one of the developmental paragraphs (or sections).

Let's take a second example. Suppose the opening had been, "We are interested in the proposal outlined in your June 4 letter. We would like to probe further into your services. We have some questions about your availability, your fees and the nature of your interface with our own employees."

Again we know that there will be three supporting subsections, probably three paragraphs. In this case, however, the writer gave the reader a "sneak preview" of the supporting elements. This is often helpful, especially in long documents, or when writers want to share their value systems. (They list the most important issues first.) In the example, the writer has probably indicated that the biggest concern is "availability." This is just another manifestation of that Principle of Primacy. When developing subpoints, it is generally wise to do the most important one first. People ordinarily get things off their chest in the order of urgency, and readers expect to read first about the most significant issues. Even if this doesn't hold true in *every* case, there is evidence that readers *remember* what they read first. That in itself is sufficient reason to use the Primacy Principle when sequencing subsections.

If you are writing to express your own viewpoint, then your own order of urgency applies. If you can empathize with the reader, then the reader's order of urgency should become the sequence in which you develop subtopics, or in which you present evidence in a paragraph or items in a list.

Importance (urgency) is the most typical sequence. But we don't always know what the other person will regard as urgent. What do we do then? We find an alternative, such as:

- MOST ACCEPTABLE TO LEAST ACCEPTABLE—Useful when we know or can predict what the reader is apt to accept or reject.

- CHRONOLOGICAL—Especially useful when explaining processes or preparing action plans.

- FAMILIAR TO UNFAMILIAR—Helpful when explaining new concepts or processes, or when "selling" a concept that may threaten the reader (perhaps for no other reason than that it is new and strange).

- GEOGRAPHICAL—Rather mundane, but useful when analyzing systemwide performance or an organization's activity, area-by-area.

- CAUSE-TO-EFFECT—Useful in an audit report, or in any document which seeks to alter an existing condition in order to solve a problem or produce improvement.

- EFFECT-TO-CAUSE—Helpful when there is considerable resistance to change. If readers can agree with the description of the "effect," they can better accept the analysis of the cause—and of the suggested solution. Solutions always mean change, and cannot be expected to "sell themselves." Sequencing can help gain acceptance; it cannot guarantee it!

- SIZE—Largest-to-smallest, or smallest-to-largest. Useful in explaining some processes, or in "selling" some change programs.

- ORGANIZATIONAL UNITS—Especially helpful in reports in which members of certain units (Sales, Manufacturing, Accounting) would like an isolated picture of their own operation, or would like to concentrate on the data about their own sphere of responsibility.

Some writers like a "sandwich" psychology. They reason that there are *two* key positions in any document: first and last. They therefore sequence their subsections in one or the other of these patterns.

1. MOST IMPORTANT TO THE READER
   LEAST IMPORTANT SECTIONS
   SECOND-MOST-IMPORTANT SECTION

2. MOST ACCEPTABLE/POPULAR FROM THE READER'S VIEWPOINT
   LEAST ACCEPTABLE OR UNPOPULAR SECTIONS
   SECOND-MOST-ACCEPTABLE/POPULAR SECTION

Activity 7, on page 63, provides a chance to analyze a letter which uses this "sandwich" method.

No matter what sequence we select, the point is to have a rationale. It amounts to a basic principle.

> PRINCIPLE 4. ARRANGE THE SUPPORTING SECTIONS IN A METHODICAL ORDER.

When we have decided on that methodical order, we may have used logic as our basis—or we may have used psychology. In either case, it is helpful to our reader to share our plan by listing the topics in messages which are long, complex or distasteful. We needn't give the reason for the sequence—just a preview of what to expect as the document develops.

Activities 8, 9, 10, 11, and 12, on pages 64 through 70, provide lots of practice in analysis and decisions about effective sequence.

Of course there are other ways to give readers "previews" of what is to follow. One simple device is titles. These are useful in long documents. But the standard way to give previews for the next part of any written document is the good old topic sentence. This is the basic way we help readers set up expectations and gain insight into the flow of our ideas. The topic sentence tells the reader what the paragraph is about. It is so important to writing that it becomes a big principle.

> PRINCIPLE 5. WELL-ORGANIZED PARAGRAPHS BEGIN WITH A TOPIC SENTENCE.

Readers are accustomed to a conventional structure for paragraphs. It looks like the figure outline next page.

Why not capitalize upon that expectation to help your reader and to help yourself as you develop each paragraph. There are exercises for developing skill in creating topic sentences in Activity 13, page 70.

Writing the sentence is one thing; assuring the relevance of everything you put into the paragraph is another. That is unity. Maintaining the unity of each paragraph is vital; all clear writers do it. (This issue is so

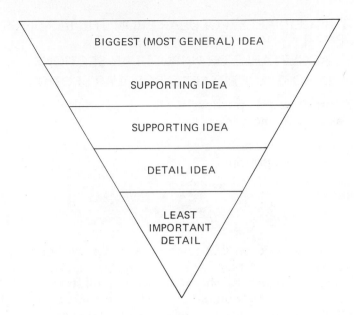

important that you'll see this Principle of Paragraph Unity stated again and again in this chapter!)

When readers start to read a paragraph, they expect everything in the paragraph to relate to the topic sentence. (That topic sentence is usually the first sentence.) In a paragraph about an applicant's education, they don't expect to read data about experience; they don't expect deficiency data in a paragraph about achievements; economic data should not appear in a paragraph about legal issues.

We can destroy paragraph unity by including too much detail as well as destroy it by including irrelevant information. That is to say, over-communication can destroy unity—and can thus destroy clarity. For an example, let's fly across the Atlantic and read this announcement, a poster in the London underground:

"Now that the Charing Cross Underground Station has been renamed Embankment, there will be no Charing Cross on the underground until the new Charing Cross (combining Trafalgar Square with the former Strand Station) opens with the Fleet Line. For economy's sake destination boards on trains going via Charing Cross, and the platform indicators and departure lists on the Northern Line will continue to show 'Charing Cross' during this period. Passengers travelling to Charing Cross British Rail Station should continue to change at Embankment until the new Charing Cross Underground Station opens."

As we quickly see, too much data can destroy the unity—and muddy the message!

The paragraph is a major unit of thought. Readers know this, and expect each paragraph to stand alone, covering *one* subject adequately.

We sometimes forget that white space also has meaning to readers. When white space comes between paragraphs, it indicates a transition. Such a signal makes the topic sentence all the more important; the reader wants to know as soon as possible (after each transition) what new topic comes next.

White space shares our structure in other ways: for example, it can mean subordination. When white space appears at the left side of the page, the indented items are presumed to be subordinate to the ideas which have immediately preceded. These indented items develop, in detail, the more general statements which appeared just before. Thus the white space used for indented lists permits the reader's mind to work just as the writer's mind worked during the organization process.

That takes us to another principle. We can add it to our list:

> PRINCIPLE 6. LET THE LAYOUT ON THE PAGE REFLECT
>   YOUR ORGANIZATION PLAN.

This principle translates itself into three techniques: titles, white space between paragraphs, and white space for indentations. None should be overused. Too many titles are a nuisance, even in a long document. Any title at all seems heavyhanded in a short document. Too many levels of subordination, or long parades of "short-short" paragraphs seem similarly "heavy."

Let's consider subordination. One or two levels of subordination will be about as much as your readers can handle. When you find yourself starting to type at the center of the page, or when you begin to wonder whether the next index symbol should go inside brackets or double-dashes . . . well, you've indented a few too many times! Besides, think of your poor reader! How many levels of subordination can the poor person be expected to keep in mind?

Indented lists are especially helpful to readers who must reply to your letter. If you are requesting information or short opinions, the indented list with plenty of white space for a reply permits the reader to make a "jiffy response" right there on your own letter. At any rate, if you ask your questions one at a time, you give your reader some attractive options:

1. To send your own letter back to you, with the responses intact on the original sheet of paper. Readers who need a copy for their own file are few in number—but those who do can make a copy on standard duplicating machines faster and cheaper than they can produce a letter.

2. To use your letter as a "notepad" for their dictation. They have the entire transaction in front of them. They can match your sequence—and thus match your priorities—by just going down the letter point-by-point.

That brings up another important device. You too can use the inbound letter as a notepad for your reply. You will save lots of time because the people you write to have already revealed their priorities. You need only respond to them in the same sequence they used when they wrote. What's more, they have revealed a great deal about their vocabulary; by using the same words your readers used, you are sure to be "talking their language." Besides, you'll need notes of some kind. Even gifted experienced writers dictate or draw up their actual products from some kind of notes.

Activity 14, on page 72, will give you some experience in using indented lists to make things easier and clearer for your reader. Activity 15, on page 74, will give practice in effective use of indented lists as well as other organizational techniques acquired in this chapter. In the "Chris Dawson In-Basket," available at the end of this book, you can practice both indented lists and use of inbound documents for a reply.

For the moment, let's just summarize by reminding ourselves that several great values result from using indented lists and the inbound letter as a notepad. They both help make the letter psychologically appropriate, and save time for writer and reader alike.

When should we stop? Well, unfortunately there is no magic formula to tell us when we have said enough to get our reader to respond as we wish—but that's the basic principle involved in stopping.

> PRINCIPLE 7. INCLUDE ONLY WHAT YOUR READER MUST KNOW IN ORDER TO UNDERSTAND OR AGREE.

That really translates to this: Include sufficient explanation or argument, sufficient logic or evidence to get people to say, "I see," or "I agree," or "I'll do it." The reader's responses govern what we include and what we exclude. Only our best estimates of our reader tell us when to stop. When we don't know anything about our reader, the best we can do is *ask what it would take to get the response out of us if the letter were directed to us?* This means that at times we have to put our own value systems out of our mind in order to be empathic with the value systems which motivate the people we wish to motivate through business writing. As anyone who ever had a difference of opinion with another human being will tell you, "T'aint easy!"

When our purpose is to inform or document we want to include enough to make things clear—but not so much background or so much detail that our readers lose the big picture. When our purpose is to persuade or get action, we want to include enough reasons to motivate and enough evidence to prove. Of course, what we want to prove is the validity, reasonableness, or urgency of the desired action. But in no case do we want to write so much that the reader gets bewildered, bored, overwhelmed, or trapped.

Writers often put readers to sleep when explaining. They often "protest too much" when persuading. When a reasonable person would accept your requested response, stop writing.

Another way to decide when to stop writing is to apply this very empirical test: *when you don't know what to say next, sign your name.* That will sometimes work for the end of a paragraph as well as for the end of a letter or a report. You catch yourself wondering how to bring this section to a close. You wonder if you've explained enough or if you've offered enough "proof." Yet you can't decide what to say next. Chances are it's time not to say *anything* next . . . just to go on to the next point—or to sign your name.

For some practice in putting an entire body of data together into a well organized business letter, you might like to try Activity 15, on page 74.

PUTTING THE PRINCIPLES INTO PRACTICE

✳ Activity 6

For each of the following, indicate which qualify as statements of purpose for a business letter:

A. Will you help us get information on small computers?

B. The rapid development of the computer industry.

C. Candidates for promotion.

D. I want to let you know which of my subordinates I consider eligible for promotion.

E. Which of the employees in your unit are eligible for promotion?

F. Training needs.

G. This will confirm our plans for the next meeting of the Management Club Steering Committee.

H. There are three reasons why you should approve this proposal.

I. Management Club: Plans for our next meeting.

J. Jay Kraemer is subject to disciplinary action as a result of three infractions of safety regulations.

L. Our most urgent training need is for knowledge about the new contracts with the AFL-CIO.

M. Steps we can take to cut costs.

N. Fourth-quarter goals.

O. Revised employee performance evaluations.

P. Our fiscal goals for next year include reducing the total budget, closer controls on travel costs, and increased expenditures for employee development.

Q. Here is my reaction to your proposal for staggered starting times.

R. I would really like to make three comments about the proposed training in Time Management.

S. Rae Smith, James Allen, and Clara McBride have met the requirements for classification as Accountant A.

Review

A, D, E, G, H, J, L, P, Q, R, and S do qualify as potential purposes; they could be developed into complete messages. The remainder are titles, not purpose statements.

✱ Activity 7

Underline the words which state the purpose of this next letter.

February 23, 19XX

Dwight Howell
720 Richmond
Rockwell, Wyoming 83666

It's my great pleasure to extend my thanks and congratulations on your recent purchase of a new Major Motors vehicle. When you chose Major, you expressed a trust which we deeply appreciate.

You, the individual owner, provide us with guidelines on which our business lives. Our products are designed and built with you in mind at all times. Accordingly, we take a sincere interest in the enjoyment you will get from your new Major Snowsled.

Speaking for myself, for your local Major dealer, and for the 12,000 people who make us Major Motors, I would like to express appreciation for your purchase.

Cordially,

Laura Grimes

Laura Grimes, Director
Corporate Sales

Do you like this letter? _____ Would you send it out over your signature? If you received it as a customer, how would you react?

If you dislike it, why? _____

The major purpose is stated twice, with "goodwill" comments sandwiched in between. The effect may be a bit effusive . . . an overstatement. Can you think of a way to share the idea that there are 12,000 employees who stand behind the project—yet introduce a *new* dimension in the last paragraph?

_____

Some organizations like to *welcome* the purchaser to the world of owners; that would be one way to vary the last paragraph.

In what ways is the format inconsistent with the friendly purpose? Or with the normal Block or Simplified guidelines?

_____

_____

✳ Activity 8

Analyze the letter below by answering these questions:

A. In which paragraph is the main purpose stated? _____

B. Underline the actual words which express that purpose.

C. What possible reasons can you find for the writer's decision to place the purpose in this location?

_____

_____

_____

D. If you were relocating the Purpose Sentence, where would you put it?

_____

E. If you reworded the Purpose Sentence, how would you express that idea?

_____

_____

MERCHANDISERS, INC.
Box 3451-A
Byers, Oklahoma 74532

Dear Customer:

Occasionally good customers like you may overlook payment of their monthly credit card statements.

Since we did not receive your payment last month, your remittance by return mail would be greatly appreciated.

If you have already sent us this check, please disregard this letter and accept our thanks.

Very truly yours,

P. Garrett

P. Garrett, Manager
Credit Card Division

✱ Activity 9

Here is another collection letter, written after a longer lapse in payment. Let's analyze the tone and technique by contrasting this letter with the one we analyzed in Activity 8.

In Activity 8, what details are included only to add a friendly tone?

_____

_____

In this letter, what details serve that same "friendly tone" purpose?

_____

Mr. G. L. King
967 Broyden Place
Lewis, Texas 75678

Dear Mr. King:

    This requires your immediate attention.

    Your Merchandisers Credit Card account is now two payments past due. Even so, I note that you have recently made use of your card to incur additional charges. Under these circumstances, prompt and substantial payment is imperative.

    Unless your check for $87.75 is received within the next ten days, I will be forced to suspend your account and declare the full balance due and payable.

Thank you.
Yours truly,

P. Garrett

P. Garrett, Manager
Credit Card Division

This letter is written as if the purpose were to inform. However, the actual purpose is to get _____ . What do you think of the approach Mr. Garrett took? Why? _____

_____

Explain and evaluate the placement of the Purpose Statement:

_____

_____

✳ Activity 10

Read these questions so you will know what to look for as you analyze the letter printed on this page:

This letter's purpose is To INFORM ____, to REQUEST ____ or to DOCUMENT ____? Quote the Purpose Sentence:

In what type sentence is the purpose framed? _____

What rationale might the writer use for this format of the Purpose Sentence?

Is the purpose sentence placed in the most advantageous position? ☐YES ☐ NO

THE SUN-VAL COMPANY
55 Lee Road
Ames, Maine

July 1, 19XX

Mr. D. E. Dabney
Box 334
Vesta, Vermont

Would it be possible for you to speak to our Sun-Val Management Club at our October 15 meeting?

We are a relatively young, very informal group which welcomes any innovative approach to managing people. We know your reputation in this field, and hope you will give us the chance to hear your well-known remarks on "Tomorrow's Manager."

If you are interested and available, won't you phone me collect at 802-555-6667 whenever convenient? When we chat on the telephone we can discuss financial arrangements—and I'll be delighted to answer questions you might have.

Hope to see you on October 15.

D. L. Kaynes
D. L. Kaynes, President
Sun-Val Management Club

DLK:bh

✱ Activity 11

These exercises will give you practice in recognizing sequences and in deciding what sequences are appropriate.

A. In what sequence are these supporting ideas (or Areas of Discussion) now arranged?

> Corporate Problems
> Departmental Problems
> Section Problems

B. How might you arrange these sections of a letter or report? (Put numbers alongside them to show your decision.)

> New England Region
> Southeast Region
> Mountain State Region
> Middle Atlantic Region
> Upper Midwest Region

C. Suppose your letter needed to share these three ideas. Arrange them in a satisfactory psychological sequence.

> The absenteeism problem continues to plague us
> There have been no industrial accidents in the past quarter.
> There is still a considerable amount of pilferage; this problem gets worse every month.

D. From the following, select the Purpose Statement for a letter which informs, and then sequence the remaining elements into a pattern that's both logical and psychological.

> The January-March period accidents were up just 1 percent over the same period a year ago.
> In the fourth quarter accidents were 18 percent below the previous year.
> This year's safety record was encouraging.
> During the peak summer period there were no disabling accidents.

Review

In Example A, size would probably be the basis on which that sequence was established.

Geographical sequences seem logical: East to West (or vice-versa) for Example B.

How about putting the best news first? If so, industrial accidents, absenteeism, and pilferage would be the sequence. If you choose importance as your plan, it would be pilferage, absenteeism, and industrial accidents.

The third statement in D is the Purpose Statement. It should come first. Good-news-to-bad would indicate summer, fourth quarter, then January-March. Of course one might also use a chronological pattern—but that's a bit dull.

* Activity 12

First, read the following paragraphs and select the purpose paragraph. Put a "1" alongside it.

Indicate with the numbers 2, 3, and 4 the appropriate sequence for each of the remaining paragraphs.

A. Another problem at Quincy is communication with the rest of the company. Inbound mail sometimes arrives as many as seven days after leaving the home office. Recent economy measures removed Quincy from the Administrative Private-Line Telephone.

The Quincy Station is to be commended for its effective safety program, for the progress it has made in meeting production quotas; it needs corporate assistance in improving communications with the rest of the company.

There have been no disabling accidents to employees at Quincy in the last eighteen months; this is the only station in the entire company with so enviable a span of accident-free operation.

Although production this year is still slightly below quota (98.9% of goal) the trend is upward. A year ago the plant accomplished only 97.8% of its quota; as recently as three years ago the production was as low as 94.6% of established goals.

Now do the same for the paragraphs of this next letter.

B. Upon arrival at the airport, Tony DeVanna will get in touch with you. Tony is our local Chief Sales Representative, and will personally escort you to the Host Hotel for check-in.

We feel that you know more about the flights you wish to use between your home and Onawa, so we will leave reservations in your hands. As you know, the corporation will reimburse you for tourist class travel on a round-trip basis, and for ground transportation in your own city. You can just submit the air fare and ground costs, with the billing for your professional fee.

We are delighted that you will be speaking to our Annual Sales Rodeo in Onawa next month! I wanted to let you know as soon as possible about the arrangements for your trip.

All the food expenses in Onawa will be taken care of for you. Luncheons are buffets in the large ballroom—just go in and help yourself. When you register at The Host Hotel you will receive tickets for dinner on the day of your appearance. Won't you just sign your breakfast bills so we can pay them with your hotel bill?

Perhaps we have forgotten some detail of your appearance. May we count on you to phone me collect if you have other, unanswered questions? You can reach me at area code 444, phone number 555-9992, extension 45.

Select the Purpose Paragraph, label it #1, and then indicate an effective sequence for the remaining paragraphs in this next business letter:

C. Ralph Grogan is a serious contender for the position: he was our second choice when we filled a similar position last year. He meets all the qualifications specified in the job description, and is highly regarded in his present work as a Planner.

Terry Robbins is a real "comer," and you will certainly want to talk to her before you make your final decision. She lacks the college degree specified in the Practices Manual, but has attended related extension courses at the University. She has accumulated over 25 credit hours in Accounting and Financial Management.

Slightly less ready for promotion is Bertha Davies. I say "slightly less ready" because she has been in the Planner classification for less time than the others. However, Bertha holds both a B.A. degree in Accounting and an M.F.A. in Business Administration.

Sid Warner cannot truly be regarded as a serious contender for this position, but you would do all of us a big favor if you would give him a courtesy interview. Sid's morale is pretty low just now, so I think you can see what I am driving at.

I am pleased to nominate three people for your consideration in filling your opening for Senior Planner.

Review

In Example A, the indicated sequence is 4, 1, 2, and 3. This is based on the order in which the topics are listed in the Purpose Paragraph.

In Example B, the third paragraph ("Welcome!") states the purpose. Thus the sequence should probably be 3, 2, 1, 4, 5. That last parapraph strikes us as an effective way to maintain two-way communication . . . and to close this letter.

In Example C, the last paragraph states the purpose. The candidates should probably be listed in an objective sequence—except for Sid Warner, whose inclusion on this list represents a questionable practice. How about alphabetical? In that case we would have 3, 4, 2, 5, 1. That gives us a problem with Bertha Davies—at least with that first phrase that she is "slightly less promotable." We would need to find a new transition. If you felt that you wanted to list them in the order of your preference, then we only know that the last paragraph would be 1 and that the fourth paragraph would be 5. The rest is up to you.

✱ Activity 13

We have discovered the importance of good topic sentences. In the space at the top of these paragraphs, add a topic sentence:

A. _____

  _____

The first element is known as unity; it says that each element in the writing will apply to the central topic of the writing—that nothing irrelevant will appear. A second element is known as coherence. This simply means that the elements are congruent, that one leads logically to the next. Finally, good writing has emphasis; the prose itself makes clear which are the most significant ideas.

B. _____

  _____

It is imperative that the unit be economical; we cannot invest more than ten dollars. Next in importance is size; the unit must fit into a cubicle one foot by one foot by two feet.

C. _____

  _____

One of the most important reasons is that the reader wants to know just as soon as possible what topic he is reading about—and what position the writer takes toward that topic. This is especially important when the writer wants him (the reader) to take action. Another big reason is that he can more easily write or dictate his reply if the first paragraph reminds him of the purpose of the inbound letter. Finally, he can better evaluate the merit of the supporting ideas if, when he reads them, he already knows the frame of reference in which they are presented.

D. _____

_____

The five years of experience may seem a great deal, but we have found that our successful Planners do have this much company experience behind them; men with less experience just don't seem to work out. We would waive the college degree for a candidate who had at least three years of college and extra related experience with another firm. The intelligence (average or better) is an absolute "must."

E. _____

_____

In the first place, the unit exceeds fluctuation tolerances by at least 10%. Of next importance, the sound levels are distracting—would prove extremely uncomfortable for the packing personnel who would work alongside this unit. And finally, the costs are prohibitive; we budgeted $25.00 per unit and these average out to nearly $40.00.

G. _____

_____

When I first saw Trabert that afternoon, he seemed a trifle unsteady on his feet. Later I decided he must have been drinking, because I could detect the odor of alcohol whenever I approached him. The situation seemed really serious at approximately 1:20 p.m. when I saw him lurch toward the water fountain. He was leaning against the wall when I got over to where he was. My exact words were, "Do you feel okay?" This question apparently angered him considerably, for Trabert then came out with the profanity. (I prefer not to put it in writing, but will testify to the exact words, if necessary.) The profanity caused me to decide to send Trabert to the office. As you know, he refused to do as I requested, so I made it into an order. What I actually said was, "This is an order, Trabert. You are relieved or your duties here and are to report to the General Foreman's

Office at once." He told me where I could go, so I immediately went to the nearest telephone to call General Security.

Review *(Possible wordings)*

A. Good writing consists of three elements: unity, coherence, and emphasis.

B. We have two criteria for this unit: economy and size.

C. There are several reasons why the basic purpose should appear in the first paragraph. (In this example, the reasons are too long to be listed—especially in so short a paragraph.)

D. Candidates should have three qualifications: five years of experience, a college degree, and average intelligence.

E. The unit fails to meet our needs on three points: excess fluctuation, noise and cost. (To build up an emotional response, you may have chosen to repeat the word "excessive": "excessive fluctuation, excessive noise, and excessive cost.")

F. Here is my summary of what happened that afternoon, OR:
Here is my description of Trabert's behavior that afternoon.

✳ Activity 14

On the facing page, rewrite these paragraphs so you effectively use indented lists to share your structure with your reader:

Before we can issue a replacement or a refund, we will need some more information from you.

For example, we need to know the store in which you purchased the knife. That should include the name and the address. If you have a sales slip we need the date. If you have lost the sales slip please estimate the date as closely as possible.

You might want to send the sales slip instead of copying the information.

Would you also tell us the date on which you first noticed the defect, and the name of the exact store where the dealer told you there were no warranties on our cutlery. We want to prove that there are valid warranties and that we stand behind our product.

Please include a complete description of the precise problems you have experienced.

You'll probably want to do a complete overhaul, so the reader sees you and your organization as logical and considerate! There is room for your version here in the workbook.

✱ Activity 15

Arrange these elements into a coherent, well-organized letter to the local vendors of your products. It will be a bit "hard sell," but it's closely modeled on a real letter. Above all, it will give you a pleasant exercise in arranging ideas so they are both logical and psychologically sequenced for your reader.

KwikKleen Powder eliminates any danger of spillage.
HiHue Colors are absolutely fadeproof.
Skidless Karpet will retail for $4.95 per square yard.
We are happy to announce three new products this year.
There are four exciting details for the HiHue Color series.
Skidless Karpet is an improved version of the old Stayput line.
HiHue includes ten colors marketed by no competitor.
Far and away the most exciting is the HiHue line.
These three products are HiHue colors, KwikKleen Powder and Skidless Karpet.
KwikKleen is 30% more effective than any liquid cleaner.
HiHue products are guaranteed for life against spotting from water.
Now let me tell you a bit about KwikKleen Powder.
HiHue Colors are available in both carpeting and throw rugs.
Doesn't HiHue seem the most promising seller in a long, time?
KwikKleen Powder will sell for less than any liquid competitor.

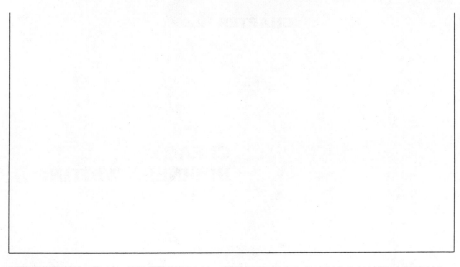

Review

Of course there is no "absolutely correct" way to arrange those ideas. However, the version listed here uses as many of the organizational techniques as possible.

We are happy to announce three new products this year. These products are HiHue Colors, KwikKleen Powder and Skidless Karpet.

Far and away the most exciting is the HiHue line. There are four exciting details of the HiHue Color series:

1. *(Note:* Several sequences make good sense for
2. the items in this list. The items to be
3. included are "Absolutely fadeproof," "Ten colors,"
4. "Guaranteed for Life" and "Available in Carpeting and throw rugs."

Doesn't HiHue seem the most promising seller in a long time?

Now let me tell you about KwikKleen Powder. KwikKleen is 30% more effective than any liquid cleaner. KwikKleen Powder will sell for less than any liquid competitor. KwikKleen Powder eliminates any danger of spillage.

Skidless Karpet is an improvement of the old Stayput line. Skidless Karpet will retail for $4.95 per square yard.

As we mentioned before you started arranging the ideas, this is a "hard sell" letter. That becomes painfully apparent when we see the final version with that incredible repetition of the product names. Those were there as signposts to help you identify the relationship of items in the list. You can now edit the final version so that nauseous redundancy is eliminated. (You might also like to change some of those "clever" spellings of the products!)

CHAPTER 3

CLEAR
BUSINESS WRITING

IN A NUTSHELL

There are several reasons why we write, and there are certain criteria for effective business writing. If we write well, our messages will be well-organized, clear and friendly. In this chapter, we will pay special attention to the techniques for writing clearly.

Clarity consists of putting a minimum number of words together to express a complete, concrete thought. As a writer, you have three basic tools to use in expressing yourself clearly: sentences, words and punctuation.

First, let's look at sentences.

It may be helpful to think of a sentence as a bridge . . . a bridge that takes your readers from what they already know to what they didn't know.

A child builds very short bridges, and puts just a few words on each. Thus children speak a kind of pidgin English: "Me love you" or "Danny

wants cookie." Children's sentences are cute—but tiresome. They also tend to be very clear.

Understandably, as adults we try to escape the simplistic monotony of the childlike sentence. There is some evidence that we overcompensate; we develop some incredibly complex sentences . . . structures which confound even the shrewdest of our readers!

The lesson seems obvious: that short sentences tend to be clearer than long sentences. So, in order to write clearly, should we avoid all long sentences? Not necessarily! A sentence doesn't get confusing simply because it's long. More often, sentences are obscure because they try to take a reader in too many directions. Good bridges get people to one specific destination; good sentences convey just one basic idea.

A sentence is too long if readers can't grasp the idea when they finish reading the sentence the first time. Stated positively, sentence length is satisfactory when the reader gets the message on the first reading . . . after just one trip "across the bridge."

How about the sentence at the top of the next page? Do you think it is too long?

"When you have finished reading this sentence, you will know three things: that short sentences are not necessarily good; that long sentences are not necessarily bad; and that the test of a good sentence is whether the reader can get the message on the first reading."

We would call that a good sentence. It has both unity and continuity.

What do those words mean? Unity means that the entire sentence expresses one central idea—and only one. Continuity means that the parts fit together in a logical pattern and in a logical sequence: the subject, then the action, and sometimes the object of that action.

Let's study continuity a bit more. Continuity makes a sentence in which the readers easily find the subject and the verb. In the sentence we just examined, "you" and "will know" are adjacent and early in the sentence. Readers can also see (literally *see*!) that there are three objects to the verb "will know." The colon tells the reader to expect a list of those three things.

How about this? Is it a clear sentence?

"A run deck has been developed to allow programmers to upgrade test versions of their program from the online file where the test version resides to the absolute file relative to the online file of the element the test version will replace."

Well, it starts out clear enough. But then it gets heavy with efforts to specify—and we lose the thought! Our efforts to specify and describe are commendable. But there's a better way to do it. We'll learn the technique by examining a sentence which doesn't use it:

"The products which were defective were returned to the section which did the welding which was faulty."

After one reading we want to go on a "which hunt"! That's because the writer used clauses—not adjectives—to describe. We can say "defective products" and save words; "The welding section" and "faulty welding" would also clarify the message. We focus on the key words, and achieve clarity by using adjectives instead of clauses to specify and describe.

Adjectives do another nice thing: they show up right alongside the words they describe. Clauses may show up in some funny places. Like this one: "I admire Thomas Jefferson because of his integrity who wrote the Declaration of Independence." Adjectives can also avoid dangling participles like this classic: "Being in a dilapidated condition, I was able to buy the house very cheap." Reduce that to an adjective, and you'll put the word "dilapidated" alongside the word "house"—not leave it as a description of the pronoun "I."

Sometimes we want to describe, or limit actions. An English teacher once told us to do that with adverbs. Adverbs tell how an action is done, or how it should be done. Is that what the author did in this sentence?

"We must complete the task with great dispatch, making certain that all the work is done with total accuracy."

No. Those are phrases—not adverbs. "With great dispatch" and "with total accuracy" are prepositional phrases. Your first clue is words like "with" and "at" or "in." Those words are certain signs of prepositional phrases, just as words ending in "ly" are signs of adverbs. Remember: phrases are the long, expensive way to describe actions; adverbs are the short, economical method.

If we use adverbs, that sentence will read "complete the job quickly, making sure all the work is totally accurate." See. One word does the work of three each time we use an adverb instead of a phrase.

Our entire sentence structure is important. Research at Harvard in 1962 proved that the time taken to respond to a sentence varies according to the grammatical structure. Readers can process active, affirmative, declarative sentences most rapidly. A declarative sentence is just a sentence that makes a statement. Affirmative sentences are positive statements. The first sentence below is an affirmative, the second a negative statement.

"You know, Sam, this is a good letter!"
"You know, Sam, this isn't a bad letter!"

Now let's look at two more sentences:

"The order will be granted by the task force to the lowest bidder."
"The task force will grant the order to the lowest bidder."

The second is the active version; the former is passive. If readers prefer active voice, there may be two reasons: the "upbeat" quality and the lesser number of words. To keep your sentences active, find the action ("grant" in the example) and then start your sentence with the *actor*—the person or element taking the action.

How about this sentence. Is it clear?

"The irrelevance of the midsectional components contributes to an ambiguity about the viability of the total conceptual framework."

Of course it isn't clear! It tells us nothing. What tool did the writer use badly? Words.

Words are tools—and surely we can select better tools to express our ideas than those in that last example. Let's look at a few rules for making good choices when we select words.

Suppose you ask a friend, "How much golf do you play?" And suppose she replies, "Sometimes." "Sometimes" is vague, rather up in the clouds. To one person it might mean "quite often" and to another "seldom." A bit more definite is the word "occasionally." But we would still have to ask, "How often?" Unless our friend replied "weekly" or "daily," we wouldn't know the exact answer.

So, our first rule about words is SELECT SPECIFIC WORDS.

On that ladder of ambiguity in the accompanying picture, anything higher than "him" is getting a trifle foggy, isn't it? When we use words like "they" we risk total misunderstanding. Readers may think we're talking about totally wrong "them's." Remember, words are about as clear as they are specific.

But what if we must use a specific word which is so specialized that we're certain our reader has never heard of it? Take the word "andragogy." If you want to talk about the science of adult learning, "andragogy" is the precise word you need. And don't despair—even if you're certain your

reader has never heard the word. Go ahead and use it—but define it within parentheses the first time you use the word in any document. Just say something like this:

"One topic on our agenda at the Supervisory Development Seminar is andragogy (the science of how adults learn)."

In that example, we've learned our second rule: BE SURE TO USE WORDS WHICH ARE FAMILIAR TO YOUR READER. IF THE WORD ISN'T FAMILIAR, DEFINE IT THE FIRST TIME YOU USE IT.

Clear writers also follow a third rule: USE AS MANY SHORT WORDS AS POSSIBLE. This doesn't mean that long words are bad; it only means that too many long words close together are hard to read. Look at this sentence:

"The efficacy of hydrochloric acid is indisputable, but the corrosive residue is incompatible with metallic permanence."

Legend has it that this was the reply given to a plumber who asked the Bureau of Standards about using hydrochloric acid to clean out pipes. There is, of course, no way to avoid the long technical word "hydrochloric," but words like "will rot out the pipes" would surely talk more clearly to the plumber who wanted information. (The legendary version has it that after further inquiry, the plumber was advised: "Don't use hydrochloric acid. It eats the hell out of the pipes!")

Long words are problems for readers when there are too many of them too close together, and when a short word would say it just as clearly.

There's one more function for words: we can USE WORDS AS SIGNPOSTS TO SHARE OUR STRUCTURE WITH OUR READERS. This is a great aid to clarity.

Words can tell a reader to link successive ideas, or to contrast them, or to expect an example. Words, used as signposts, can be important aids to your reader on the trip through your ideas.

Among the commonest signposts are "linking" words. These are words like: "and" and "also" and "too" and "next" and "third" or "fourth." Such words help your reader link ideas when you put these words at the start of paragraphs and sentences, and between your clauses inside sentences.

However, other signposts communicate contrasts. They announce sharp turns in your thought pattern; they help your reader change viewpoints with you. A few common "turn signals" are "however," "but" and "yet." Phrases like "on the other hand" or "in opposition to this" can also be helpful.

Readers sometimes have trouble knowing whether an idea is a generalization or a specific example of that general statement. We can help them by giving signposts like "for instance" and "for example." This type of transition is like the "Point of Interest" signs along a highway.

Words can also signal such logical processes as drawing a conclusion from previous statements. "Therefore," "thus," "so" and "hence" are helpful when you draw an inference *after* presenting the data.

And so we have accumulated four ways to use words so they contribute to the clarity of our business writing:

RULE 1 FOR WORDS: USE SPECIFIC WORDS.

RULE 2 FOR WORDS: USE FAMILIAR WORDS—OR DEFINE NEW TERMS

RULE 3 FOR WORDS: USE SHORT WORDS WHENEVER POSSIBLE.

RULE 4 FOR WORDS: USE WORDS AS SIGNPOSTS TO SHARE TRANSITIONS.

Our third tool for clear writing is punctuation. In its simplest form, punctuation tells readers that they are starting across a new bridge . . . beginning a new sentence. Then punctuation tells them they have crossed it. A capital letter tells them that the sentence is starting. A period tells them that the sentence made a statement. An exclamation mark tells them that there is great feeling associated with the statement. A question mark indicates that some sort of response, actual or rhetorical, is expected.

Sometimes there are two lanes of traffic across the bridge. These may be parallel thoughts going in the same direction, or contrasting thoughts traveling in opposite directions. (In that case the unifying principle of the sentence is that very contrast.) In either case we use a semicolon to separate the clauses.

Let's look at an example to show thoughts in parallel:

"Training is useful in acquiring new behaviors; feedback systems are useful in maintaining those behaviors."

Here is an example where two clauses show contrast:

"Training is useful in giving people new behaviors; it is of no value when they can already do what the training teaches."

When we give lists or examples, we need to use colons. Readers quickly comprehend lists. But when we use the end of a sentence to explain the first part of the sentence, we're being rather sophisticated: we're giving an immediate "illustration." The official name for this is "explication."

This transition is a tricky one, so it's wise to use both the colon and the words "for example" or "for instance" or "to illustrate."

And of course there are ideas we wish to include as "asides" . . . little extra related thoughts which enrich the main message of the sentence. These are relevant, but they are subordinate to the main thought. Thus we put them inside parentheses. Defining jargon is another good use for parentheses, as in the example we saw earlier about "andragogy."

You can get the opposite effect—give emphasis—by using dashes to sur-round or precede an element. The sentence you just finished reading is one example of that. Here is another:

"When subordinates write effective letters—let them know!"

It must be apparent now that punctuation provides a "signpost" function for our readers. Punctuation, like transition words, contributes to clarity in writing.

Remember, as writers we want our reader to understand our message with just one reading. A good organizational plan, which we share, can help achieve this effect. In addition, we have three other tools: sentences, words and punctuation. If we use these tools wisely, we will create clear business writing.

IN GREATER DETAIL

What do we mean by clarity? Clarity is the quality of business writing which permits our reader to say "I see" after just one reading.

Clarity results in part from good organization—provided we share that good organizational plan. It also results from intelligent use of three other tools of language.

Those three tools are sentences, words and punctuation. The rest of this chapter will examine each tool in some detail. We will first discuss theory and techniques for each; then at the end of the chapter there are practice exercises. Let's start our study with sentences.

Sentences

In our English classes we learned that a sentence expresses one complete thought. We also learned that a sentence starts with a capital letter; that it ends with a period, question mark, or exclamation mark. That "one complete thought" concept is a useful technical definition, and the details about punctuation provide a useful technical description.

But it is also useful to look at a sentence from a non-technical point of view. Just think of what sentences do for your reader. Once you do that, you can picture a sentence as a bridge . . . a bridge which gets your reader from the unknown to something known. Such bridges are strong enough to carry only one complete thought; they don't get to the opposite shore unless they are a *complete* thought; punctuation tells the reader at the "other side" whether the trip made a statement, asked a question, or expressed great feeling.

It's vital that there be a complete thought. "In a moment," or, "When we have more information," or "Hmmmm" can be sensible thoughts in face-to-face communication; we do our readers very little good when we put them into our business writing. They are just *parts* of a thought; they do not stand alone. Our facial expressions and vocal inflections add meaning to such fragments when we are speaking, but it's hard to add such inflection to the printed page, so fragments are rarely useful to business writers. When such partial sentences are useful, it's to add informality—not clarity—to our messages.

What about the requirement that a sentence contain *just one* complete thought? Does that precept also hold up in business writing? You bet it does! Now this doesn't mean that sentences must be childlike in their simplicity—only that they be clearly unified.

Children build very simple sentences. Childish sentences often have a subject, a verb, and an object—and nothing more. Thus we parody childlike sentences when we say, "I have a dog. My dog is Spot. Spot can run. Run Spot run. See Spot run."

The ideas we need to express in business writing are far more complex than that, so we build more complicated bridges. Instead of using an entire sentence to establish the fact that we have a dog, another to announce the dog's name, and a third to explain Spot's skills, we link these ideas into one sentence. We can thus develop a unified sentence with several dimensions. Thus adult sentences try to define and describe simultaneously, to show dependencies and linkages, conditions and relationships, parallels, series, and contrasts; they establish sequences and processes, criteria and judgments.

But when any single sentence tries to express too many of these things, the reader gets lost. The sentence has lost clarity. That's why clarity depends upon clear-cut "one-ness" for every sentence . . . with a minimum number of words. Way back in 1893 L. A. Sherman's *Analysis of Literature* noted that the written sentence is growing shorter year by year. Flesch quotes this in his *The Art of Readable Writing* (p. 122) and then asks, "Have we arrived at the end of the process? A typical magazine article now runs to less than 20 words per sentence." Then Flesch regrets, "But as soon as we get the itch to appear more serious and dignified, up it goes . . . "

As Flesch implies, in our adult effort to avoid the simplistic monotony of "Run Spot run" we overcompensate with some incredibly complex sentences . . . with sentence bridges which collapse of their own weight.

The lesson seems obvious: to write clearly, write only short sentences. Well, it isn't quite that simple. Sentences don't get confusing merely because they are long. They get confusing when readers cannot see the relationship of the parts. If a sentence doesn't take the reader in just one direction, the reader is certain to grow confused—probably to get lost. If a sentence does go in just one direction, but uses too many words to get there, the main idea and the reader both get lost.

Business writing is unfortunately full of cumbersome, confusing sentences. Why? Surely the writers aren't trying to hide their meanings. Probably they once wrote mature-but-clear sentences in high school or college compositions. Could they be trying to impress someone? If so, they succeed only in seeming pompous. And if they are trying to impress someone, who is it? Surely not their readers. More likely, it's their bosses they want to impress.

If we study the prose style of people at various organizational levels, we get some evidence that the effort to sound impressive produces pompous, unclear business writing. Let's look at it graphically. In our figure, the vertical direction indicates position; the horizontal placement indicates complexity of prose style: big, abstract words in long, complex sentences. Note the "Middle-Management Bulge." Those writers are either trying to impress the people "at the top," or are incredibly gullible about the myths of "how they want you to write around here"!

PROSE STYLE — AND ORGANIZATIONAL PLACEMENT

TOP MANAGEMENT

EASY TO READ   HARD TO READ

UPPER-MIDDLE MANAGEMENT

MIDDLE MANAGEMENT

FIRST-LINE SUPERVISORS AND STAFF SPECIALISTS

NEW EMPLOYEES ON EARLY WRITING ASSIGNMENTS

The tragedy is twofold: the obscure messages and the deterioration of writing skill in new members of the organization.

A sentence is too long when the reader cannot get the sense after just one reading. The federal government has discovered this. In an effort to cut down on the paper explosion, it formed the Federal Paperwork Commission. There were dreams of cutting down on paperwork —especially with forms which citizens must complete. The results were discouraging. Recently the Office of Management and Budget announced that although the number of forms had been reduced, citizens had to spend an added 13,000,000 man-hours in filling them in! The lesson? Simplicity probably starts with the sentence unit.

Readers can get the sense of sentences, no matter how long, when those sentences have both unity and continuity. What do we mean by "unity" and "continuity"?

Unity merely means that a sentence has one idea—and only one idea. Continuity means that the parts of the sentence fit together in a visible, logical sequence. Here is a long sentence which has both qualities.

"Our July meeting will try to develop an action plan for changing employee performance, and to assign key responsibilities for each phase of that plan, with realistic deadlines for each phase; it will not revisit the question of what the desired performance standards should be, because we agreed on those at our June session."

There is unity: the entire sentence defines the scope of the July meeting, including what it will *not* involve. There is continuity because the subjects of each clause ("meeting" and "it") come directly before the verbs ("will try" and "will not revisit"). The semicolon clearly divides the two main clauses. The second object of the verb "will try" is focused by repeating the word "to." The words "will not" appear early in the second clause, letting the reader know immediately that this clause contrasts with the first one.

How important is unity? In business writing it is very important. It reflects an organized mind and shares a total thought clearly. In *The Careful Writer*, Bernstein says: "The one-idea-to-a-sentence dictum is designed for those kinds of writing in which instant clarity and swift reading . . . are dominant desiderata." Bernstein gives newspaper articles and technical papers as examples; he might as easily have mentioned business letters and reports. What businessperson, confronted with 6000 pages of desk reading each year, wants to read those pages twice in order to make sense of them?

Activity 16, on page 112, gives you practice in recognizing unity by distinguishing between unified and non-unified sentences.

One symptom of unity and continuity is the visibility of the Subject-Verb-Object elements. When readers can clearly identify the main elements as they read, they can respond to the logic of the sentence dynamically. In the sentence "Haste makes waste" there can be no doubt about those three elements. Structurally, that sentence is just about like "Spot is a dog." The concepts are vaster, but both structures are simple Subject-Verb-Object sentences.

That should make two things clear:

1. That structure as well as words share meanings, and

2. As we add words between the Subject, the Verb and the Object, we make our readers work harder to get the sense of our sentences.

A reasonable amount of mental effort by readers isn't entirely a bad idea. Look at the examples on the next page:

"Our goal, a 17 percent increase in gross sales, seems reasonable."

"Our goal for next year, a 17 percent increase in gross sales, seems reasonable to those of us who have faith in our product."

"Our corporate marketing goal for next year, a 17 percent increase in gross sales, seems reasonable and feasible—especially if you have just a little faith in our product, our sales people, and the national economy."

By that last version, the reader is probably asked to work about as hard as readers ought to have to work. The extra descriptions in the first part, the parallel judgments ("reasonable" and "feasible"), the parallel objects of "if you have just a little faith"—all these things approach an overload. It's time to stop.

What might we learn from that example? That you can control the clarity of your own business sentences . . . and that you do so partly by clearly revealing the Subject-Verb-Object pattern.

Activities 17 and 18, on pages 113 and 114, will help you refresh yourself in what is probably a forgotten skill: recognizing these important elements: Subject-Verb-Object.

We can help readers see the main words of our sentences without writing short, choppy sentences. In other words, we need not—and should not—subject our readers to the "Run Spot run" type of sentence. By finding the essential relationship between ideas, and then by communicating that relationship, we can link ideas into mature-but-readable sentences. On page 116, Activity 19 provides a chance to practice doing just that.

Complexity comes to sentences in part by adding elements and in part from specifying or describing elements already there. Thus in that last example, even the simplest version expands the basic subject ("increase") to "a 17 percent increase in gross sales." In making certain that the reader shares exactly the same concept as the writer, we add descriptive, limiting words. There are two ways to do this: the simple way is to use adjectives; the complex way is to use clauses.

For example, we can say "outstanding managers," or we can say "managers who are outstanding." We can say "significant achievements," or we can say "achievements which are significant." If we link these concepts into a single sentence, our choices are:

"Outstanding managers make significant achievements," or

"Managers who are outstanding make achievements which are significant."

The second is obviously a cumbersome way to share our description.

Our efforts to limit, define, or describe can get us into funny predicaments. Take this puzzler from a cafe menu: "One of the delectable, relatively new dishes to our shore has captured the American palate." (Have you tasted any palatable shores recently?) Or another: "They will make the nomination at the convention in August which is scheduled to take place in Houston." (Where else would August take place?) Or there is the contribution from a consumer advocate who deplored " . . . toys you buy for your children that break at the end of the week."

Words like "who," "that" and "which" are symptoms of adjective clauses. Now adjective clauses are not cardinal sins, but they are obstacles to clarity—especially when writers over-use them! All adjective clauses use extra words: helping verbs and those linking-words such as "who" and "which."

Another problem: adjective clauses tend to show up in awkward places. There are the examples we've already noted. Here are more:

"We salute the rank and file employees who spoke out against the strikers, who were appreciated."

"The Landrum-Griffin bill, designed to end corrupt labor practices and which are prevalent in the country, was approved by the committee."

The second example is from Bernstein's wonderful book, *The Careful Writer*. He gives another great example of the wandering clause when he quotes:

"Mr. Hoffa represents the combination of devious dealings and dictatorial, overweening power in some of the leading unions, exposed by the McClellan committee, and which calls for curbs."

The real secret of sharing description is to find the essential quality you wish to share—then to *select one adjective* which says it for you. Now sometimes the problem goes deeper: the need to find the essential *action*. Take that first example. You may very well decide that "salute" is not really the main verb; then it must be "appreciate." In either case, if you locate the object as soon as possible after the verb, you come up with a clear sentence. It may be "We salute the rank and file employees who spoke out against the strike," or "We appreciate . . . " or both verbs: "We salute and appreciate the rank and file employees who spoke out against the strike."

Activity 20, on page 117, and Activity 21, on page 119, provide practice in recognizing and converting the long "clause approach" to the shorter, clearer format.

There are times when we try to describe our verbs. We want people to know "when" or "why" or "under what conditions." Here are some sentences which do it quite effectively:

"When your check has cleared, we will ship your furniture."

"As soon as your previous employers verify your tenure there, we will process your application."

This next sentence expresses the condition in awkward ways:

"Tucked away in the filing cabinet, the personnel clerk found your employment application."

That's an awkward position for anyone to get into—even a small personnel clerk! Here's another example of misplaced modifiers:

"Trailing the national average by nearly 10 percent, we find our company in an unfavorable marketing position."

In these cases the non-clarity is simply a matter of position. We can reverse the one sentence so it reads, "The personnel clerk found your original employment application tucked away in the filing cabinet." You can clarify the next example by saying, "Our company is in an unfavorable marketing position: it trails the national average by 10 percent."

From those examples we can distill a principle of clarity:

> PUT ALL MODIFIERS DIRECTLY BESIDE THE WORDS THEY MODIFY OR LIMIT.

Another form of "describer" is the participle. That's the technical term for phrasing starting with "*ing*" words. Examples are phrases like "pending further information," or "awaiting the election returns," or "wondering what decision to make." These can be terribly troublesome for writers —to say nothing of the trouble they cause readers. For example:

"Awaiting management's response, the decision seemed very late in coming."

"Hoping you will accept this proposal, the benefits will continue to accrue through the next three years."

"Believing that the demand would quickly surge upward, the drill press production was accelerated last quarter."

What, exactly, do those "ing" words describe? Surely the decision isn't "awaiting" anything. The benefits obviously cannot be "hoping." And it's a rare drill press that is "believing." These are almost as bad as the newspaper columnist who wrote: "He sat in the sun at a table with a vase of flowers on it smoking a cigarette."

There is a basic principle here, and it comes from that master of prose style, William Strunk, Jr. On page 8 of *The Elements of Style* he enjoins writers: "A participial phrase at the beginning of a sentence must refer to the grammatical subject."

His classic examples: "On arriving in Chicago, his friends met him at the station." And "Wondering irresolutely what to do, the clock struck twelve." (By the way, the 1972 edition also includes another classic: "As a mother of five, with another on the way, my ironing board is always up." This particular sentence often appears in lists of the "purple passages" that supposedly have been mailed by indigent people to government relief agencies.)

On page 120, Activity 22 provides practice in the proper location of modifiers.

Now sometimes the words we wish to limit or specify are verbs. In those cases, the efficient way to describe is to use an adverb. The inefficient way is the prepositional phrase. Prepositional phrases are not wrong; they are just cumbersome. They expend more words than do adverbs. They thus obscure the main words of the sentence. That raises an important point: the more words we put into the sentence, the less clearly key words stand out to snare the reader's attention.

Let's examine some examples:

"Management took this step with great reluctance," is less efficient than "Management reluctantly took this step."

"We read the proposal with great enthusiasm," is the expensive way to say, "We read the proposal enthusiastically."

Why not focus on the main idea? Just say "We hope you will read your new warranty carefully and file it where you can easily retrieve it." The alternative is the clumsy "We hope you will read your new warranty with care and file it where you can retrieve it with ease."

We should probably review the relationship between conciseness and clarity. In fact, we need to examine the whole issue of conciseness in business writing. By definition, the word "concise" means "cut short, brief . . . free of all elaboration and superfluous detail." Of course we want to get rid of anything that's superfluous, so conciseness seems a worthy goal. But we don't always want to get rid of elaboration. Furthermore, if we use the "cut short" or "brief" definition, then we certainly don't always want to be concise. To leave out key ideas is a foolish conciseness: readers will not agree with our position. To omit useful details is equally foolish: readers will not understand.

For our purposes, conciseness can be tied in with clarity. Unnecessary words get in the way of the really necessary words. Such intrusions obscure our important meanings. To that degree, non-concise writing detracts from clarity.

That may be just another way of saying that *the clear sentence permits the reader to see the structure while reading.* This ability to sense structure aids the reader toward the ability to put ideas into a total "big picture." It's small wonder that those Harvard researchers discovered, in 1962, that the time taken to respond to a sentence varies according to the grammatical structure of the sentence. Readers can read declarative, active, affirmative sentences most rapidly and easily. If we can use one adverb instead of three words in a prepositional phrase, we contribute to this clarity. Activity 23, on page 121, gives you practice in identifying adverbs as opposed to the longer prepositional phrases; Activity 24, on page 122, provides practice in changing phrases to adverbs.

Now let's examine the exact nature of something else that Harvard study urged: affirmative, active sentences.

First, Affirmative Sentences. There isn't much to say about these—but remembering to use them is a different matter. So often our thoughts come out with emphasis on the negative rather than the positive. The slogans say "AVOID ACCIDENTS" rather than "THINK SAFETY!" Why plant the idea of breaking the law with slogans such as "DON'T SPEED!" when the simple positive statement of the speed limit has the same effect?

There are a couple of problems with negative statements. They are just naturally more "downbeat" and less action-oriented. They give the wrong impression, the wrong image. A second fault is that when readers see the negative words, they may think they are being denied or criticized. Now this doesn't mean that if you are denying you must avoid negative words. If you are telling your reader that the answer is "No," then "No" is the proper word to use. But if you are telling your reader that the answer is "Yes," then for goodness' sake don't say that the answer "isn't 'No.' "

That last bit of advice may seem farfetched, but there are documented occasions on which the use of negative words caused unfortunate misunderstandings. A large transportation company was closing its offices in a city where it would no longer operate. Naturally this meant closing out some local bank accounts. Their letter of explanation stated: "This action is in no way due to any dissatisfaction with your services." What happened? A senior bank officer made a long-distance phone call to find out what the bank had done to "dissatisfy" their customer. Another example: in its printed statement about certificates of deposit, another bank placed an asterisk alongside certain account numbers. In the fine print below, the explanation read: "If your account is not accompanied by an asterisk, it is not subject to automatic renewal." There were two predictable results: a great many inquiries about what the terms actually were, plus a large number of disappointed depositors who thought the message meant that certificates would be automatically renewed. Small wonder! Remember how difficult double negatives were for you when you first confronted them in arithmetic classes? Well, readers have less time to remember how they convert. Bernstein notes this inherently negative approach in his *The Careful Writer* when he cites that clumsy phrase, "cannot help but."

Activity 25, on page 123, will give you experience in finding ways to express ideas from the positive, rather than the negative approach.

Next let's consider that other finding from Harvard: that active sentences give meaning faster than passive sentences.

What's the difference between an active and a passive sentence? It's a technical difference, but it has a great effect on the tone and clarity of our writing. English teachers call the technical difference a difference in *voice*. When we arrange sentences so the action-taker is the subject of the sentence, that's the active voice. (It's not the same thing as *tense*. Lots of business writers have long forgotten the difference between the "passive voice" and the "past tense." Nor does the active/passive distinction apply to sentences where the verb "be" is the main action word. Our examples will not involve sentences with the words "am" or "are," "was" or "were" or "been.")

Let's take two examples:

"Management example exerts a powerful influence on employee behavior." Or:

"A powerful influence upon employee behavior is exerted by management example."

The first is the active version; the second is passive. How do we know? To answer that (and to learn the difference between the two voices) we need first to *find the central action word*. In both sentences the action is "exerts." The second step is to identify the action-taker. Again, in both sentences the action-taker is "management example." But in the first sentence "management example" is the subject of the sentence; the second uses "A powerful influence" as the subject. Which of these actually does the "exerting"? Obviously, the answer is "management example." Because it is the subject of the first sentence, that sentence is in the active voice. In the second sentence, the real action-taker *receives* the action. This obscures the message, adds needless words, and puts the subject into a subordinate role as the object of the proposition "by."

Two shorter sentences will demonstrate the same results:

"Strikes cost money."

"Money is cost by strikes."

These short sentences reveal even more clearly the awkwardness of the passive voice. Again, the key element (the action-taker "strikes") appears late in the sentence. It's in an emphatic position, last—but it comes too late to help the reader. The reader doesn't find out the true subject until the sentence is over. Readers should know the subject just as soon as they possibly can. These sentences reveal the strength of the last-word-position. Note how powerful "money" is in the first version? "Strikes" also has a strong position; it comes first. Even in the passive version "strikes" occupies a powerful position; the trouble is that it comes too late.

As Strunk says in *The Elements of Style*, "Place emphatic words at the end of the sentence. The proper place . . . for the word or words the writer wishes to make most prominent is usually the end." (Strunk did it himself in that very sentence.) Nevertheless the first word is important too: it establishes the reader's expectation about what the subject deals with. As such, the subject should come first. The active version tends to ensure that primacy.

If you want a good example of how "dead" the passive can be, examine a check from the U.S. Government. On the back of their datacard checks they give a great many descriptive comments, ending with the admonition: "It is suggested that this check be promptly negotiated." (Maybe they know what they're doing. By putting this advice into the deadest possible wording, they may keep their funds on deposit and drawing interest longer!) Note that the action-taker, "you" doesn't appear in the sentence at all, and that the key concept ("promptly") doesn't occupy a position of any significant strength.

But back to our examples:

"Strikes cost money."

"Money is cost by strikes."

Note that there are two extra words ("is" and "by") in the second, passive version. There will always be at least two extra words in the passive voice: a helping verb and a preposition. Thus the passive hides key words among supporting (really needless) words . . . words which do nothing to push the thought forward into the reader's consciousness.

On a very few occasions the passive voice is appropriate. If you wish to imply inaction ("The issue was never discussed by the Steering Committee until the last meeting of the year.") or to obscure the real actors, then the passive voice is available to you. But since clarity is their constant goal, good business writers use the active voice whenever they can.

For some exercise in recognizing the active voice, turn to page 124 and Activity 26. Activity 27, on page 125, will give you experience in converting from the passive to the active voice.

Before we leave the subject of sentence clarity, let's review some of the techniques and principles we can follow in making our sentences easy for our reader to follow:

1. Maintain the unity of each sentence: just one central idea.

2. Maintain the continuity by visible Subject-Verb-Object patterns.

3. Describe nouns and pronouns with adjectives, not clauses.

4. Describe your action words with adverbs, not prepositional phrases.

5. Put your modifiers right alongside the word they limit or describe.

6. Participial phrases at the start of the sentence must refer to the subject.

7. Positive statements are easier to read and to remember than negative statements.

8. The active voice is easier to read, and is clearer than the passive.

9. Cut words that don't do any work for you.

These nine suggestions will help make your sentences clearer. They thus help your reader get the meaning at the first reading. That is, they help your reader get the meaning if the reader knows what the words know.

That takes us to our second tool for clarity, words.

Words

Words are about as clear as they are specific. They are about as useful to readers as they are familiar. They are about as popular as they tend to be short. Thus we have established the criteria for effective words in good business writing.

We have already noted that words exist on a kind of "ladder of ambiguity." The words "a lot" are less specific than "over 500 cases." But "over 500 cases" isn't as definite as "547 cases." "Unmotivated" doesn't share as much definite information as "consistently tardy and absent," but even that judgment is less revealing than "absent without approved cause 14 days last year" or "tardy on 19 days."

Let's see what sort of message, and what image the next letter communicates. Where does it exist on that "ladder of ambiguity?"

Dear Mr. Kalucci,

You are invited to become a member/participant of the ExecUClub and as such, meet one day per month with eleven other people.

A pool of 101 professional resources persons are drawn from to chair host meetings providing technical insights, while members provide life experiences. Customarily, within a few hours after the first meeting, the relationships among the members have coalesced so that the durable ties they have created move the theoretical outlines to concrete action in the form of social, economic and political applications.

As a result of your participation the interests and concerns of your life see new solutions, promise a new entrepreneurship of intentions in action, demonstrate that things and ideas can multiply, and prove that your interests as an individual are not in contradiction with those of the Group, rather indeed are complementary. Finally, as you grow in knowledge and wisdom, so then will that which is within your sphere of influence, be it your family, your organization or your society.

Please give this some thought and I will be getting in touch with you in about a week.

Cordially,

R. Brian O'Leary

R. Brian O'Leary
President, ExecUClubs

Do you know what Mr. O'Leary is talking about? Well, maybe you do in the first and final paragraphs. He wants you to join a group and he's going to get in touch with you. But what about the middle of the message? Those abstractions certainly lack something in clarity. On the basis of this letter, readers are supposed to buy a pig in a poke—or more aptly, a pie in the sky!

The words which do the most to make our meanings clear are the verbs and the nouns. Indeed, Strunk advised his college students to "write with nouns and verbs." He goes on to say, "The adjective hasn't been built that can pull a weak or innaccurate noun out of a tight place." He doesn't disparage adjectives and adverbs: "They are indispensable parts of speech." Generally, however, it is "nouns and verbs, not their assistants, that give good writing its toughness and color." *(The Elements of Style,* Second Edition, p. 64)

The point is that we want to find the accurate noun and the precise verb to communicate our ideas. The search is often worth a few moments of our time. If there is any possibility that a reader won't know what "program" we mean, then we should not refer to "programs" in general or even to "that program." Best we should say "the IBEDS Program" or the "Empathic Listening program for new supervisors."

Some words assume meanings peculiar to a given organization or locality. The word "timely" is an example. In most circles it means coming early, or at an appropriate time. In many U.S. federal agencies it means "meeting the deadline." Or again, the word "flimsy" is usually an adjective meaning "weak." In business offices it is also a noun meaning lightweight paper used in multiple copies.

When we must convey an abstract concept to our readers, it's often wise to use an example. We give an example when we go from the known to the unknown. Here is a classic example of using an illustrative example to clarify an abstraction . . . a concept so vast that readers couldn't be expected to "get it" without special help. Benjamin Franklin felt that a citizen's rights should not depend upon property. People who agreed with Franklin expressed their creed in these words:

"It cannot be adhered to with any degree of intellectual or moral certainty that the inalienable right man possesses to exercise his political preference by employing his vote in referendum is anything other than man's own nature, and is, therefore, properly called a natural right. To hold . . . that this natural right may be limited externally by making its exercise dependent upon a prior condition of ownership of property is to wrongly suppose that man's natural right to vote is somehow more inherent in and more dependent on the property of man that it is on the nature of man."

Franklin found that pretty abstract. According to *Gobbledygook Has Got To Go* (pp. 45–46) he explained it this way:

"To require property of voters leads to this dilemma. I own a jackass; I can vote. The jackass dies; I cannot vote. Therefore the vote represents not me but the jackass."

So we learn that good business writers select concrete words, or give concrete examples, to add clarity to their writing. There are exercises in identifying specific words in Activity 28, page 127.

Of course it isn't always a question of concreteness; a word may be specific and still be inappropriate. As Strunk says, the sense of our writing is communicated by precise, specific nouns and verbs. There's a foolish joke about the patient who couldn't communicate to his psychiatrist why the patient's marriage was childless. "It's like this, Doctor," he said. "My wife is inconceivable." The doctor was baffled. "Don't you mean she's impregnable?" he asked. "Well, to tell the truth, Doctor, she's unbearable!"

Or there is the actual case of the St. Louis Police Academy chief who bought 180 dictionaries. "I hope," he said, "never again to read that an accident victim had his foot decapitated."

How long must you search for "the right word"? That's up to you. You know how much you value your reader's making the precise response.

Some writers seem to seek ambiguity. Edwin Newman cites this trend: "Experts in certain fields . . . are using language to suggest that what they're saying is far more complex and difficult than what it is. They make it next to impossible for the person outside the discipline to understand what's being said." (*Flightime,* March, 1977, p. 15) The article cites an architect's comment: "The exhibition makes transitionally visual the omni-intertransformings of convergently, divergently coordinate processes." Cautions Newman: "The reader must be careful not to see content where there isn't any."

Technical words are often precise at birth, but time gives them generalized, analogous meanings. If your youngsters behave well under stress, you call them "little soldiers." Yet they are years away from enlistment. The word "straight" describes more than an unbending line. People drink their liquor "straight"; they have "straight" morals and social codes. Housekeepers set rooms "straight" and sages set our thinking "straight." In elections we may vote a "straight" ticket, and in the 1970's "straight" started to describe our sexual preferences.

What has this to do with business writing? The lesson is this: when we use specialized technical terms, or when we use words in specialized ways, we want to make sure our readers are familiar with those special terms and those special usages.

That gets us to our second criterion for words: they must be familiar as well as specific. What good is a specific word to a reader who has never heard it before? Good writers make new words familiar by defining them the first time the word appears in any document. Suppose you want to talk about a nemesis to someone who never heard of one. Use the word, then inside parentheses say "a formidable, victorious opponent." (If you'd like to know more about this word, it's derived from a Greek goddess who punished extravagant pride. Maybe that's why fancy, show-off words are "the nemesis" of some business writers!)

Define new words inside parentheses and you tell readers what those funny words mean. The technique works for technical terms, specialized meanings, and acronyms. Here are examples of each type:

"We hope to soothe the acrophobics (those who fear great height) by using both a glass enclosure and a five-foot grill."

"Frankly, we think the idea should be filed in File Q (our nearest wastebasket) along with the blueprints for the endless belt that was going to stretch from Chicago to Buffalo!"

"The IBAFS program (Internal Budgets And Fiscal Services) will be online in our computer by March 15."

Of course, if a specific familiar word and a specific unfamiliar word are available, use the former. You haven't been appointed a missionary, charged with responsibility to expand your reader's vocabulary; you haven't been selected to write just so you could call attention to your own fabulous command of words. In fact, there are those who feel that a thesaurus is a dangerous weapon for business writers: synonyms are a rich resource for the creative writer, but a potential liability for the clear business writer.

We have now noted two criteria for words: that they be specific, and that they be familiar. The third criterion is that they be short.

This isn't an invariable criterion. When we urge short words we are not saying that a short word is always preferable to a long word. It must be apparent that a great many precise technical terms are rather long. They are the right word just because they are precise. The thing about big words is that readers are bothered by too many of them. Thus the basic principle is simple:

> RESTRICT YOUR LONG WORDS TO TECHNICAL TERMS—
> AND THEN DEFINE THOSE.

Long words are not bad words. However, when there are too many long words in business correspondence, those long words diminish the clarity. If the percentage of big words gets too high, readers have been known to "turn off." Studies show that words of three syllables begin to strike the eyes of readers as rather long. Too many words with three or more syllables give readers a problem.

When do you have too many tri-syllabic words? There is no arbitrary rule, but writers will not generally seem sluggish if they limit their "long words" to 17 to 18 percent of their total.

That isn't always easy to do, but you are especially helpful to your readers if you form the habit of selecting short words for non-technical concepts. Writers can say "firm" instead of "corporation"; they can write "office" instead of "facility" or "installation" or "operation"; they can "expect" instead of "anticipate." All of us can "end" things or "finish" them a good deal more easily than we can "terminate" or "finalize" them.

What's the general principle?

> FOR FAMILIAR, NON-TECHNICAL TERMS, USE THE
> SHORTEST POSSIBLE WORD.

We can save our long words for those precise concepts which have no short, familiar name. We can resist current fads such as adding "ize" to words that are already rather long. Thus "finalize" and "prioritize" and "familiarize" become "finish" and "rank" and "acquaint."

Activity 29, on page 128, will help you consider short versions for some of the characteristic big words which haunt lots of business writing.

To make the point about the value—and the power!—of short words, here is an excerpt from a wonderful little message. The original source is unknown, but you'll note that only the title uses any multi-syllable words.

ONE-SYLLABLE WORDS

When you come right down to it, there is no law that says you have to use big words when you write or talk. There are lots of small words and lots of good words that can be made to say all the things you want to say—and they say them quite as well as the big words say those things.

It may take a bit more time to find these small words at first—but it can be well worth the search; for all of us know what these words mean. Some small words (more than you might think) are right with just the right feel, the right taste; and if made to, they help you say a thing the way you want to say it . . . the way it should be said.

Small words can be crisp, neat, terse. They can go to the point like a knife. Do not try to gauge the depths of one's thoughts by the size of one's words. Big words do not mean big thoughts.

And so we have set up three criteria for choosing effective words to use in our business writing: they should be specific, familiar, and short.

Activity 30, on page 130, will help you cut down the pomposity of typical sentences by substituting short words for the long ones in those examples.

When we talked about positive sentences, we could have made the same point about words. Writers respond better to positive words than they do to negative words. This involves a certain semantics, and thus goes beyond clarity, which is our focus in this chapter. It's important to remember, though, that the precise word we select probably does carry an "aroma" or a "bouquet." This involves what we call connotations . . . semantics. It involves the associations which readers unconsciously re-experience when they see words on the page. There is a longer analysis of this in the chapter on Friendly Writing, and Activity 42, on page 182, deals specifically with selecting positive words.

But for the moment, let's concentrate on clarity. Specifically, let's turn to another way in which good business writers use words.

> CLEAR WRITING USES WORDS AS SIGNPOSTS TO SHOW HOW IDEAS RELATE TO ONE ANOTHER.

What do we mean by "using words as signposts"? Merely that we put some words into our letters and reports for no other reason than to show the relationship between ideas. Throughout this workbook we have stressed the importance of *sharing our structure with our reader.* When we use words as signposts, we are doing just that. In other words, we communicate our transitions by including words whose sole function is to ensure that the reader experiences the transition just as we planned it.

For instance: we want a reader to know that the next idea links to the previous idea as a further explanation. Words like "and " or "then too" or "also" are useful at such a transition. We might also use more formal transition words such as "first" or "second" or "finally." We may use such coded transitions as numerals or alphabetic signposts like "A, B, C and D." These coded symbols are really most helpful when we think the reader may need to reply to only certain parts of our letter. They can use the codes as a reference to direct our attention.

A more difficult transition for our readers is the "sharp turn." This represents a complete change in viewpoint—and we must be very careful to share that change with our reader. We need to use words like "however" and "but" and we need to use such words *before* the transition. This means that we will sometimes start a sentence or a paragraph with these "contrary" conjunctions.

Why not? You may have heard somewhere in an English course that conjunctions at the start of sentences were "no-no's." Nonsense! Great writers—and *clear* writers—have been doing it for centuries. Shakespeare had Lady Macbeth tell her husband, "But screw your courage to the sticking-place and we'll not fail." He had Mark Antony tell his Roman countrymen, "Yet Brutus says he was ambitious."

We can and should put the transition words where our readers need them. When we are making sharp turns in thought, that means we should start the new direction by transitions such as:

"On the other hand"   "To take an opposite viewpoint"
"Contrary to this"   "Contrariwise"
"Despite this"   "Yet"
"Nonetheless"   "Nevertheless"
"On the contrary"   "Opposing this"
"Opposite to this"   "But"
"However"   "Otherwise"

Readers often have trouble knowing whether an idea is a generalization or an example. We need to tell them. Thus, whenever we make the transition from a generalization to a specific application, we should use phrases like "For example," "For instance," "To illustrate" or "A case in point."

The same need exists, but in reverse, when we draw an inference from specific data. Useful words and phrases for this type of transition are:

"Therefore"	"Thus"
"And so"	"So we can see that"
"The conclusion is"	"The conclusion? That . . ."
"Our conclusion: . . ."	"The conclusion: . . ."
"What does this prove? That . . ."	

Other useful phrases show cause-and-effect relationships. Clear business writing often uses words like "Because," "Since," "This causes" or "This results from" or "The effect of."

Structure can be shared by other helpful "signpost" words and phrases:

"Next"	"First"
"Second"	"Finally"
"At the center"	"In the upper corner"
"In the lower left"	"Directly beneath"
"Directly opposite"	"Above"

Activity 31, on page 132, gives a number of chances for you to select helpful signpost words to share the relationship of ideas.

So what have we discovered about the words we select for our business writing? Let's summarize. First, we know that there are not "special business words" on which we draw. Rather, words are selected because they meet certain criteria:

1. Effective business words are clear because they are specific.
2. Effective business words are clear because they are familiar—or because we make them familiar with parenthetical definitions.
3. Effective business words are clear when about 82 to 83 percent of the words are short (fewer than three syllables.)
4. Words contribute to clarity when they serve as signposts, sharing transitions with readers.

Now that we have discussed sentences and words, let's look at punctuation as a tool for clarity.

Punctuation

To punctuate clearly, we really don't need to master a great many types of punctuation. A few basic punctuation marks can do a lot to communicate the relationship of the parts of our sentences.

Of course we know that a capital letter is the simplest form of punctuation. Capital letters tell our readers when a sentence is beginning, and that certain words are proper nouns. We're already masters of this type of punctuation.

Periods are equally easy to master: they tell readers that a statement is complete, or that a word is abbreviated.

Commas are far more ambiguous. They can indicate the division of words in a list; they can mean the end of a phrase within a list; they divide dependent clauses from the rest of the sentence; they can also divide independent clauses if those clauses are connected by a conjunction. But sometimes we don't put in a comma between independent clauses connected by conjunctions. Have you had enough? Are you confused? So are many of your readers. No—make that read "So are *most* of our readers." In short: the comma can do so many various types of work that its appearance on the page isn't really very helpful to most readers. We would do better to concentrate on less ambiguous punctuation marks. As Bernstein notes: "The tendency these days is to use a minimum of commas." This doesn't mean that commas are bad; they're just ambiguous.

Now to the more specific types of punctuation.

First, let's deal with the semicolon.

Semicolons are valuable to us whenever we want to show parallels or contrasts. Here is a sentence using a semicolon to convey parallelism:

"The procedure solved the maintenance problem; the manuals explained the procedure to the using departments; now we need a training program to ensure implementation."

Here is a sentence in which the semicolon divides contrasting independent clauses:

"The accountant detects infractions of procedures, analyzes causes and suggests solutions; the auditor challenges procedures and recommends improved approaches."

Those examples, as well as the one in the illustration on the next page, study semicolons from the viewpoint of the writer's intention. We might also look at them from a technical viewpoint.

Both of the printed examples and the illustration have more than one central independent clause. Yet semicolons contribute to a unified sentence. They show the parallel functions in the first example, and in the illustration; they show the contrasting responsibilities in the last printed example. Since there are no connecting conjunctions between any of

these independent clauses, the semicolon is appropriate punctuation. Let's remember that usage:

> TWO INDEPENDENT CLAUSES WHICH USE NO CONNECTING CONJUNCTION NEED A SEMICOLON TO CLARIFY THE TRANSITION.

By independent clauses we mean merely sub-sentence units which have their own subject and their own verb. Not all clauses are independent; some depend upon the other clauses in the sentences. An example would be "if we are looking for clarity." The word "if" is the symptom of *dependence*. Well, we normally divide an independent clause from a dependent clause with a comma. Example: "While the manuals were in the printshop, the instructors were busy preparing visual aids." Now suppose we had said "The manuals are in the printshop, and the instructors are preparing the visual aids." In that version we have two independent clauses—and once again we use a comma to communicate the transition between them. The transition is short, and the comma works very well.

But let's be realistic; let's complicate our message just a little bit. Let's decide to say: "The manuals are in the printshop (a process requiring three weeks); and the instructors are preparing the visual aids, but without the actual scale drawings used in the manuals." The presence of that parenthetical expression leads us to put a semicolon between the clauses. It really should "compel" us to use a semicolon. The relationship between the ideas has not changed, but the structure has changed. If we used commas at both our transitions (after the parenthesis and before the word "but") our reader would be unable to find the major transition between the independent clauses. The comma is asked to do two remarkably different tasks within a single sentence. It simply is not strong enough for those dual roles! We want our punctuation to match the transition. So we come up with a policy:

WHEN ANY CLAUSE CONTAINS INTERNAL PUNCTUATION, USE A SEMICOLON TO SEPARATE THE CLAUSES.

You may find a few exceptions to that, but you will rarely confuse your readers if you follow the policy. It's merely an extension of what we always do when there are commas inside the items in a list. For example:

"Madison, Wisconsin; Des Moines, Iowa; Omaha, Nebraska."

If you didn't use semicolons, think how confusing that list would be! The commas between punctuated clauses are no less vital. Just remember that semicolons divide elements with interior punctuation, and you will add a lot to the clarity of your writing.

There are exercises to build your skill in using semicolons in Activity 32, on page 133.

So much for semicolons. Now let's talk about colons.

If we can remember just two common uses for colons, we can help our readers a whole lot. Colons denote lists and examples.

USE COLONS TO START LISTS AND TO SHOW EXAMPLES.

For example: "We have audited three plants: Moline, Paducah and Greenville." That was a very short list with very short items. When you have longer lists, or many words within the items in the list, consider indenting the entire list.

Secondly, we use colons for examples. "There are many bits of evidence that our employees sense a new pride in their organization. For example: Mr. Kevin Lade's spontaneous speech at R. V. Kinkade's retirement dinner." You'll note that we gave our reader two signals: the colon and the words "For example." This is probably a good idea. It may seem a trifle heavy-handed, but there is much evidence that readers have special trouble with the transition from a generalization to an example of that generalization.

Bernstein says, in *The Careful Writer* (p. 359), that the colon "heralds fulfillment of a promise implied in what precedes it. It sometimes says 'for example' and it often says 'that is' or 'this is what that means.' " This potential ambiguity is just another reason for including both the punctuation and the transition words.

The Bernstein comment reveals that we sometimes mean a special kind of example. Some people actually put a name on this usage: they call it an "explication." (How's that for fancy jargon?) It stems from the explicit example supplied in the words following the colon. How about these examples?

"We have noted a remarkable trend recently: in October complaints were down by 24.7 percent !"

"There are many evidences that our employees sense a new pride in their organization: Mr. Lade's spontaneous speech at R. V. Kinkade's retirement dinner; Deborah Lakey's comments in the *Evening Courier* of November 14."

Since the explication following the colon is just an independent clause, it is not normally capitalized. Of course if the first word is a proper noun (as Mr. Lade in the second example) the explication begins with a capital letter.

Activity 33, on page 134, gives lots of chances to decide where to put colons in actual sentences.

Oh, by the way: we have inherited a Latin derivative of some transition words which do the work of colons. There is the Latin "e.g." meaning "for example." We often see this in business writing. There is also another Latin derivative, "i.e." This second abbreviation means "that is," or "that is to say." Unfortunately, most readers of modern English do not know which is which. So why don't we write English? Anything that needs to be translated can hardly qualify as clear communication!

Another useful mark of punctuation is the parenthesis.

We have already noted how helpful parentheses are in defining technical jargon or acronyms. Parentheses are also very helpful in sharing added data which will enrich the message. They constitute a kind of "aside," a way of lowering the voice, of saying "by the way." Thus material inside parentheses includes background which isn't familiar to all the key readers of a report. It includes background which readers can skip if they already know it—but which less informed key readers find useful. (Don't put in material which you're certain your letter reader doesn't need; but if you're uncertain, this is a nice way to be sure you're giving enough facts to be clear.) Here are examples:

"The Boyden Plan (so-called because Hal Boyden, then a manufacturer's representative, suggested the first application) eliminates preventative maintenance with TARAN (Test and Replace as Necessary) policies."

In the first usage, the material is supplementary and subordinate; in the second, a necessary definition of new jargon.

"The Basic Supervision program (until recently known as Supervision I) contained nothing about non-directive counseling; we do not understand how Mr. Craine got the impression that these skills had always been expected of our very new supervisors."

In this example, the material is clearly subordinate ... . pure enrichment. Its inclusion is probably the result of the writer's estimate that the reader might confuse programs whose titles had recently changed.

We want to remember that parentheses have the effect of subordinating what they contain. Sentences should therefore stand alone without the material inside the parentheses. The words enclosed tend to have secondary impact—just the opposite of the dash.

However, before we study the use of the dash, let's look again at the first example of parentheses:

"The Boyden Plan (so-called because Hal Boyden, then a manufacturer's representative, suggested the first application) eliminates preventative maintenance with TARAN (Test and Replace as Necessary) policies."

That example may teach us two things about parentheses:

1. It's an awfully long afterthought; perhaps it separates the subject from the main verb by too great a distance.

2. It's possible to overwork any technique. Did you feel that two parenthetical comments within the same sentence was just about one too many?

Activity 34, on page 135, allows you to exercise some judgment about sensible use of parenthetical comments.

Now let's discuss effective use of the dash to clarify our messages.

The dash is used rather seldom in business writing—and that's good. It isn't that the dash is a bad type of punctuation—far from it! It's just that the dash, when used most effectively, gives emphasis. If you use too much emphasis, you'll sound overbearing. What's worse: you'll lose emphasis.

Dashes secure emphasis in one of two formats: (1) by enclosing the idea we want to stress, and (2) by preceding the element we want to emphasize. You can reason it out that if dashes are emphatic, and if the end of sentences are emphatic, the more effective use of the dash is to place it before the accented element—at the end of the sentence.

The reason dashes should be a rare punctuation mark is just that when too many things are emphatic, nothing is emphatic. Why not look at the next sentence for proof? Sometimes we use ALL CAPITAL letters to emphasize; IF WE CAPITALIZE ALL THE LETTERS OF EVERY WORD, WHICH WORDS ARE REALLY EMPHATIC? They all look just the same, don't they? In case you need still more proof about the futility of too much emphasis, just observe the speed with which tiny children teach their parents to shout! Mother or father shouted one command to give it special stress. Baby ignored. So they shouted louder. Baby again ignored. Pretty soon they were shouting everything—and trying to dream up still more creative, more effective ways to get baby's attention. Everything is shouted—but nothing is emphatic.

But in business letters the dash can give emphasis. Place an emphatic "aside" inside dashes and readers will notice it more than if you put the same words inside parentheses. Put a dash before key words at the ends of your sentences, and those words will be doubly stressed. Just don't do it too often.

Activity 35, on page 136, lets you make decisions about when to use a dash or a parenthesis.

There are really four basic punctuation marks (besides capital letters and periods) which add clarity to our writing. Let's review the key uses:

- SEMICOLONS properly divide independent clauses where there is no conjunction.
- SEMICOLONS properly divide any clauses containing interior punctuation.
- COLONS introduce lists.
- COLONS precede examples, including "explications."
- PARENTHESES enclose definitions of technical jargon and new terms.
- PARENTHESES enclose helpful (but subordinate) ideas.
- DASHES emphasize the words they enclose or precede.

Activity 36, on page 137, lets you practice use of all types of punctuation. Activity 37, on page 139, is a "fun" exercise: rewriting a very unclear letter.

Although clarity and conciseness are two very different things, they do go hand in hand. If we are concise, including only what our readers must have in order to understand or accept our purpose, then we'll also have a better chance of being clear.

Perhaps we should take a tip from Alfred E. Kahn. When he became chairman of the Civil Aeronautics Board in 1977, he took direct aim at the paper profusion and at the gobbledygook which goes with it. Kahn wrote a memo urging his staff to "Try reading aloud some of the language you use, and ask yourself how your friends would be likely to react. (And then decide, on the basis of their reaction, whether you still want them as friends.)"

Reading our letters and reports aloud might help all of us. It might reveal where we most desperately need to apply techniques for clarity. And we have discussed a number of techniques for achieving clarity. These techniques involve the way you build sentences, select words, and punctuate your ideas. No technique will replace lucid thought on your part—but technique can implement your clear thinking so your business writing is as clear to your readers as it is to yourself.

The rest of this chapter offers you lots of practice in the techniques of clarity.

PUTTING THE PRINCIPLES INTO PRACTICE

✳ Activity 16

A. Starting with this sentence, indicate whether these sentences have unity by writing YES if the example does, NO if the example does not express a single idea.

B. Until the local offices have indicated their preferences for the format of the new correspondence manual, the committee can take no action; until the committee takes action, I am unwilling to insist that the project continue.

C. Your attention is directed to two major responsibilities of the local manager in administering personnel policies: adherence with all ethnic ratios required by the federal government, and maintenance of a complete roster of key positions.

D. We appreciate the extra hours of hard work you invested in meeting this deadline, and we congratulate you on the innovations you implemented in accomplishing your goal.

E. We hope you understand our logic, and if there is any other information which will be helpful to you, we trust that you will not hesitate to call upon us for such services.

F. The electrical flow is shown in red; the hydraulic in green; the pneumatic in blue.

G. Psychiatry has an explanation for every behavior: if you are early for an appointment, you are suffering anxiety; if you are late, you demonstrate your rejection; if you arrive on time, you're being compulsive!

H. Road maps lead to ordinary goals—they do not lead to creative solutions.

I. I would like a style of writing in this office that reflects the clarity of thinking we want to adhere to and economy as in our other operations.

J. The senior engineer assigned to this project has requested that all requests for expedited shipments carry the initials of that senior engineer or designated alternates, Kay Klein, Herold Newman, or G. J. Snow.

Review

Cases E and I are questionable. The offer for help probably *is* related in Example E, but it hides in so many clichés that the unity is hard to find.

The economy issue probably *does* relate to the central idea in Example I, but the structure hides that fact and makes an awkward sentence. Let's say that they just barely do achieve unity. All of the other examples represent mature, unified sentences.

✱ Activity 17

Identify the SUBJECT, ACTION, and OBJECT in each sentence.

A. The scarcities create higher prices in services as well as commodities.

B. We will supply you raw materials for the exhibit if you will supply the design.

C. You may send your answer to Box 234, Media, Ohio.

D. Dun and Bradstreet publish the materials you are seeking.

E. Attention to both detail and quality control can solve this problem for us.

F. We must consolidate our losses and increase our profits within six months if we expect to maintain the respect of our stockholders.

G. The Longview Plant met its quota exactly as assigned; Thermopolis fell below quota by nine percent; Ringstead exceeded quota by three percent.

H. You have probably already identified the promotable people in your section.

I. Dividing the tasks into simpler assignments will only compound the problem, reducing whatever motivation the workers already have for doing good work.

Review

	SUBJECT(S)	ACTION(S)	OBJECT(S)
A.	scarcities	create	prices
B.	We	will supply	materials
C.	You	may send	answer
D.	Dun and Bradstreet	publish	materials
E.	Attention	can solve	problem

F.	We	must consolidate	losses
		(must) increase	profits
G.	Longview Plant	met	quota
	Thermopolis	fell	
	Ringstead	exceeded	quota
H.	You	have identified	people
I.	Dividing the tasks	will compound	problem

✲ Activity 18

After locating the SUBJECT, VERB, and OBJECT in each of these sentences, indicate whether the sentence DOES or DOES NOT have continuity.

A. We believe that we should not hire the person for what type of person the person is but rather for the ability to do a job well, in accordance with published standards of performance.

B. Maintaining a balance between production and concern for employee welfare requires sensitivity.

C. Only sensitive managers can maintain a balance between production and concern for employee welfare.

D. Operating statistics often reveal to managers where training is needed.

E. We must ask ourselves what we can do to prevent future accidents and providing assistance to injured workers.

F. To prepare a new employee for proper on-the-job performance is one thing, but maintenance of these requisite skills requires a totally different set of skills and circumstances by the manager.

G. Now, if you wrote DOES NOT for any sentence, revise that sentence so it DOES have continuity.

Review

	SUBJECT	ACTION	OBJECT
A.	We	believe	that we . . . performance.
B.	Maintaining	requires	sensitivity
C.	managers	can maintain	balance
D.	statistics	reveal	where training is needed
E.	We	must ask	what . . . workers
F.	To prepare	is	thing, AND
	maintenance	requires	set
G.	(You)	revise	sentence

Although all the sentences have continuity, it's awkward and hidden in examples A, B, D, E, and F. Example C gives a good model of improving example B. In D the objective clause "where training is needed" can become "training needs" to make the continuity clearer. In example E, try a parallel form: "to prevent" and "to provide." That gives the desired continuity, doesn't it? The same parallelism would help in example F: "To prepare" and "to maintain" would clear things up a bit.

✳ Activity 19

Build some mature, unified sentences from these overly simple examples.

A. Sales produce profits. Economy in manufacturing contributes to sales. Good incentive programs increase sales. They also can make workers in the manufacturing operation cost conscious.

B. We formed a committee to investigate. The accident was the most costly in the history of the Antioch shop. Tom Hartford was chairman, and Erna Logan and Harry Senn also served. All members were freed from any other responsibility.

C. Arson was one possible cause. Substandard wiring was another possibility. Possibly the inspections had been careless. The thought that it might have been arson was upsetting to management.

Review

There is always more than one good way to express an idea. So these suggested combinations of those jerky sentences are nothing more than models.

A. Good incentive programs contribute to profits in two ways: they produce sales and cost-consciousness in workers.

B. Tom Hartford chaired the committee to investigate this costliest accident in the history of the Antioch shop. He and members Erna Logan and Harry Senn were freed from any other responsibility.

C. Possible causes included substandard wiring, careless inspections and arson—an upsetting possibility for management.

* Activity 20

In the space at the right you can create an "adjective description" of the adjective clauses listed at the left:

A.   Plugs manufactured by Ajax   _____

B.   Your letter of June 12   _____

C.   Letters which were well organized   _____

D.   Ideas that are clearly phrased   _____

E.   For positions where public contact is involved   _____

F.   People who are courteous and considerate   _____

G.   The brochure which is enclosed will answer the questions which you ask which are vital.   _____

H.   The theory that Mr. Milliken promulgated is the one that is most vulnerable of all the theories which we heard at the convention held in Atlanta.   _____

I.   The idea that you submitted for our investigation has been approved.   _____

J.   We have promoted all the employees who were recommended.   _____

K.   We can now count a total of 14 acres which are devoted to experiments.   _____

L.   There are very few demands which are negotiable in the document you submitted on June 14.   _____

M.   The case is full of decisions where the manager used judgment that is questionable.   _____

N.   The TV commercial which proved
to be the most productive for us
had no slogan that was recogniz-
able as such.   _____

Review

A.   Ajax plugs

B.   Your June 12 letter

C.   Well-organized letters

D.   Clearly phrased ideas

E.   For public contact positions

F.   Courteous and considerate people

G.   Enclosed brochure . . . your vital questions

H.   Mr. Milliken's theory . . . most vulnerable of all theories heard at the
Atlanta convention.

I.   Your idea has been approved.

J.   All recommended employees

K.   Fourteen experimental acres (This may change the meaning somewhat: if you felt that it did change the meaning, you probably merely
omitted the words "which are." That doesn't change structure, but it
sure helps clarity.

L.   Negotiable demands . . . your June 14 document.

M.   Questionable decisions by the manager OR: decisions with questionable managerial judgment

N.   Most productive TV commercial . . . recognizable slogan. (Note
that the last alteration gets rid of that gobbledygookish "as such.")

NOTE: Of course there are other ways to write the sentences so the
words all become functional. The revisions shown here reflect only the
specific task of this activity: converting adjective clauses to adjectives.

✳ Activity 21

Revise this paragraph so you have eliminated all those adjective clauses.

When we consider all the accomplishments which have been made by the men and women who are employed by this organization, we can easily understand why there was such good news in the report which was presented to last week's Board of Directors meeting. We are most appreciative of the great diligence which must truly be called "beyond the call of duty" and the perseverance during these times which have been so trying. The men and women who are leading this organization have asked me to convey to you the appreciation which they feel for the splendid work which has been done by the people who work for you.

✳ Activity 22

By relocating the distracting elements, convert these poor sentences into clear messages.

A. Dated May 24, the Manager of Accounts Receivable located the request for extended payment.

B. Obscuring the real issue, I found the committee members full of slightly related, trivial objections to the proposal which you had made.

C. Believing in the essential justice of the Fair Employment Practices legislation, the debate was lively and informative between Mr. Adams and Ms. Grainer.

D. Caught between company loyalty and union allegiance, the policy is distasteful to many salaried, senior employees.

Review

There are several ways to make sense out of each of those examples. It depends upon what you decide the original writer was trying to say! How do you like these?

A. The Manager of Accounts Receivable has located the May 24 request for extended payment.

B. The committee members obscured the real issue, I felt, with trivial, slightly related objections.

C. The debate between Ms. Grainer and Mr. Adams was lively and informative; it reflected their belief in the essential justice of the Fair Employment Practices legislation.

D. The policy is distasteful to many salaried, senior employees, caught between company loyalty and union allegiance. OR: Caught between company loyalty and union allegiance, many senior salaried employees find the policy distasteful.

✳ Activity 23

For each set of sentences below, check the one which uses an adverb (not a prepositional phrase) to describe, limit or specify the action.

A. A writer should express all ideas clearly.
B. A writer should express all ideas with clarity.

C. The idea was adopted with great enthusiasm by the committee members, but rejected quickly by the Board of Directors.
D. The committee members enthusiastically adopted the idea, but it was quickly rejected by the Board of Directors.
E. The idea was enthusiastically adopted by the committee members, but rejected with great speed by the Board of Directors.

F. This metering device must be designed for an operation without error for a period of one full year.
G. This metering device must provide error-free operation one full year.

H. At the end of this training our managers should be able to read their inbound correspondence with maximum speed and retention.
I. The training should provide managers who read speedily and retain with maximum efficiency.
J. The training should produce managers who read fast and retain well.

K. Good organization in business writing depends upon thinking logically.
L. Good organization in business writing depends upon logical thinking.
M. Good organization in business writing depends upon thinking with logic.

N. The campaign, under the guidance of the advertising agency, came off with great smoothness.
O. The advertising agency conducted the campaign smoothly.

Review

A, D, G, J, K, and O use adverbs rather than prepositional phrases. Example K contrasts with example L; L does not use a prepositional phrase, but converts the "quality" to an adjective. Thus "logical thinking" becomes a useful way to express the same idea.

Example G may concern you. The original version contains three prepositional phrases: "without error," "for a period," and "one full year." In the revision, there are really no adverbs—although the absolute phrase "one full year" denotes time and fills the function of an adverb.

✱ Activity 24

Change the following sentences so the verbs are limited, defined or specified with adverbs rather than with prepositional phrases.

A. We need to reply to their inquiry with total candor.

B. If we depict the instructions in visual form, we can do it with the maximum effectiveness.

C. The complaint should be treated with delicacy.

D. He replied in a short period of time that his organization could not meet our specifications.

E. We must proceed with great caution if we are to achieve our task with effectiveness.

F. The lines drawn with red crayon indicate electrical flow.

G. The application was completed with such careless penmanship that we were inclined to treat it with very little interest.

H. NOTE: Did you change any of these without using an adverb in the new version?

Review

There are several ways to change most of the sentences. One version would be:

A. candidly.

B. visually . . . most effectively.

C. delicately.

D. He soon replied . . .

E. cautiously . . . effectively.

F. Red lines indicate . . .

G. The application was written so carelessly that we weren't very interested.

H. The typical correction for Example F does not use an adverb; rather, the prepositional phrase "with red crayon" is changed to an adjective modifying the noun "lines."

✱ Activity 25

Convert these sentences so they are affirmative and positive:

A. The shipment had nothing missing.

B. There was nothing mediocre about the employees in the assembly room.

C. Her appraisal contained nothing derogatory from any previous supervisor.

D. The writing was not cluttered with gobbledygook or with such extra words as clauses doing the work of adjectives.

E.   There is no reason to think that the scheme would not work unless it were delegated to people who did not understand its purposes and its methods.

F.   We are unable to offer any objections to your proposal.

Review

You probably have your own versions—and they're probably excellent! One way to express those ideas positively is:

A.   The shipment was complete.

B.   The assembly room employees were above average.

C.   Her appraisals from previous supervisors were satisfactory.

D.   The writing was free of gobbledygook and such extra words as clauses doing the work of adjectives.

E.   We have every reason to think that the scheme will work if delegated to people who understand its purposes and methods.

F.   We like your proposal.

✳ Activity 26

From the following sets, select the active version:

A.   All suggestions should be submitted to committee members before June 1.

B.   Submit your suggestions to committee members before June 1.

C.   The filing clerks stamp the orders, then keep a tally on each type of transaction.

D.   Each order is stamped by the filing clerk, then they tally each type of transaction.

E.   Each order is stamped by the filing clerk, and then the type of transaction is tallied.

F.   Mary Tyson developed this famous recipe, which is envied now by our competition.

G.   Mary Tyson developed this famous recipe, now envied by our competition.

H.   Mary Tyson developed this famous recipe, and now our competition envies it.

I.   Your statement will be mailed to you by our auditors on May 15.
J.   Our auditors will mail your statement to you on May 15.

K.   The inconsistency of our promotion with industry standards was pointed out by the Director of Personnel as early as last January.
L.   As early as last January the inconsistency of our promotion policy with industry standards was pointed out by the Director of Personnel.
M.   As early as last January, the Director of Personnel pointed out how our promotion policy is inconsistent with industry standards.

N.   Theory Y advocates participative management and employee involvement.
O.   Participative management is advocated by Theory Y; so is employee involvement.

P.   Employee participation in decision-making is advocated and practiced by Theory Y enthusiasts.
Q.   Theory Y enthusiasts advocate and practice employee participation in decision-making.

R.   The costs will be borne by the tax preparer if any errors are committed.
S.   If there are any errors, the costs will be borne by the tax preparers.
T.   Tax preparers will bear the costs if any errors are committed.
U.   In case of errors, the tax preparer will bear the costs.

Review

The *totally* active versions are B, C, H, J, M, N, Q, and U.

✸ **Activity 27**

Convert each of these passive sentences into the active voice:

A.   Your replacement battery may be picked up at the nearest Quik-Ware store.

B.   Sincere regret is expressed over the inconvenience which was recently experienced by your purchasing agent.

C. It is recommended by the Accounting Department that all forms be filed according to existing procedures until the computer installation has been completed by the EDS Division.

D. Indefinite and ambiguous safety precautions have been communicated by a great many line managers to new assembly-line workers.

E. Our dealer has been advised of this change in policy and you will not be subjected to such misinformation in the future.

F. It is recommended that this check be promptly negotiated.

G. Your patience is appreciated.

H. The recommendation of the task force was that the user specifications be submitted to a central steering committee where they could be put into proper priority.

I. Insulation inspection will be required before our approval can be forthcoming.

J. The attention of the addresses is directed to the necessary answers by them.

Review

A. You may pick up your replacement battery at the nearest QuikWare store.

B. We are sincerely sorry that your purchasing agent met this inconvenience.

C. The Accounting Department recommends that we use existing procedures to file all forms until the EDS Division completes the computer installation. (Note that there are three conversions.)

D. A great many line managers have communicated indefinite and ambiguous safety precautions to new assembly-line workers.

E. We've told our dealer of this policy change; he will give you accurate information in the future.

F. Please negotiate this check promptly. OR: We suggest that you negotiate this check promptly.

G. We appreciate your patience.

H. The task force recommended that users submit specifications to a central steering committee which would put them into proper priority. Or, if you like the word "prioritize," it might read " . . . to a central committee for prioritizing."

I. We can approve this after insulation inspection.

J. We call your attention to the answers you need to supply.

✱ Activity 28

From each of the following sets, label the most specific word as number 1, then on down until the least specific word in the list carries the highest number:

A. Community _____

Peoria _____

Inhabited area _____

City _____

B. They _____

Humans _____

Women _____

Joan Lincoln _____

Supervisors _____

C. Phaeton _____

Vehicle _____

Automobile _____

1945 Phaetons _____

My '45 Phaeton _____

D. 274 _____

Scads _____

Many _____

Many dozen _____

Too many _____

E. Indefinite   _____   **G.** Employees   _____
    Abstract   _____   Managers   _____
    Confusing   _____   Ken Pyle   _____
    Fuzzy   _____   Personnel
F. Troublesome   _____   managers   _____
    Complex   _____

Review

A. Community 3; Peoria 1; Inhabited Area 4; City 2
B. They 5; Humans 4; Women 3; Joan Lincoln 1; Supervisors 2   OR
    They 5; Humans 4; Women 2; Joan Lincoln 1; Supervisors 3
C. Phaeton 3; Vehicle 5; Automobile 4; 1945 Phaetons 2; My '45
    Phaeton 1
D. 274 1; Scads 5; Many 4; Many dozen 2; Too many 3
E. Indefinite 2; Abstract 1; Confusing 3; Fuzzy 4
F. Troublesome 2; Complex 1 ("Complex" identifies the nature of the
    trouble.)
G. Employees 4; Managers 3; Ken Pyle 1; Personnel managers 2

✱ Activity 29

For the long words at the left, think of a short, familiar translation. Put
your clearer version at the right.

Alienate   _____   This facility   _____

Categorize   _____   Finalize   _____

Conflagration   _____   Location   _____

Controversy   _____   Human resources   _____

Delineate   _____   Incompatability   _____

Employ   _____   Instigate   _____

Equipment   _____   Malfunctioning   _____

Examination   _____   Occasion   _____

Facility   _____   Objective   _____

Organization	_____	Utility	_____
Perpetuate	_____	Unusual	_____
Prioritize	_____	Viability	_____
Referring to	_____	Whereabouts	_____
In reference to	_____	Whosomever	_____
Scenario	_____	ADD YOUR OWN:	_____
Subsequent	_____	_____	_____
Termination	_____	_____	_____
Trepidation	_____	_____	_____

Review

Alienate = anger/displease
Categorize = sort
Conflagration = fire
Controversy = dispute/issue
Delineate = define/explain
Employ = use/hire
Equipment = machine/tool
Examination = test
Facility = ease
This facility = this site/office/place
Finalize = end/finish
Location = site
Human resources = people
Incompatability = mismatch
Instigate = start/begin
Malfunctioning = not working

Occasion = date/day/event
Objective = goal
Organization = firm/agency/group/unit/section
Perpetuate = maintain/retain/keep
Prioritize = put in order/rank/select
Referring to = about
In reference to = about
Scenario = plan
Subsequent = next
Termination = end/finish
Trepidation = fear
Utility = use
Unusual = rare
Viability = alive/living
Whereabouts = site
Whomsoever = who

✷ Activity 30

Edit these next sentences so each contains fewer long words:

A. A preponderance of the remittances are improperly prepared: illegibility, inaccuracy, and incompleteness are primary areas of central concern—and can be attributed to carelessness in the preparation.

B. Indisputably and undoubtedly the preponderant problem in our own organization is indubitably overblown phraseology and ponderous vocabularies.

C. Ingenuity, innovation, and creativity are unquestionably extraordinarily desirable attributes in computer programmers.

D. Radioactivity is no longer a remote possibility; it has become incredibly imminent, with the omnipresent preponderant possibility of excessively dangerous exposure for the overmost plurality of the citizenry of this commonwealth and this civic entity.

E. The incongruity of the established procedural guidelines cannot be adequately reconciled with standard safety practology, and is understandably of overwhelming concern to the undersigned.

Review

There are many good ways to cut down the overblown vocabulary. We hope that you noted the real need for some of those words. In Example C, how else can you tell your readers what traits you want than the first three words? But the other big words can be shortened.

For example, in A:

"Preponderance of the remittances" can become "most" or "many remittances."

Why have both a "central" and a "primary area" of concern?

Attributed just means "blamed on."

Is "in the preparation" really a contributor to the message? Cut it.

In B:

You don't need both "indisputably" and "undoubtedly." In fact, "Clearly" would share the idea just as effectively.

"Certainly" is just as certain as "indubitably."

"Grand" or "pompous" say it just as well as "overblown."

"Heavy" is probably as apt a description as "ponderous" in this case.

For C:

Since the subjects of the sentence are long (but specific) concepts, how about "surely special qualities" or "surely special assets" instead of those big words in the original?

And after all, is "attributes" a better word than "traits"?

In D:

There is some need to express urgency. But how much?

"Omnipresent preponderant possibility" is hardly more frightening than the word "threat." That word has heavy connotations.

One must wonder why they fret about "excessively dangerous" exposure. Isn't it bad enough if there just "danger of exposure"?

A commonwealth is usually called a state; a civic entity is best known as a city. Why not use those words? And why not "most citizens"?

For E:

Some people would write, "Our procedural guidelines are not congruent with standard safety practice. I am very concerned!"

✱ Activity 31

Add some linking words to help your reader make sense of these ideas:

A. Senior citizens often dream of the past. _____ youngsters tend to dream of the future.

B. When many traders try to sell their stock, the prices tend to go down; _____ when lots of traders seek to buy stock, prices tend to rise.

C. _____ the tendency is toward informality in business writing, legal writing still uses formal wordings.

D. We had to look at a great many factors. _____ we were concerned with the economy. _____ we thought of civic responsibilities. _____ we felt that there were social implications.

E. The economics of the investment are staggering: _____, a single central processing unit can cost as much as $90,000,000.

F. Clear writers select words which meet three criteria: _____ the words are specific; _____ they are familiar; and _____ they are short.

G. The form is not really that complicated. _____ you will find the place for your name, address and vital statistics. The actual figures for your computer appear _____. Directly _____ that is the place for your signature.

Review

Of course there are lots of useful words to provide "signpost services" for your readers. We might suggest:

A. However
B. But OR however
   The important thing in examples A and B is to signal the "sharp turn" in thought.
C. Although

D. First . . . Second/Next . . . Third/Finally
E. For example/For instance
F. First . . . second/next . . . third/finally
G. "In the upper _____ corner" OR: "at the top," "in the center" OR: "beneath" OR: "at the left"—wherever you decided to put those elements. The point is that by giving "directional signals" you can assist your reader.

✳ Activity 32

Where would you put the semicolons to clarify these next sentences?

A. The person who makes inputs to the computer must follow a rigid format however if one is writing the program one must observe even stricter rules.

B. Among the mass media television has the largest audience the daily newspaper is a close second.

C. The comma is perhaps the weakest of the punctuation marks used within sentences the semicolon is a stronger signal to readers the colon is the strongest of the three punctuation marks.

D. If there is any reason for optimism it lies in Ms. Brown's concern for the employees and if there is cause for pessimism (and we feel there is!) it lies in her inability to find time for individual counseling with those subordinates.

E. We have always encouraged employee teams in intercompany athletic leagues however under the present circumstances we are unable to supply funds for uniforms.

F. The word "macro" indicates large routines the word "micro" indicates small routines.

G. Although the project is late, we are optimistic and we will continue to do everything we can to get back on schedule.

Review

A. . . . format; however . . .

B. . . . audience; the daily . . .

C. . . . sentences; the semicolon is a stronger signal to readers; the colon . . .

D. . . . employees; and if there is cause . . .

E. . . . leagues; however, under . . .

F. . . . large routines; the word . . .

G. . . . optimistic; and we . . .

In Examples D and G there is some argument about the need for any semicolons. For clarity, we recommend them as shown. When either clause contains internal punctuation, a semicolon between clauses clearly identifies the main break for the reader.

✱ Activity 33

Supply colons as needed in these next sentences; change existing marks as needed.

A. The report covers three aspects of the problem, economic, social, and legal.

B. Specifically, we will need to know the office at which you bought your razor, the model number of your razor, and the date of purchase.

C. The cost is computed this way;

> Determine the total number of trainees
> Determine their median hourly salary, then
> Multiply those two figures.

D. Good letters have at least three qualities, clarity, friendliness, and conciseness—to say nothing of relevance.

E. Let's review punctuation marks and their uses;

> Periods indicate the end of a sentence
> Semicolons indicate the end of independent clauses
> Colons indicate the start of a list or an explication.

F. Downey gave this explanation, the agent was distracted by a personal crisis while packaging your shipment.

G. The author makes several assertions in this article, namely that new employees need very little in the way of task training, that they are not well informed about organizational policies, and that they are more interested in being professional than they are in being loyal.

H. There have been alarming instances of organizational sabotage, the presumed abduction of two supervisors during the strike is merely one of the more flagrant.

Review

A.   . . . problem:

B.   . . . to know:
> The office . . .
> The model number . . .
> The date . . .
> (This indented list makes it easy for the reader to reply on your letter.)

C.   The cost is computed this way: *etc.*

D.   . . . qualities: clarity . . .

E.   . . . and their uses: *etc.*

F.   . . . explanation: the agent . . .

G.   . . . article: that (omitting the word "namely") OR: article, namely: that

H.   . . . sabotage: the presumed abduction . . .

✳ Activity 34

Where would you put parentheses in these sentences?

A.   We must report, unpleasant as it is, that all costs continue to soar.

B.   The trend is stronger in the western states. See chart on page 43.

C.   The sales curves, except in the international division, are encouraging.

D.   Jargon, technical terms and definitions is acceptable when the writer is certain the reader knows the terms.

E.   The CAB Civil Aeronautics Board has restricted airline use of such promotional fares.

F. We are happy to announce that Ms. Eleinor Swayne, who first joined our organization as a receptionist and who has later served as Employee Relations Representative, Customer Service Representative, Supervisor of Personnel, and Employment Manager, has been named a member of the new Employee Policy Board.

G. The original request—you will recall it was then known as the Fund for Basic Education—was tabled nearly as soon as it was received because of the recession in the early part of the decade.

Review

A.   . . . (unpleasant as it is) that . . .

B.   . . . states. (See chart on page 43.)

C.   . . . curves (except in the international division) are . . . OR: leave it as it is.

D.   Jargon (technical terms and definitions) is acceptable . . .

E.   The CAB (Civil Aeronautics Board) has . . .

F.   . . . Ms. Eleinor Swayne (who first joined . . . Employment Manager) has been named . . .

G.   . . . request (you will recall is was then known as the Fund for Basic Education) was tabled . . . NOTE: This seems an "aside" rather than a stressed point; thus we feel the parentheses are clearer than the dashes.

✳ Activity 35

Where would you put parentheses or dashes in these sentences?

A. One precaution, perhaps the most important one, is to wash your hands each time you leave the laboratory.

B. One idea, if you have nothing better to do, is to stop by the Office of Accounting to pick up their proposed new payroll certification forms.

C. The Employment Representative has many responsibilities including the interviewing and bookkeeping and most important of all the compliance with EEO legislation.

D. The creosote is absolutely vital, let me repeat, absolutely vital to the lifespan of the sidewalk.

E. We have had a number of cases, such as the episode in Catawba County and the general decay of performance at Rawlins, proving our need for modern motivational techniques.

F. The details for this task are outlined in regulations—see page 35 of Chapter 12—and in placards along the input slots on the Condensing Machine.

Review
A. precaution—perhaps the most important one—is to wash . . .

B. . . . idea (if you have nothing better to do) is to stop . . .

C. . . . bookkeeping and—most important of all—the compliance OR: bookkeeping—and . . .

D. . . . vital—let me repeat, absolutely vital—to the . . . OR: . . . vital—let me repeat—absolutely vital to . . .

E. . . . cases (such as . . . Rawlins) proving our need . . .

F. . . . regulations (See page 35 of Chapter 12) and in placards . . .

✳ Activity 36

Punctuate these sentences so they will be just as clear as possible for the reader:

A. if we are going to accomplish this objective and I cannot stress enough the importance of doing just that then we must make substantial improvement in three things productivity punctuality and innovation

B. it is entirely possible that the competition will begin to market a similar product before we reach the stores with FixBurn

C. the decision to proceed with octal based representation was based on these considerations it is the most economical of storage space it is already a familiar process to our staff and it was urged by the computer vendor

D. would you please have your proposal in my hands by May 23rd by the 22nd if at all possible

E. the obligation to meet these specifications is our main obligation we have no alternative but to give it our total energy

F. when we have considered all the variables including the cost of labor and materials we conclude that option a is the most desirable it involves fewer complications than options b or c

G. his indifference i might even call it a what you are going to do about it attitude prevented any effective counseling

Review

Of course there are lots of good ways to punctuate these sentences. What do you think of these versions?

A. If we are going to accomplish this objective—and I cannot stress enough the importance of doing just that!—then we must make substantial improvement in three things: productivity, punctuality, and innovation.

B. It is entirely possible that the competition will begin to market a similar product before we reach the stores with FixBurn.

C. The decision to proceed with octal-based representation was based on these considerations:
1. It is the most economical of storage space;
2. It is already a familiar language to our staff; and
3. It was urged by the computer vendor.

D. Would you please have your proposal in my hands by May 23rd —by the 22nd if at all possible?

E. The obligation to meet these specifications is our main obligation; we have no alternative but to give it our total energy. (Some might use a dash before "we," OR use two sentences.)

F. When we have considered all the variables (including the cost of labor and materials) we conclude that option "A" is the most desirable: it involves fewer complications than options "B" or "C."

G. His indifference (I might even call it a what-are-you-going-to-do-about-it? attitude) prevented any effective counseling. OR: (I might even call it a "what you are going to do about it?" attitude)

✳ Activity 37

On a separate piece of paper (because it provides more space than a blank page would), revise this letter so it is clear. Use as many techniques as you possibly can from those acquired in your study of this chapter.

We do not disagree with the viewpoint which you outlined in your communication of May 3. It has always been StrongSteel's position that outstanding workmanship should not be ignored and there are definite ways in which this policy is implemented. Our policy has always been to "Promote From WITHIN."

Our PFW policy is stated with great emphasis in the Personnel Practices Manual, Chapter 16, Page 23, Par. 17. When any supervisory/management position is vacated by reasons of resignation, promotion, termination, or expansion, first consideration is mandatorily given to employees who are already on the employment rosters.

Of the 87 (eighty-seven) promotions in StrongSteel's Drury Division last year, 67 were thus assigned to incumbents. By which we mean people already on our payrolls.

Working diligently in their present positions we find many employees who are dedicated and able. Skill in performing present assignments does not guarantee equal skill in supervising or managing the work output or processes of others which is after all the definition of management, getting work done through other people.

Fourteen (14) new supervisors last year requested replacement to former positions, apparently they were uncomfortable directing the work of others, many of whom may have been former associates.

The desire for promotion and the ability to discharge supervisory or management responsibilities are not, in our conclusion, one and the same thing.

We trust that this explanation has explained our position in selecting Ms. Louise Larwick rather than yourself as Supervisor of Time Systems.

G. E. Grey
G. E. Grey
Personnel Specialist
GEG:jkp

CHAPTER 4

FRIENDLY
BUSINESS WRITING

IN A NUTSHELL

What makes writing seem friendly? The essence of the answer seems to be just this: writing is friendly when the thoughts are presented so they *focus on the reader*. Many writers like the term "reader-centered" as a way to describe friendly business writing.

As in achieving clarity, writers have sentences, words, and punctuation as tools for achieving friendly writing.

First, let's see how sentences can help make writing seem friendly.

The first sentence is prime time. It gives your reader a first impression and an insight about the entire unit. So we stress first sentences of letters, of reports, and of paragraphs.

Which of these would seem the friendlier opening of a business letter?

"In order to process your refund, please answer these questions."

"Could you help us process your refund quickly by giving us some more information?"

The second sentence expresses more concern for the reader, doesn't it? The writer and the reader have found a mutual goal: settling a refund request *quickly*. This is something the reader cares about—something the reader will recognize as a friendly concern on the part of the writer. Then also, phrasing the request as a question rather than as a command adds to the warmth of the second version.

We sometimes have to give our readers bad news. When this happens, it's best to come to the point tactfully. Here's an example:

"We are sorry your application reached us after we had already selected Ms. Mavis Hartley as our Credit Manager."

That certainly isn't a welcome message—but it's expressed in a reader-centered manner: it states the purpose quickly, contains a brief but concrete apology. The reader doesn't need to cope with paragraphs of "protesting and apologetic explanation" to get the news.

So, we've discovered that special attention to the first sentence is one way to create friendly writing. State the purpose from the reader's point of view.

The closing is the next most important sentence. It's your last chance to sound human. Studies show that readers remember best the first and the last ideas of things they read and of messages they hear.

Now a "thank you" or an offer of further assistance *can* make an effective closing. However, such closings are friendly only if they are personalized. Let's test that by selecting the friendlier of these two closing sentences:

"If there is any way I or the members of my staff can be of further assistance in this matter, please do not hesitate to let us know." OR:

"We want to help you solve your equipment problem. When future troubles arise, do call us at 404-987-6665."

Our choice is the second version. Why? Because the writer did three friendly things:

- Related the last sentence to the specific purpose of the letter and to the specific topic the reader cared about: equipment problems.
- Included new, specific helpful information (telephone number) and
- Avoided the old clichés like "further assistance" and "please do not hesitate."

Openings which state the purpose from the reader's viewpoint, and closings which offer specific help can increase the friendliness of business writing.

There's another important thing to say about closings. They should come as soon as the purpose has been developed. How often have you, as a reader, grown frustrated because the writer didn't stop writing? How often have you, as a writer, grown frustrated wondering how to close a letter?

When you wonder how to stop writing, you've probably developed your purpose adequately. So don't ponder. Do the obvious thing: stop writing! If you have written a well-organized letter clearly, and presented the purpose from the reader's viewpoint, why waste time (yours or the reader's) by going on and on searching for a "snappy ending"?

Now and then a very short sentence helps your reader. Short-short sentences (three to five words) give a breather . . . a break in the heavy workload that goes with reading compound and complex sentences.

Sentence structure *can* make a difference. For another thing, active sentences tend to be friendlier than passive sentences. That's especially true when you can put a "reader-centered" word as the subject. Note how that works:

"You will receive your furniture as soon as your check arrives."

"The merchandise will be forwarded upon receipt of proper payment."

Even when you can't use reader-centered words like "you" or "your" as the first sentence did, your use of the active voice puts the action-taker in the main role in your sentences. In the next examples, note the position of the subject, "claimant," in the passive (first) and in the active (second) version:

"The reply must be prepared in triplicate by the claimant."

"The claimant must prepare the reply in triplicate."

If "the claimant" is your reader, then go one step further: combine the active voice and the reader-centering by saying,

"You, as claimant, should prepare the reply in triplicate."

Another friendly sentence is the interrogative. Ask questions. We do so when we face people; why not when we write them? When we speak directly to people, we ask questions to get at facts, to get at feelings, and just to show our concern to know "where they are." We can use questions for these same purposes when we write.

Let's consider making a request in business writing. "Please let us have your answers by March 5." That's polite enough: the word "please" and a definite deadline are there. Yet it may sound terse, brusque, domineering when it appears on the printed page.

Now let's phrase it as a question: "May we have your answers by March 5?" It is a request—not a command. We just phrased it as a question.

There are several reasons why questions make the printed page seem a little bit friendlier. First, they take the curse off our requests. Second, they mold thinking when we want to get information from readers. By phrasing the request as a question, we are better able to *specify* what we want. In the third place, questions are more conversational . . . warmer. Finally, questions imply or secure the involvement of the reader.

Before we leave the subject of sentences, let's remind ourselves that when our readers can sense the Subject-Verb-Object pattern they "get the message" easily. This is, of course, one element in being friendly.

So to summarize, we might say that sentences contribute to friendliness when:

1. The opening sentence states the purpose from the reader's viewpoint,
2. The closing comes as soon as the purpose has been developed,
3. There are occasional short-short sentences,
4. The active voice prevails, and
5. The Subject-Verb-Object pattern is easy to find.

Next, let's look at words as symptoms of friendliness.

First, there is the matter of connotation . . . roughly related to semantics. Some words, because of their usage, carry connotations they cannot shake. Connotations may be positive, warm, friendly—or they may be negative, unattractive.

Among those "loaded words" here are just a few often seen in business writing:

POSITIVE CONNOTATIONS	NEGATIVE CONNOTATIONS
Capable	Cheap
Confident	Dispute
Enjoy	Liable
Satisfaction	Marginal
Stability	Inflexible
Success	Unfortunate

Here are two sentences which will help us see how words create feelings in our readers:

"We always enjoyed your services, but will no longer be operating in the Boston area."   OR

"Our cancellation of this account is in no way due to any dissatisfaction with your previous services.

Both sentences express a friendly idea—but the first is much friendlier. It does what we should do if we want to be friendly: use positive words to express positive thoughts. It really makes no sense to use negative words to express positive ideas. If you express yourself positively, your readers will appreciate your vigor and understand your message at one and the same time.

When you wish your writing to center on your reader, you need to try to put yourself in the reader's position. *There is no substitute for that empathy or for the effort to achieve such empathy!*

Unfortunately even when writers are empathic, they sometimes fall into the trap of expressing their ideas from their own, rather than from the reader's, point of view.

So the magic word "YOU" can be a great help. Let your writing express that "YOU ATTITUDE" by using the words "you" and "yours" to show that as a writer, you've looked at issues from the reader's viewpoint. It's no good saying "You should do what we want"—but it *is* friendly to say "Your interests lie in . . ."

The word "you" isn't the only way to reflect your empathy for your reader. In these sentences, you'll find another way to bring your reader into the focus of your business writing:

"The aforementioned shipment of vegetables should arrive early next week."

"Mr. Barnes, your vegetables should arrive early next week."

The second uses the reader's name. That's a helpful technique. (It is especially useful when writing in the Simplified Format, where there is no salutation.)

The "Magic of the Proper Noun" deserves our attention. It helps in reports as well as in letters and memos. In reports you can talk *about* specific people (They like to see their names in print!) and organizations and products and places; in letters and memos, you can use the name of the reader and of the reader's associates to add personality, humanity and friendliness to your writing.

Most of us want to "see our name up in lights." There is a little of the ham in all of us. That's why the names of people, their organizations, their products, their home towns and home states all help to ease the coldness of the printed page . . . to put some friendliness into our business writing.

When we cannot use specific names, we can use personal pronouns. "I" and "we" are quite acceptable in modern business letters and reports. There are times when writers take individual responsibility for opinions; in those cases, "I" is the appropriate pronoun. At other times writers speak for their offices or their organizations; in those cases "we" is appropriate.

Of course, modest writers avoid over-use of either first-person pronoun. But that's less a matter of technique than a result of looking at the issues from the reader's viewpoint . . . of the "second person" attitude. Another thing: when you slip into the third person, beware of assuming that people are masculine. In today's liberated business writing, plurals help solve the dilemma. So do the rather awkward "he or she" and "he/she" and "person"—as in "chairperson" or "salesperson." What do you think of the proposed new "s/he"?

But remember: it takes more than technique to make friendly writing. To be truly friendly, look at issues and ideas from your reader's point of view. After all, understanding is what you want from your reader. Understanding starts with you!

We've noted the power of words to evoke feelings as well as meanings. There is a regrettable cluster of words which hinder both feeling and meaning. We call these words gobbledygook. Gobbledygook consists of clichés . . . stereotyped, meaningless expressions. There are two examples in the sentence, "Please return the referenced samples to the undersigned."

You can eliminate both clichés ("the referenced samples" and "the undersigned") merely by changing that request to a question: "Will you just return the samples to me?"

So, to our list of effective words, let's add the phrases "Can you . . .?" and "Will you please?" In a way, this technique helps both your words and your sentences to be friendly: *use interrogative sentences occasionally.*

And so we have seen how sentences and words can contribute toward friendly business writing. Now let's see how our third tool, punctuation, can help us seem friendly on the printed page.

Punctuation creates friends when it contributes variety to our writing. Variety is important. It lends a conversational tone to the writing—not so much that the letters, reports or manuals are "colloquial," but enough so they sound like a document between human beings.

Most business writing tends to be strictly declarative statements. Did you ever notice that—or ask why? The answer probably boils down to just this: "Because that's the way business letters are supposed to be." Who said so?

Well, we can change that—at least we can change it for our own letters and reports. And the big reason for doing so is that we want to sound like a friendly person. That's hard to do on the printed page, but it's possible.

IF WE USE A VARIETY OF PUNCTUATION, WE CAN COME AS CLOSE AS POSSIBLE TO SHARING THE VOCAL INFLECTIONS WHICH GIVE WARMTH TO OUR MESSAGES WHEN WE SPEAK TO PEOPLE FACE-TO-FACE.

Let's test it with another request. One version, the typical version, goes like this: "Write me as soon as the material is available." That sounds stern and harsh and dictatorial. It's a request, but it can be read as a command. A better version would be: "Will you write me when this material is available?" Notice how the question mark takes the sting out of the request . . . how it *specifies* the intention? It's a friendlier way to express the idea. It asks rather than dictates. (By the way, when you move toward questions for your requests, you may have to retrain typists. They probably learned in school that these should be punctuated with periods. Just remember, it's *your* letter and it should reflect the style *you* want! If it's a question, insist on using a question mark.)

Of course there is a wide array of punctuation available to give those exact feelings we want our reader to get . . . to show that we are people. Let's review some of the most useful punctuation.

The dash is effective because it adds emphasis. Such emphasis gives your reader another friendly signal from you. By using a dash you communicate your concern for certain ideas; you let your reader know which ideas you consider most important. Dashes help you share your values.

An opposite effect comes when you use parentheses. Parentheses say "By the way." The parenthesis is especially helpful to show that an idea is subordinate to its surroundings, to define technical jargon, and to break up long sentences. For example, the parentheses in this next example break up what would otherwise have been a long, rather unwieldy sentence.

"These work habits have grown up over a long period of time and are (we suspect) the result of rumors about how the work should be done more than the result of approved performance standards."

Exclamation marks rarely appear in business letters—but there is no law against them! They can add interest and variety as well as emphasis. Now remember: this device (like any technique) can be overworked. It's important to use all emphasis-getting devices sparingly. If you stress many things, nothing will seem emphatic. So, go easy with those exclamation marks and those dashes.

Quotation marks are helpful in two ways: to indicate quotations and to reflect forced meanings.

When you quote someone else, you're borrowing material to share a fresh viewpoint or another approach. That's friendly. Sometimes you quote someone else just to expand, or to share the "best possible wording." Again, that's a friendly thing to do. So is the "proof" included inside quotation marks.

Sometimes we use quotation marks to make mental comment . . . to signify a forced meaning, as "the circular file" for the wastebasket, or "on the beam" for good thinking. A bit of this adds to the warmth and friendliness; too much would make our writing a bit too "cute" for business communication.

Contractions give informality and warmth. They're perfectly acceptable, and have been common in business writing for at least the past century. Top executives and military leaders alike have said things like "isn't" and "don't" in memos, letters and reports.

In an earlier chapter we learned that semicolons and colons add clarity; they also add friendliness because they reflect variety in our sentence patterns.

That's the point about punctuation: VARIETY IN PUNCTUATION REFLECTS A VARIETY OF SENTENCE STRUCTURE AND A VARIETY OF FEELING ABOUT THE CONTENT. Thus a wide variety of punctuation is a symptom of your "human-ness." It's an element in the friendly image you send your reader.

Let's summarize. By using effective sentences as openers and closers, by varying sentence length and structure throughout your writing, you can sound like a human being—not a business machine. By using positive, reader-centered words you share your concern to see things from the reader's viewpoint. By using a variety of punctuation, you can reveal your own personality . . . give some "inflections" to the printed word . . . add more warmth and friendliness to your business writing.

IN GREATER DETAIL

We are always concerned to create a good image when we write. We want our readers to regard us as logical, so we seek organization and clarity. But we want more: we'd also like our readers to think of us as warm human beings . . . friendly people doing business with them. We want to sound like a person dealing with a person—not like a business machine.

We sometimes fail. As Flesch points out (*The Art of Readable Writing*, p. 220) "We write stilted English because we unconsciously assume that this is expected of us in the position we happen to fill in the organization we belong to."

Why friendliness is so important

What sort of person emerges in your mind as you read this next letter? It is designed for people who are attending training sessions in the headquarters building of a major organization.

This announcement applies to every class, for the information of every participant, including the instructor. With the exception of emergencies, when a person is asked to call home or the office immediately, office telephones are not for the general use of others. These telephones are business telephones for the use of local office personnel in the conduct of official business.

All persons who wish to call home, their office or to conduct personal business, should use the pay phones located on the ground (cafeteria) level or the third floor. Because of a particular project or other top priority work there is a possibility that your office may need to contact you. If this is the case, you may want to check with them during your coffee break or at lunch time. Under no circumstances are persons to wander in and out of private offices in other offices.

We have had a number of complaints from local employees and the general public concerning the tie-up of our telephone lines. We have also had a number of thefts from local offices. We must keep our telephone lines open for business and we do not want to have innocent persons suspected of taking things. To avoid either of these situations, your complete cooperation will be appreciated.

Thank You,

Raymond Kester

Manager of Building Services

What a welcome! A far cry from the friendly image we would like to create with our own business writing.

Of course we must send such messages now and then. But need we sound so persistent? . . . so authoritarian? . . . so petulant? Surely a polite, brief request would produce the cooperation more effectively. At the same time it would maintain our image as a friendly person doing an unpleasant piece of business in the friendliest possible way.

How do we make business writing seem friendly?

First, last, and always, friendly writing results from trying to put ourselves in the reader's position. We cannot always say what our readers would like us to say, but we can say unpleasant things less harshly if we have tried to examine the issue from the reader's viewpoint. What benefits accrue to them if they accept our recommendation? What will they gain from doing as we ask? What detail will let them understand why we have bad news for them? What specific words indicate that we considered their feelings before we reached our decision?

And then when we have considered their thoughts and their feelings, we can use words and structures which make the bad news as bearable as possible. Our words and our structures *do* make a difference. But unfortunately, some writers send even their friendly messages in cold, impersonal fashion.

This relationship between viewpoint and technique is very important. Let's restate it this way:

> NO TECHNIQUE CAN REPLACE OUR EFFORT TO PUT OUR-
> SELVES INTO OUR READER'S POSITION. BUT ONCE WE HAVE
> LOOKED AT THE ISSUE FROM OUR READER'S VIEWPOINT,
> WE CAN USE TECHNIQUES TO SHARE OUR EMPATHY.

Thus techniques implement intention. Whether the news is good or bad, a few simple techniques can add some warmth and friendliness to business writing. In this chapter we will consider those techniques.

Friendly organization

What about organization? How can it contribute to friendliness?

For one thing, good planning and organization leads to concise-ness—and conciseness is friendly. "Talk to the busiest tycoon on Wall Street, or to the spinster who owns the least visited antique shop in New England. Both will tell you that they have been 'extremely busy.' . . .This has a direct influence on . . . reaction to letters; the shorter they are, the better." (*Level-Headed Letters,* Laird and Hayes, p. 115) This assumes, of course, that the letter isn't so short that it omits critical data; this assumes that the letter includes at least one positive statement of concern for the reader's feelings or opinions.

Once again, let's look at the organization of business writing from two approaches: the logical plan and the psychological plan. Logical organi-zation is friendly because it contributes to the conciseness and continuity; it makes sense of the purpose and the content. The reader learns at once what response is expected, and then finds supporting ideas developed in a methodical order. Psychological organization assures that some state-ment of concern or understanding appears with the statement of purpose. Psychological organization sequences ideas so they are as acceptable as possible. We might put it this way: logical organization produces friendliness indirectly; psychological organization is directly concerned with being friendly.

Friendly writers also keep their readers in mind when they express those supporting ideas. They select words, build and punctuate sentences so ideas are clear and acceptable to readers. Thus our study of techniques for friendly writing will examine the same tools which make our writing clear. We will look again at sentences, words and punctuation—but this time we'll be considering how to make them warm rather than how to make them clear.

Friendly sentences

First, let's see how sentences can convey warmth to our readers.

Remember always that the first sentence of your letter or report is "prime time." It gives your readers their first signal about what to expect and about what is expected of them. It gives them their first image of you, the writer. Readers want to know at once whether they are reading to get information, or to get signals about an action you want them to take or an opinion you want them to adopt. If they are reading for information, is it so they will acquire new facts? Or so they will be persuaded to a particular viewpoint? If they are expected to take action, exactly what action is it?

The sooner they know, the better. The sooner and clearer the statement of purpose, the friendlier the writing. Even when the news is bad; even when the position is controversial or unpopular; the sooner they know, the better.

But it isn't enough merely to *state* the purpose. We need to state it from the reader's point of view. We might do that with a sentence that reads, "You will have to send us more information if you want to be considered for employment." Or again, "There is no way we can answer the questions you asked in your March 21st letter. As you can well imagine, that information is confidential." Or we might just say, "You have to appear at a hearing on June 13 at 1:30 p.m. in the General Foreman's office." All of those sentences state the purpose—from *our* viewpoint.

In each of those cases we could improve the tone by being just a little bit friendly. For example: "We want to consider your application fully—and to do so we need more information." We could have said, "We're sorry we can't send the information you requested on March 21st. Unfortunately, those matters are confidential." Or we could have written, "We feel you will want to clear up the question of your liability in the May 3 accident as soon as possible; so we have scheduled a hearing at 1:30 p.m. on June 13 in the General Foreman's office."

None of the three revisions holds a friendly message—but they are reader-centered because they state the purpose quickly and give the readers a motive for their response. These reader motives should appear in the first sentence. They are sometimes called "carrots" or "jellybeans." Those are colloquial ways to say that people will more readily do something when they see "what's in it for them." Thus a "carrot" for sending information is to complete some transaction originally requested by the reader. A potential "jellybean" for late payments is "to maintain your good credit rating." But writers often fail to mention these motivators. They make demands like "Please tell us. . ." or "You must. . ."

Or they make impersonal, gobbledygookish statements like "Reference is made to your current Purchase order #2785-673-2A in which you specified that . . ."

When writers find mutual goals with readers, they are ready to write their first sentence.

Another tip before we leave the subject of first sentences: if you are having lots of trouble finding the motivator, or trouble wording that first sentence, try writing the rest of the letter first. That's right! Compose the rest of the letter, and then come back to write the first sentence. It's amazing how often your work with the remaining ideas will unlock your creativity, revealing the wording or the "carrot" you need to mention to your reader.

When we introduce bad news, or request unwelcome responses, we especially need to show the benefits of responding:

"To speed your order, will you send us some additional credit references?"

"We will ship your merchandise as soon as we receive. . ."

"We wish we could grant your request for.extended leave. However. . ."

The point about giving bad news is just this; nobody likes to be kept dangling. . . to be the mouse in a cat-and-mouse game. Only on very rare occasions do you make your message friendlier by postponing the inevitable. We can prepare our readers for the denial with phrases like "much as we would like to" or "after careful consideration" or "We tried to look at both sides." Such "planting" has a positive effect much like ideas planted by social leaders. Many current practices are realities today because someone planted them years ago: Equal Rights for Women, space travel, the 32-hour week, legal holidays arranged to comprise three-day weekends.

If you feel there are very, very special reasons to state the purpose late in the letter, then your first sentence still needs to provide an "objective generalization." This plants the possibility of bad news without being specifically negative. How? By implying that the issue can go either of two ways. For example:

"This letter reviews your request for extended payments."

"To evaluate your proposed new minimum salaries, we asked if they were both feasible and competitive."

"This letter analyzes your recent job performance and outlines steps for improvement."

"We have carefully considered your qualifications for the position of . . ."

When the news is good, you obviously want to share it in the friendliest possible way at the earliest possible moment. How would you evaluate this computer-generated letter from a large utility company?

Dear Customer:

You have reached the anniversary of your levelized monthly billing plan. A comparison has been made between your actual metered usage and the amount you have been billed with the following results:

Total billing 12 months	$ 436.00
Less: Total Usage 12 months	$ 305.39
Less: Amount outstanding from previous year	$ .00
Overbilling	$ 130.61

Since your billing was greater than your actual usage, plus any outstanding amount from the prior year, the credit has been applied to your current service bill. Any remaining credit of $1.00 or more is refunded to you through the enclosed check. If the remaining credit is less than $1.00 it will be applied to your next monthly bill. It is not necessary to make a monthly payment this month. Your next bill will be revised based on your usage the prior year.

Should you have any questions about your account, please call us. We appreciate your business and are always glad to help you.

M. D. Calvin

Customer Billing Manager

Cold and mechanical—yet it has such good news! By putting the background in the foreground, and by arraying the evidence before the findings, the writers add chill and confusion. Only the last paragraph seems really warm and friendly—and it could be written to anybody. One just has to ask, "Why take so long to give good news?" We aren't Agatha Christie, writing mystery novels; let's tell our readers "whodunnit" in the very early sentences!

This last example raises the issue of computer-generated letters. When they can be typed on normal typewriters with normal type fonts, these letters can *look* just as personal as any other letter. The style of the writer determines how friendly they are. When they are printed on highspeed computer equipment, they often look routine and dehumanized. To ease this pain, some organizations insert the reader's name and local data (like home town, home state, job title) at discreet intervals. This helps—but not much. The printing gives it away. Besides, the amount of data that can be stored in the computer's limited memory is too tempting to programmers: they use it too often. Result? You get your name and your home town "dragged into" the letter every few sentences. The probable moral is this: if a computer will print your message, then be especially careful to arrange and express the ideas from the reader's viewpoint. Be very sure to show your readers the benefits of your recommendation, or what they have to gain from accepting your position or purpose. Find out—and express—"what's in it for them." Look at every issue from their point of view. That is psychological organization.

This psychological organization, reflecting our concern for our readers, is sometimes called "reader-centering." That's because friendly writers put their reader(s) in the center of their attention and are guided by that empathic urge when they arrange ideas.

Activity 38, on page 176, helps you locate friendly opening sentences.

"Openings" are important. So are "closings." The closing sentence isn't really prime time—but it's "next to prime time."

Part of the secret of friendly closings is a principle which emerged in our study of how to organize:

> WHEN YOU HAVE SAID WHAT YOU HAVE TO SAY, JUST STOP WRITING.

Friendly closings are purposeful. It's simply not a friendly thing to keep your readers reading while you "wind down" by repeating yourself or adding polite, irrelevant details. Your final sentence is your last chance to sound relevant and human. It probably boils down to just that: you best show your humane-ness by being relevant. Quit while you're ahead.

Business letters and reports do not normally need a summary as do lessons, speeches or sermons. Teachers, speakers and ministers find it necessary (or wise) to use a three-step process: they tell people what they are going to tell them, then they tell them, and then they tell them what they have told them. In business writing such repetition is unnecessary and unwise. It's unnecessary because the words are already there on the page for reference in case anyone needs them. It's unwise because it makes the writing seem so pedantic, ponderous, and pontifical. Pedantic urges explain the summaries in this workbook; themes are repeated to drive them into your consciousness. Such summaries really can contribute to friendliness if used *inside* the report to provide transitions from one section to another. They tend to say, "And now we have completed our study of Point A; let's go on to Point B." However, a final conclusion or summary is seldom necessary or wise.

Friendly messages are often concise. Remember, the warmest message you can send anyone takes just three words: "I love you."

What would constitute a purposeful closing paragraph? In most letters, the final supporting idea makes a satisfactory last paragraph. In most reports, the last paragraph needed to develop the final Area of Discussion makes a satisfactory last paragraph. When the logical plan has been developed, it's time to stop. Only in very long, very complex, or very controversial documents need you consider a summary.

Over the years, letter writers have fallen into the habit of putting on a "final paragraph" which they defend on the grounds of courtesy, politeness, friendliness. These paragraphs tend to be trite. For example: "If there is any way we can be of further assistance to you, please do not hesitate to call on us." The clichés give it away. The paragraph is a sincere, but extremely ineffective way of signing off. If the letter hasn't already established its warm concern, it's too late now. Such paragraphs are really just expansions of what the complimentary close was originally designed to do: to signal our sincere concern.

If you use a simplified format (with no complimentary close), or if you feel an overpowering need to have a "sign-off" paragraph, then let that paragraph do one of these things: offer a mental comment about the entire letter, or offer concrete help. Some examples of mental comment would be:

"We trust this adequately explains our reasoning."

"Does this strike you as an acceptable position?"

"We hope this clears up the matter."

Examples of offers for concrete help might be:

"If you have other questions, give us a call at (404) 981-8582."

"The full file on this transaction is available if you'd like to check it."

Many creative business writers say these kinds of things in the complimentary close. They avoid the traditional "Truly" and "Sincerely." Instead they express their comments or offers of help. When they do this, the wording tends to be crisp, informal: "Hope this clarifies things." "See you on the 12th." "Give us a call." "Do you agree?" "Hope you agree." "Call me on the 10th."

When we thank people in writing, we face the problem of the coldness of the printed page. A "Thank you" is about as friendly as it is complete and concrete. The mere words "Thank you" at the bottom of a letter don't carry as much warmth as we might wish. We've all heard cashiers who have problems making their "Thank you!" sound real: sometimes a recording might sound more human. That's why we need to be specific when we thank someone in a business letter. We need to thank people for their interest, for their questions, for their payment. Better to say "Thanks for giving us your opinion" or "Thanks so much for the sketches," than "Thanks for your help." Better say "Thanks for waiting six weeks for our reply," than just "Thank you." "Thanks for understanding," makes an effective way to thank a reader—and to end a letter.

The same need for personalized comment applies to offers of further help. Which of these is the friendlier closing?

"If there is any way this office can be of further assistance, please do not hesitate to contact us," OR:

"Won't you call me at (404) 981-6745 if you have any more problems with your StatOMatic?"

The second sentence gives a telephone number to use. It uses the first and second persons; it admits frankly that there have been problems. It avoids the clichés like "this office," "further assistance" and "contact." Such personalized, concrete closings are the difference between a warm handshake on the one hand—or a brushoff on the other. They're the difference between a nice smile or a door slammed in the face. Even the words "Thank you" can sound like a closing door when they appear alone on the pages of a business letter. Personalization by being concrete is the best way to handle the closing—when you feel there is some compelling reason to have a paragraph devoted to nothing but closing the letter. That is the antidote for those preprogrammed, trite "winding down" paragraphs which appear again and again, word-for-word, in too many business letters . . . letters where the writer has said everything there is to say but just hasn't quit writing yet!

Activity 39, on page 177, gives you some practice with closing sentences.

Although written sentences tend to be shorter than spoken sentences, business sentences tend to be longer than readers like. At least there is a tendency to overload the sentences we write in letters and reports. This costs us some clarity: readers find it hard to follow Subject-Verb-Object patterns, and they thus lose the thought. For this reason, it's friendly to keep the average length of our sentences as short as possible . . . around 15 to 17 words. Now remember, we're talking about the aver-

age. That means that some sentences will be somewhat longer than 17 words. But it also means that some sentences should be considerably shorter.

In fact, there is much to be said for deliberately using a short-short sentence now and then. By short-short, we mean from two to five words. Wayne Dyer uses this device in his best-seller, *Your Erroneous Zones:*

"Perhaps you've adopted a stance that the self (you) is fragile and easily shattered if you enter areas where you've never been before. This is a myth. You are a tower of strength. You are not going to collapse or fall apart if you encounter something new."

See how those short-short sentences work for the author? "This is a myth" directly confronts the preceding comment. "You are a tower of strength" has such vitality that its very structure tends to convince us. And both these sentences, nestled among rather long sentences, seem like a person talking to us . . . not like a dull discourse.

One big reason for short-short sentences is the relaxation they give our reader, like a landing on a long flight of stairs. Another reason is the variety they give to the rhythms of the prose. Variety is no small part of apparent friendliness. W. H. Auden, a celebrated poet whose comments don't always apply to business writing, makes one comment that applies directly: "The ear tends to be lazy, craves the familiar and is shocked by the unexpected; the eye, on the other hand, tends to be impatient, craves the novel, and is bored by repetition." (From *The Dyer's Hand.*)

Active sentences tend to be friendlier than passive sentences. There is a very simple reason for this: active sentences put key words (subjects and objects) into key positions. The subject of an active sentence tends to come at or near the start; the object at or near the end. The passive voice often traps us into the impersonal "it": "It was decided," or "It is felt." In the active voice we say "Ms. Briggs decided . . .," or "I feel." That's good. If you want to be friendly, give credit by naming names—not by naming "It."

Activity 40, on page 179, gives drills in using the active voice as a tool of friendliness. It thus differs from earlier activities about the active voice.

Interrogative sentences contribute to friendly letters and reports. Questions achieve several friendly results. First, questions take the curse off a request. Suppose you were talking face-to-face with an associate. If you said, "Please give me your decision," you could inflect your voice so it sounded like a courteous request. But on the printed page, there is no way to give it that same warmth; your request sounds like a command. By phrasing it as a question, "May we have your decision?" we make it seem what it really is—a request and not an order.

When we request, we are being both courteous and businesslike to add a date. For example, "May we have your answer by July 15?"

Commands such as "You must," or "You are required," get very little result when used in business writing. They are better than the third person ("Employees must," or "All taxpayers are required," or "All recipients of this letter are requested") but they still don't get much result. The third person format allows the readers to escape: it talks about "employees" or "taxpayers" or "recipients"—it isn't talking to them! The command, such as "You are required," or "You must," just becomes a challenge. Readers tend to ignore such commands; they thus win the challenge!

A second value of questions is that they mold thinking—ours and our readers'. When we must phrase the request as a question, we are more apt to pin down exactly what we want from the reader. The use of the question format can thus lead us to add a date to our request for a decision, or to include a criterion when requesting a product. Perhaps our original idea was to "ask for some more background." By moving into the interrogative viewpoint we translate that to a specific set of questions which pin down the precise type of background data we need: "What schools did you attend?" "How many credits did you earn at each?" "What degrees have you earned?" That's far more helpful to our reader than just, "Please supply us with details of your education." (And note that stuffy word "supply"! We might use it in a request; we'd weed it out of our direct questions.)

Then too, questions tend to be more conversational. They are the method we use when we want information in face-to-face communication. We say, "Tell me, what school did you attend?"—not "Education!" Questions imply an interchange, and lend to the printed page at least the *illusion* of people talking to people.

Finally, questions imply or secure the involvement of our readers. This sense of participation can be important, particularly when we are trying to arouse the reader's interest to a level that produces action or support. There are lots of occasions when our purpose is just that, and on these occasions the question is a useful method. We need to ask our readers for their opinions. We need to ask them how they feel. We need to show our concern for their views if we want a mutually profitable activity. Put yourself in your reader's shoes. If someone wanted your opinion, would you be more responsive to the request: "Please state your opinions and your feelings," or to the question, "How do you feel about this issue?"

Which would you think friendlier? To be told "State your opinion," or to be asked "What's your opinion on this?"

Activity 41, on page 180, will give you plenty of practice converting commands and orders into effective, friendly requests.

Remember: the phrasing is just part of this technique. If you are going to make a request in the form of a question, then follow through. Older texts still say that requests should be punctuated with a period; however, when you phrase them as questions, the question mark is the logical, appropriate and friendly way to punctuate.

Let's summarize about sentences and their contribution to the warmth of our business writing:

- The first sentence states the purpose and provides a motivator.
- The closing sentence has a definite function (mental comment or offer of specific help) or it's omitted!
- The Subject-Verb-Object pattern is clearly visible.
- There are occasional short-short sentences.
- You use the active voice.
- You use questions to specify, to elicit feelings, and to get some reader involvement.
- Any of these techniques is just a way to implement the concern you really feel and the time you spent in considering your reader's position.

Friendly words

Next, let's consider the words we choose as friendly writers.

Words can do two things simultaneously: they can denote a specific meaning, and they can arouse associated feelings in readers. That second process is called connotation. It's closely related to semantics, and it impacts heavily upon our behavior as business writers. We want words which denote precision and connote warmth.

One way to create a friendly image is to concentrate on words which carry warm, positive connotations. Let's examine this process by looking first at a word which has just the opposite impact. Take the word "cheap." It has negative connotations. Your service or your product may cost less than those of your competitors—but you're not about to say, "Our product is cheap." So you escape by saying "Our price is cheap." You've become more accurate—but you have planted that negative word "cheap" in your reader's consciousness.

Just a short search for the positive word can pay big dividends. You end up saying that your service is "inexpensive" or that your product is "a bargain." (If that strikes you as connoting the hard sell approach, then you probably use a word like "reasonable" or "economical.") The point is that you select an accurate word with positive connotations. But by avoiding the negative word, you also get to talk about what you really want to talk about: your product or your service, not your price.

Which of these lists communicates the more positive images in your minds—and in your spirits?

Unimportant	Significant
Neither	Both
Neglect	Attention
Not uncomfortable	Easy
Not rude	Polite
Not at all	Very
Heavy	Important
Somewhat	Considerably

Obviously the list at the right carries the cheerful connotations. But the interesting thing is that each word appears opposite an alternative way to express the same idea . . . to describe the same thing. Writers have choices. You can say that something is "significant" or that it is "not unimportant." You may opt between "somewhat better" or "considerably improved." When given such options, writers have often selected the negative approach. It's amazing how often we describe things as "not bad" instead of "downright good."

We can "plant" the wrong impression by saying that something is "not unimportant" or we can create friendly responses by saying it is "significant." We want to find a way to use the positive words when we write . . . just as we want to express ideas positively. Consider these two approaches to reviewing an employee's recent job performance:

"Your production and accuracy have improved considerably in the past six months," OR

"Neither your production nor your accuracy is as big a problem as it was six months ago."

The first version sends positive stimuli with the words "improved" and "considerably." The second sentence sends the negative verbal stimuli: "neither," "nor" and "problem." Once the employee sees those words, defenses are up. Only a careful reading will undo the damage. Even when (or if) the correct message is received, the employee has a right to wonder why the praise came so grudgingly.

A large soap company has applied this to its advertising. For years, its advertisements implied the negative threat: Maybe your best friends aren't telling you! Could you possibly have body odor? Today their television commercials picture a husband putting his arms around his wife and beaming, "Gee, honey, you smell good."

As reader-oriented writers, we want to use positive words in positive sentences to express positive thoughts. We say, "We will ship your order immediately," instead of, "The referenced shipment will be forwarded at the earliest opportunity." If we have bad news we say, "We will ship your materials just as soon as possible," rather than, "We will not be placing your materials into the mails until the present backorder problem has been eliminated." Even if the delay is considerable, we will name a time. It may not be soon—but it is at least positive and definite. Thus the best positive approach would probably be, "We will ship your materials as soon as possible—probably on or before May 1."

Here is an example of an extremely positive approach. Is it too positive? It is an actual letter from a merchandising-by-mail firm. They sent this as a form letters to members who were a little bit tardy with payments:

Dear Member:

Don't pass it up—the opportunity to purchase the wide range of books and records that are made available to you.

Just take care of the enclosed billing today, and we can continue to send the merchandise you request.

Yours truly,

Diane Coberly

Diane Coberly, Director
Accounts Payable

Some will feel that this takes the positive approach too far; others will see it as a reasonable way to motivate the reader. It should prove for all of us that no one approach will work with all the people all the time. And nearly everyone will agree that it's a vastly warmer approach than that taken by another organization, which reportedly wrote one delinquent customer:

Dear Mr. Smith:

You owe us $132.56 for past purchases and there can be no doubt about it. You own a house that is attachable, and other assets that can be attached, plus salaries that can be garnisheed.

We therefore demand that you make partial payment within 10 days. Consider this: is it really worth it to you to have neighbors and relatives and employers who know how careless you are in discharging your financial responsibilities?

Awaiting your immediate action,

R.G. Sterns

R.G. Sterns

Activity 42, on page 182, lets you practice the use of positive words.

Perhaps we need to remind ourselves again that this is not merely a matter of technique. When we cannot give good news, we can at least try to look at the bad news from the reader's viewpoint. "We are sorry," or "We have examined the issue from all angles, and honestly feel . . ." may not make our readers happy—but they are a lot friendlier than no evidence at all that we tried to understand. Above all, they are a lot friendlier than those messages which don't take time to say "We're sorry," or "We understand how you feel," or "We tried to . . . but."

It isn't that the words can take the place of making the effort to understand; it's just that many times writers have tried, but didn't bother to share their effort to understand. Thus the words don't replace the effort; they just accompany it. Of course there are times when writers don't use the words because they didn't try to empathize. It's just possible that by training oneself to use the words, one can also train oneself to try to understand.

That reminds us that when we make a mistake, we should admit it. When we need to apologize, we should do so at once, and for something specific: a delay, a refusal, a mistake. Not only should we apologize at once (early in the message) and for something specific; we should apologize in as few words as possible. To repeat the apology, or to go on and on explaining it or its causes is just to prolong the negativism. Remember Hamlet: he might have believed that his mother was innocent of complicity in his father's murder if she hadn't had so many excuses. The lady doth protest too much, methinks," concluded the Prince of Denmark. Or as one psychologist put it: "When you're on thin ice, skate fast!"

In *Level-Headed Letters,* Laird and Hayes point out (p. 39): "By freely admitting errors, and by explaining corrective action, you're being positively positive—even in a negative situation."

Let's summarize how to handle apologies in a friendly fashion:

1. Apologize immediately.

2. Apologize briefly.

3. Apologize for something specific.

4. End by mentioning corrective action. You thus end the apology on a positive note.

There's one more thing: for any negative message (apologies, bad news, unpopular and controversial purposes) avoid humor. When we're face to face with friends, humor sometimes dissipates the tension. Note that word "sometimes." When we're distant (as we are always distant from our business readers) humor is far less effective. We may think it's side-splitting to call the fiscal year the "fiasco year"; it may tickle us to call our inseparable friends "insufferable friends"; we may think of the utility companies as "public senilities," or tell subordinates to use words of "one cylinder." Okay. But if you yield to such urges in your letters, be sure to enclose those forced meanings within quotation marks.

If our message is straightforward, or contains good news, humor may seem human. But beware. Light frivolous comments have a way of seeming smarty or snide on the printed page. *Now this does not mean that humor has no place in business writing—only that it has a limited place in business writing.* It has no place at all if we're apologizing or proposing purposes which our readers won't like very well.

The effort to be friendly should result in our reflecting more "YOU interest" in our writing. The word "you" isn't exactly magic—but it certainly is powerful! It won't *ever* take the place of real empathy, but if you keep the word "you" in mind as you plan your writing, you will be silently saying to your reader, "If I were *you* . . ." That produces empathy; just putting the word "you" into your letters may not do so at all. They tell the story about the mother who was worried because her debutante daughter got very few dates. After about two seasons of this, the mother decided to confront the issue. She called the daughter aside and counseled her: "Dear, the problem is that you are so self-centered. Just listen to your conversation: It's 'I did this' and 'I think that' and 'I want this or that.' You must show an interest in the young men. Talk about

them—not about yourself!" Well, the daughter listened, and believed—but forgot. On her very next date she was her usual self-centered self until halfway through the evening. Then she remembered. So
she interrupted herself: "But I've been going on and on about myself.
Let's talk about you for a change. Tell me, what do you think of me?"

The story is forced, but the point is well taken. The mere word "you"
won't produce friendly writing. But if we try to get that word onto our
pages, we will need to think of our readers . . . their values, their motivation, their stake in our purposes. When we do that, gobbledygook like
"referenced shipment" becomes "your furniture"; "Our regulations require that all employees . . ." becomes "You can secure your seniority
rights by . . ."

On page 184, Activity 43 gives you some interesting practice in converting third-person, impersonal statements into reader-centered sentences
with some "you" interest.

Sometimes a proper noun is as valuable as the word "you"—maybe
better! Perhaps the most magic word of all is the reader's name. Do you
remember Bette Davis and Ann Baxter in the movie *All About Eve?* This
story of how important it was for Eve to see her name up in lights hits at
an important human need.

This human need is so universal that the same story was later a smash musical on Broadway: *Applause,* with Lauren Bacall. You see, there's a trace of Eve in every one of us: we like to see our name. That's why some firms like the Block Letter format: the reader's name must appear in the salutation.

Whatever your format, you can use your reader's name. There's plenty of opportunity to do so at major transitions or summaries in the body of your letter. Example: "And so, Ms. Browning, we hope you will soon complete your Basic Accounting course. We can then consider your application for . . . " When we write reports we can populate our paragraphs with peoples' names: instead of saying "The Implementation Committee: we can mention at least once that Ms. Eva Luce, Mr. Glen Bly and Dr. L. E. Fry were its members. Instead of talking about "the product" we can call it by its trade name.

The names of people, companies and agencies, products and programs accompany the word "you" to make our business writing seem friendly. Business letters need not describe vague deserts made up only of things and processes, machines and concepts; they can just as easily mention people, familiar organizations, and products.

Here is an actual example of a conversion from the impersonal to a rather friendly sentence.

"Remaining basic procedural information required by field locations should be available chiefly in the form of bulletins and regulations in the not-too-distant future."

The supervisor of the writer who created that wanted a friendlier version. Together, the boss and the subordinate came up with:

"You should have the bulletins and regulations from our office by June 20. This will help you explain the new Profit-Sharing Plan to your staff."

Personal pronouns include the words "we" and "I," as well as the word "you." There is no reason why these first person words, "I" and "we," cannot appear in your business writing. They have been a common part of the business vocabulary for several centuries. Good business writers have been saying "I" and "we" for as long as there have been business letters.

There are times when you speak for yourself in a letter or a report. In those cases the word "I" is appropriate. At other times you speak for your office or your organization, your team or your committee. Those are the times when you say "we."

Mark Twain has a witty comment on the editorial "we." He once noted that technically, the only humans entitled to use such a plural were people with tapeworms! But Twain was jesting. The editorial "we" has been common communications practice long enough to be sanctioned as habit. Others have protested the use of "I" and "we" in business writing on more serious and more valid grounds: their overuse. If writers say "I" when describing a team effort, then they are indeed being egotistical. If they say either "I" or "we" too often, then probably they really *are* being self-centered rather than reader-centered. But these excesses do not change the fact that first-person pronouns are entirely proper. As a matter of fact, they add a great deal to the warmth and personalization of business prose.

Another enemy of friendly writing is gobbledygook. Remember it? Gobbledygook is wordy, unintelligible jargon. It has lost its meaning, if it ever had any. It gets used out of habit rather than out of thought; it appears out of laziness rather than out of purpose. Some writers use gobbledygook because they think it makes them sound important. Unfortunately, they merely sound pompous. People use gobbledygook to impress, not to express. It follows that gobbledygook shows up when writers haven't taken the trouble to pin down precisely what it is they want to say.

The trouble with studying gobbledygook is that the more we imprint those offensive words, the more apt we are to use them; Probably the best thing we can do is recognize gobbledygook when it accidentally crops up in our own writing—and then weed it out with some meaning-ful substitutes . . . or by omitting the material altogether. (It often hap-pens that the gobbledygook expresses non-thought, or unnecessary comment, so it really *can* be cut.)

If we exorcize the clichés from our writing, then:

- "The referenced letter" can become "Your May 26 letter."
- "The undersigned" can become "I" or "me."
- "Heretofore" can become "Up until now."
- "Take this opportunity" becomes "You can" or "We would like to . . ."

There are activities which permit you to recognize gobbledygook in Activity 44, on page 185. Activity 45, on page 186, lets you translate gobbledygook into "plain talk."

Friendly punctuation

Now that we have examined sentences and words as instruments of our friendliness, let's talk about how some punctuation marks add warmth to the prose of business letters and reports.

When we use a variety of sentence structure, we will also use a variety of punctuation marks. Long declarative sentences tend to get monotonous, and they can sound pretty unfriendly. In fact, their punctuation betrays that monotony. Readers see only capital letters, periods, and commas—and not too many of those because the sentences are so long! But what if our sentences reflect different intentions—intentions such as statements, questions, parallels and contrasts, asides and emphasis? Then we will need to use lots of different kinds of punctuation. Thus variety in punctuation is a symptom of a friendly, conversational style. (And remember what Auden said about variety: the eye craves variety; it is bored by repetition.)

First, we must establish the fact that a variety of punctuation isn't good in itself: only because it reflects a variety in our prose style.

We will examine several punctuation marks which help us communicate our friendly intentions. We can begin with ways to punctuate the Saluta-tion in organizations using the Block format.

The traditional punctuation following the Salutation is a full colon:

Dear Ms. Forsythe:

Some organizations tried to make the Salutation less formal. So a number of years ago they substituted the semicolon:

Dear Mr. Henderson;

In very recent years, other organizations have used even less formal punctuation marks: the comma, the dash or nothing at all. It's not unusual (but by no means common) nowadays to see salutations like these:

Dear Mr. Drury,

Dear Mr. Charles

Donna—

Let's just remind ourselves that question marks reflect a desire to soften requests and to get reader involvement. As such they are important marks of "friendly punctuation."

The dash is an effective way to get emphasis. Dashes say "This is important," or "Remember this!" Thus the dash signals your friendly intention to tell readers what parts matter the most; it is a friendly way to share your values with your readers . . . like speaking a bit louder or stressing certain words. The dash will emphasize words which follow, or words which are enclosed by dashes. Dashes provide a kind of inflection, showing your reader what you personally feel is important. You use dashes to tell your readers what to remember—what you hope they will value as much as you do.

Of course there are other ways to emphasize. You can simply say that something is important. You can underline. You can print words or entire ideas in ALL CAPS. You can use italics to emphasize.

If your final document will be typed, you can use both underlining and italics as different devices for emphasis. But if your document is going to a printer, your use of both devices will drive someone up the wall. The underlining is a signal to typesetters to put the words in italics. We mention this not to be technical, but to lead into an important point about emphasis. Use it sparingly. That advice has two dimensions:

1. Don't try to emphasize too many words or ideas.
2. Don't use too many emphasis-getting devices in any single document.

IF YOU UNDERLINE TOO MANY THINGS, OR PRINT TOO MANY THINGS IN ALL CAPS, THEN YOU HAVE PROBABLY OVER-STATED YOUR CASE—AND YOUR READER WILL BEGIN TO MIS-

<u>TRUST YOU</u>, <u>THINKING THAT YOU ARE MORE HYSTERICAL THAN JUDICIOUS</u>—<u>MORE EXCITABLE THAN FRIENDLY AND HELPFUL</u>!! See what we mean? That sentence with its overabundant underlining and capitalization and dashes and exclamation marks is simply unbelievable.

Emphasis must be used sparingly or it loses its emphasis. Just remember how some of your teachers had to work harder and harder to get less and less of your attention.

Here is a glaring example, a real letter which tried too hard to be informal and emphatic at one and the same time.

Dear Former Subscriber:

Well—you did it!

You kept putting it off . . . and putting it off . . . and putting it off . . . and it finally happened!

   Your subscription to ACTIVE PEOPLE has expired and you will not receive any more copies unless you send us your renewal instructions.

   Our experience has been that *most* subscribers choose to renew their subscriptions and of those few who do not, many simply just forgot to send us their renewal instructions.

   I hope this is the case with you and you will send us your renewal instructions today. If you act *immediately* it is still possible (we won't promise though) to reinstate your subscription so you do not miss a single issue.

   Please do not procrastinate any longer.

DO IT RIGHT NOW!

Sincerely yours,

Ara G. Hanley

Ara G. Hanley
Publisher

Do such letters get results? Well, it's an established fact that one "former subscriber" responded to this letter by writing on the letter itself and returning it in the enclosed postage-free envelope. Alongside the third paragraph, the customer used a red pen and wrote PROMISE?

We hope you noted the inconsistency in the style of that last letter. In all that overbearing prose, the writer still indents the first line of some paragraphs—but not all of them. It uses a formal colon at the "clever" saluta-tion. These are relics of earlier times planted right in the middle of Madison Avenue.

And let's remind ourselves that position gives emphasis. The first and the last ideas of any document, and the first and last words of any sentence, occupy "memorable" positions.

Activity 46, on page 187, gives you practice in selecting methods for emphasizing key elements of short messages.

Parentheses have quite the opposite effect of dashes. Parentheses say, "Oh, by the way." They are thus excellent symptoms of our friendly con-cern that our reader understand. They are excellent punctuation for those friendly enrichments which clarify, translate or expand key ideas. They can enrich the main thread of a sentence, or the main thread of a paragraph.

Does this imply that we can put just a few words or even entire sentences inside parentheses? It certainly does. In fact, we can put entire para-graphs inside parentheses. Why would we want to do that? Well, the content of the parenthetical paragraph might provide a history, the back-ground on a person being discussed, a further explanation of a process.

When we add parenthetical expressions, we want to be sure they are helpful to our reader. (In reports, they may be useful to some key readers but not all of them. Material which only secondary readers need should not go in the Body of the report, but in footnotes or appendices. Paren-thetical material in the Body of letters and reports must have value to key readers.) The parenthesis is a way of saying "Oh, by the way, if you need this extra explanation or background, here it is just where you need it. If you don't need it, just skip to the end of the parenthesis." For key read-ers—usually the only reader of a business letter—these comments belong in the main body of the letter. To put them in footnotes or attachments is to ask your reader to take a considerable detour. Besides, attachments and footnotes are pretty pompous for the business letter—not really too friendly.

It is apparent, of course, that the parenthesis is an excellent device for defining technical jargon. When terms express the precise concept, but may be unfamiliar to our reader, it's just the friendly thing to define the terms within parentheses.

Activity 47, on page 189, provides exercise in identifying these helpful comments and in proper placement of the parentheses.

Quotation marks can do more than merely indicate that you are borrowing some material from another source. Now, borrowing material is a fine, friendly thing to do. Borrowed material can clarify, illustrate, expand or give credibility. Quotations used just for that purpose show your consideration for your reader, and reflect your integrity in not taking credit for statements developed by others. But in addition quotation marks can indicate your informality if you put them around forced meanings or if you "fracture" your own grammar just a bit in order to be warm, informal, or human. We use quotation marks when new, unsanctioned usages seem especially apt. Thus we refer to the wastebasket as "File 13" or "File Q." We say we are "cannibalizing" when we use workable parts of broken equipment to repair other machines. We say a system is "go" when it's operating properly. This uses a verb as an adjective—a friendly thing to do provided we use quotation marks to tell our reader what we're doing. Or again, we report that we are "in the pink" when all our physical systems are "go."

These informalities enliven and warm business prose. If used moderately and appropriately (the right audience and the right subject) they are excellent ways to communicate personality as well as content. They probably are unwise in letters of condolence, reprimand, or discipline. They probably have no place in letters whose readers will find the desired response to be distasteful. We can, however, use them at other times —even if we are writing the president, the commissioner, the director or the boss. These executives are human too! They would probably welcome more "human-ness" in their reading. As a matter of fact, top executives are often quite informal themselves. The president of one company once wrote a very informal letter that a business writing instructor wanted to quote in future classes. The instructor wrote for permission, and the president replied:

SUBJECT: Your letter of August 18
Referring to my letter of June 3
Referring to your purchase order #456Z
Which we regretfully returned.

Dear Mr. Baird,

You may quote me line, verse and chapter. Who knows? Some day one of the people attending your course may become a purchasing agent—our favorite sex.

Sincerely,

Dwayne F. Lee

Dwayne F. Lee, President

That takes us to contractions. Contractions have been common in business writing for at least a century. The English language has always been particularly comfortable with contractions—in fact many forms sound constrained when we fail to contract. Words like "do not" sometimes seem sterner than "don't;" "can not" or "cannot" somehow imply greater difficulty than "can't." If these common contractions feel comfortable, use them. Unusual contractions probably won't feel comfortable. "Would've" and " 'Frinstance" show up in conversation, but they look awkward and forced on the printed page. If you were a novelist trying to replicate spoken English, you'd put such forced contractions into your character's dialog. In business writing you probably won't be comfortable with these unusual contractions. What about in a memo? Well, we can't tell for sure what you'll be comfortable with. However, funny contractions do show up every now'n then.

Contractions, and usages like that final preposition a couple of sentences ago, are obviously matters of personal preference. If you feel that such usage draws undue attention to the way you are saying things—as opposed to the things you say—then avoid such usages. However, to say that contractions are unacceptable would be as absurd as to say that they are mandatory. In using any technique, remember you use the technique to call the reader's attention to what you say—not to how you say it.

Marks of punctuation have a tendency to grow less rigid after they've been around for awhile. Take contractions: some English words have been contracted for so many decades that we no longer bother with an apostrophe. One example is the word "none." It's actually a contraction of "not one," so there was once an apostrophe there: "no'ne." But who can remember when we spelled the word that way?

New systems bring new symbols, and some of those symbols eventually become so common that they are accepted as punctuation in business writing. For example, the colon is used to show ratios in mathematics, as 4:3. The equals mark is occasionally seen in letters and reports—ordinarily in mathematical statements or fiscal tables. We seldom see the symbol = as a substitute for the word "equals" in a prose statement. However, the slash (/) is now used quite often to indicate "or" as in the word "and/or." Some people predict that there will be a common word, "andor," in a few years.

This process of assimilating new usages and dropping fine discriminations is known as "leveling," and it is very common in English. Other languages are less flexible. Another example of leveling in English is dropping the distinction between "which" as a pronoun for inanimate objects only. Today we hear established commentators say "a person which." We read established journalists saying the same thing. Language will do what its users do with it, and punctuation changes just as do words, spellings, and speech forms.

Right now, for instance, we badly need a new word. We need a uni-sexual pronoun. Habit causes us to say "he" when we are not sure of gender. But the Womens' Liberation movement has changed our comfort with that. It has also brought us words like "Ms." and "chairperson." Yet we still don't have a happy word to indicate "he or she." "He or she" seems cumbersome, and gives top billing to the male. If you're not totally "liberated," that sequence seems ungallant. A few writers have begun to use "s/he" in the hope that it will become popular . . . or that it will spur other writers to devise an even better word. The same problems occur with "him or her" and "his or hers." At any rate, friendly writers no longer assume that all managers are masculine and that all secretaries are of the feminine persuasion.

In addition to dashes, question marks, parentheses, quotation marks, and contractions, writers also have those old standbys: the colon and the semicolon. These help clarity more than friendliness. They express logical relationships and in themselves aren't especially friendly. Their presence, however, does show that there is variety in sentence structure. To that degree they contribute to the overall warmth and conversational tone of business writing.

We must also say a few things about innovation. The most effective business writers project their personality by creating stylistic details of their own invention. They do it sparingly, but these unusual ways of expressing themselves project the image of a friendly person. For one thing they use words in unusual contexts and add quotation marks to show the forced meaning. They join several words with hyphens to create new, one-and-once-only vocabularies. They use quotation marks to tell readers they have moved a word into an unfamiliar part-of-speech category. For example: we say we "position" things when we give background to provide a frame of reference; one manager referred to the "Santa-ness of our employee benefits package"; another to the "Monte Carlo aspects of our promotion policies." Finally, creative writers give their readers occasional excursions into brief-but-unusual sentence structures. Even fragments.

For some writers, the use of any "friendliness technique" seems a trifle threatening. "I've never done it" isn't a terribly good reason for not trying it now. "They've never done it that way around here" is really a challenge to the creativity and initiative of the friendly writer. There's no time like the present to set new standards. The tragedy of not trying to be friendly is that the cool, cold aloof style of so much business writing robs writers of so many good reader results. Even when writers try to see the purposes from their reader's points of view, they lack a technique for communicating that analysis or that concern.

If it's results we want from our readers—and it should be!—then we might well envision our reader while making decisions about the style and structure of our letters and reports. We can be a bit of ourselves. We can dare a little!

Activities 48 and 49 can be real challenges—and lots of fun. On page 190, Activity 48 gives you a chance to practice a great many friendliness techniques by revising a letter that requests information. Activity 49, on page 192, is a chance to revise a letter explaining a management decision. Both the original versions lack a great deal in warmth. How friendly can you make them in your conversions?

PUTTING THE PRINCIPLES INTO PRACTICE

✳ Activity 38

From each group, select the friendlier (or friendliest) opening sentence.

A. We need to hear from you immediately with your decision about our request for additional filing space.

B. Can you tell us now what you have decided about our request for additional filing space?

C. What are your plans for paying off your unpaid balance?

D. May we consider with you some plans for paying your unpaid balance?

E. Thanks so much for your prompt reply to our May 1 letter.

F. We have received your prompt reply to our earlier letter. Thank you.

G. We are confident that you will understand our position about sending your subordinates to management training workshops.

H. We would like to show you the advantages of sending your subordinates to management training workshops.

I.   You can help us clear this matter from our records if you sign the enclosed receipts.

J.   To clear up this matter, you need only sign the enclosed receipts.

K.   This letter outlines the steps to be taken by you in filing any claim.

L.   You can complete your claim by following the steps outlined herein.

M.   Your claim can be processed as soon as you complete the steps outlined in this letter.

N.   May we have a minute of your time to discuss a matter of vital importance?

O.   May we have a minute of your time to discuss the vital matter of your retirement income?

P.   We want to discuss an important issue with people of your age: retirement income!

Q.   We hope you have been thinking about your retirement income, and would like to chat with you about it in this letter.

R.   Your request for an appointment has been received and is being processed as rapidly as possible.

S.   As you requested, we will arrange an appointment at the earliest possible date.

T.   We've been delighted with your work and hope it will continue at its present high levels.

U.   We hope your work will continue at its present high levels. It has been delightful for us.

V.   Congratulations on your excellent work! And keep it up. We're delighted at the progress you've been making.

Review

Our choice of the friendly versions would be B, D, E, H, J, M, Q, S and V.

✱ Activity 39

Which of the following sentences strike you as friendly closings for business letters? If you can't decide, encircle the question mark.

A.   Thank you for your inquiry. We hope to serve you in the very near future.   YES   NO   ?

B.   Thank you for your inquiry.   YES   NO   ?

C. May we hear from you soon?   YES NO ?

D. Thank you.   YES NO ?

E. May we hear from you by the first of next
month?   YES NO ?

F. We hope that you will soon send us an order
for these improved Model K-17A recorders.   YES NO ?

G. Thanks again for calling this lapse of service to
our attention.   YES NO ?

H. Thanks again for calling this lapse of service to
our attention. As mentioned before, only by information such as you gave us can we improve
our service for others who wish to use it.   YES NO ?

I. If there is any further way that this office can be
of assistance, we trust that you will not hesitate
to call upon us.   YES NO ?

J. We appreciate your order, Ms. Shannon, and
hope you will find these books useful in your
training.   YES NO ?

K. I remain your humble servant, looking forward
to the time when we can again serve your
needs.   YES NO ?

L. We are genuinely sorry that your KenPen was
unsatisfactory. We are confident, though, that
the enclosed replacement will meet the high
standards you have a right to expect.   YES NO ?

M. We're really sorry that the warranty had expired
before your KenPen failed to operate properly.   YES NO ?

N. Do keep in touch.   YES NO ?

O. Please remit by the 16th of this month.   YES NO ?

Review

A, B, and H would get "?" marks from us. A may be a bit hard-sell. B is
perhaps just too exclusively "business-ese" to carry much warmth. H
seems too repetitious to be friendly; note the words "again" and "as
mentioned." C, E, F, G, J, L, M and N strike us as being genuinely
friendly. The rest are either too cool or too antiquated to be very friendly.

✳ Activity 40

From each group of sentences below, select the active version:

A. The reply must be prepared in triplicate by the applicant.

B. If you prepare the reply in triplicate, we will process your claim at once.

C. You should receive the applications by May 20.

D. Applications should be received in your office by May 20.

E. These decisions cannot be made without your personal involvement.

F. Your personal involvement will make these decisions possible.

G. Your personal involvement is required for these decisions.

Convert the following passive sentences into the active voice:

H. Enclosed is a transcript of the proceedings as requested by you or your office.

I. The aforementioned photographs were shot from four strategic angles and permit the viewer to get a complete picture of the machine operation.

J. If your payment is not received by August 15 the matter will be turned over to a collection agency.

K. Your attention is requested to this matter.

L. Your attention is directed to the organization's policy that all funds taken for travel purposes must be accounted for within ten days after the travel is completed.

Review

B, C, and F are active; all other versions are in the passive voice.

H. You will find the transcripts enclosed (as you requested).

I. You can get a complete picture of the machine operation from the pictures. They show the operation from four strategic angles.

J. If you send your payment by August 15 we will not need to turn it over to a collection agency.

K. Please give this matter your (immediate) attention.

L. Organizational policies require that travelers account for travel advances within ten days after completing travel.

✱ Activity 41

The requests below are stated as commands. Can you convert them to friendly requests by using the interrogative format?

A. Please pay by August 15.

B. Give your immediate attention to this matter and we will stop bothering you with these requests for information.

C. Please tell us how you wish us to dispose of the materials remaining over from your recent sales meeting.

D. We need this information soon, and cannot complete your order until we know what color cabinets you desire.

E. Please remit at your earliest convenience.

F. We require your cooperation if this program is to succeed.

G. Fill out these forms promptly so your opinion will be reflected in this survey.

H. It is imperative that we have this information by June 1.

I. Please list the nominations on the enclosed ballot.

J. Return the application as soon as you have completed it.

Review

A. May we have your payment by August 15?

B. Won't you give this your immediate attention, so we can stop bothering you . . . ?

C. How do you wish us to dispose of . . . ?

D. What color cabinets do you desire? We can complete your order as soon . . .

E. May we have your payment as soon as possible?

F. May we have your cooperation in making this program a success?

G. Will you fill out these forms promptly? Your opinions can then be reflected . . .

H. May we please have this information by June 1?

I. Why not just list your nominations . . . ? OR: Will you list your nominations . . . ?

J. Will you please return the application as soon as you have completed it?

✱ Activity 42

From the words listed here, circle the ones which have positive, affirmative connotations.

Abandoned
Ability ✓
Achieve ✓
Admirable ✓
Advantage ✓
Alleged
Ambition ✓
Approval ✓

Benefits ✓
Beware
Blatant

Can ✓
Capable ✓
Careless
Cheap
Cheer ✓
Complaint
Complete ✓
Confident ✓
Cooperative ✓
Courteous ✓
Creative ✓
Crisis

Deadlock
Decline
Definite ✓
Desirable ✓
Diplomatic ✓
Discourteous
Discredit
Distinction ✓

Ease ✓
Economy
Effective ✓
Efficient ✓
Energy ✓
Enthusiasm ✓
Exaggerated
Excellence ✓
Exceptional ✓

Fail
Faith ✓
Fault
Fear

Good ✓
Grateful ✓
Great ✓
Guarantee

Hardship
Harmony ✓
Helpful
Honest

Ignorant
Imagination ✓
Imitation
Implicate
Impossible
Improvement ✓
Inexperienced
In vain
Informative ✓
Insolvent
Integrity ✓

Judgment ✓
Justice ✓

Key
Kind

Liable
Liberal
Loyalty

Majority
Mediocre
Misfortune
Mutual

Necessary
Neglect
Not
Notable
Noteworthy

Opportunity
Optimistic
Oversight

Politic
Polite
Permanent
Poise
Popular
Precise
Premature
Prestige
Progress

Recognition
Regular
Reliable
Recluse
Rude
Ruin

Satisfaction
Service
Shirk
Simplicity
Specific
Stability
Stagnant
Struggling
Success
Superficial
Suspicious

Tact
Thorough
Thoughtful
Truth

Unfortunate
Useful

Valuable
Viable
Vigor
Vital

You
Your

Zealous

Review

Readers generally respond affirmatively to these words:

Ability	Effective	Judgment	Recognition
Achieve	Efficient	Justice	Reliable
Admirable	Energy		
Approval	Enthusiasm	Key	Satisfaction
	Excellence	Kind	Service
Benefits	Exceptional		Simplicity
		Loyalty	Specific
Can	Faith		Stability
Capable		Mutual	Success
Cheer	Good		
Complete	Grateful	Notable	
Confident	Great	Noteworthy	Tact
Cooperative	Guarantee		Thorough
Courteous		Opportunity	Thoughtful
	Harmony	Optimistic	Truth
Definite	Helpful		
Desirable	Honest	Polite	Useful
Diplomatic		Permanent	
Distinction	Improvement	Poise	Valuable
	Informative	Popular	Vigor
Ease	Integrity	Prestige	Vital
Economy		Progress	
			You
			Your

Some of the other words may deserve comment:

"Advantage," "imagination," "creative," or "majority" may be positive in some contexts, but negative in others. Unless you are certain your reader shares your values, these words are ambiguous. Best avoid them, at least if you're writing on controversial subjects. "Liberal" and "politic" carry social comment.

Some words are temporarily positive because they become "in" words. One good example is "viable." In the mid 1970's "viable" was about the best thing a businessperson or an idea could be. However, the word was so overused that it lost its lustre, eventually becoming something of a joke.

Why "specific" and not "precise"? Because the latter connotes fussiness for some people. Why not "zealous"? Because people read carelessly; the word looks like "jealous."

✳ Activity 43

In each of the following groups, select the sentence which does a better job of reflecting the reader's viewpoint:

A. Mr. Barnes, your shipment of produce will arrive early next month.

B. The aforementioned shipment of produce will arrive early next month.

C. To help us quickly locate your file, please reply on the extra copy of this letter.

D. Please answer on the second copy of this letter, so we can more easily locate your file.

E. A great many people feel as you do about this issue, and we are glad to hear from you.

F. Thanks so much for letting us know that you are one of the many who hold this opinion.

Now, convert these impersonal third-person sentences so they are friendlier and more reader-centered:

G. Subject employees, assigned to your section, have been commended on four previous occasions for close adherence to safety regulations.

H. In reference to your request for transfer, please be advised that because of the crisis in the Kenyon Plant we have been delayed. However, all effort is being made to expedite your request.

I. The enclosed Request for Adjustment must be filled in completely for further consideration of the request.

J. Consideration has been given to the report of the Implementation Committee, of which we understand you to be chairwoman, in adjusting next year's budget to provide for subject project.

Review

A, C, and F seem to be the friendlier versions.

For G, how about "Your employees have earned four commendations for . . ."?

In H, begin with "We are doing everything possible to expedite . . ." You may or may not want to include anything about the crisis at Kenyon.

Sentence I can become a question, "Won't you fill in the enclosed Request for Adjustment completely so we can consider your request?"

J. How about "We have adjusted the budget as a result of your Implementation Committee report." In the original version, it's impossible to know whether there was or was not any budget adjustment.

✳ Activity 44

From the list of phrases, pick out the ones which are NOT examples of gobbledygook . . . tired business clichés.

After reading your letter	Contents noted
Referenced letter	The aforementioned
Subject employee	The undersigned
Pursuant to	This writer
Per your request	As of this date
As you requested	At this point in time
Subsequent to	Hereinafter
In accordance with	Please find enclosed
According to	Enclosed please find
We reference your request	Enclosed are
Your obedient servant	

Review

Although they are used often, the terms "After reading your letter," "Per your request," "As you requested," "According to," and "Enclosed are" are relatively straightforward English.

✳ Activity 45

Put your "plain talk" version of the clichés at the left in the space provided at the right.

A. Referenced letter _____

B. The undersigned _____

C. We wish to take this opportunity_____

D. Pursuant to _____

E. This writer _____

F. The previously requested _____

G. Thanking you in advance _____

H. At the present writing _____

I. Your letter of recent date_____

J. Let us state _____

K. We wish to state _____

L. Inasmuch as _____

M. In compliance with your request_____

N. We acknowledge receipt _____

O. I have before me your letter_____

P. A check in the amount of_____

Q. Please be advised _____

R. Under separate cover _____

S. Please find enclosed_____

T. Attached hereto _____

U. Enclosed herein/herewith _____

V. In accordance with your request_____

W. Enclosed please find_____

Review

A. Your letter OR: Your (____date____) letter

B. I OR: me

C. We (and then state what it is you are going to do)

D. Per OR: As

E. I OR: me

F. As you requested (on ___date___)

G. This is a "no-no." Thank for what has been done, not for what hasn't yet been done.

H. Now OR: Today

I. In your (___date___) letter

J. We believe

K. We believe/We want to assure you that . . .

L. Since/Because

M. As you requested

N. We have . . .

O. Omit this; just say what you have to say.

P. A (___amount___) check

Q. Omit this; just say what you want to say.

R. In another envelope/ In another letter

S. You will find (enclosed) OR just discuss the enclosures

T. Attached

U. Enclosed

V. As you requested

W. You will find OR just discuss the enclosures

✱ Activity 46

From the sentences below, select the element or words you wish to stress. Then use the dash or relocation of key words to give the emphasis you desire. If you need to substitute punctuation—fine!

A. The employee maintains, and this is important, that he was out of the city on the day the pilferage took place.

B. I have always believed (and I want to stress this point) that adult learners are capable of more than we permit them to do in our training programs.

C. The applications must contain full salary history, with no missing entries, and three or more personal references.

D. The proposals are due in this office by March 31; they will be ignored if they arrive after that deadline.

E. One significant point I need to call to your attention is the economic saving such a system provides; it is really impressive!

F. Of course there are other benefits: less paperwork, fewer entries per applicant and above all simplicity of application.

G. We are currently considering five applicants: Josephine Rosenshire, Tom Hakely, J. G. Finch, Fred Campbell and number one in my opinion, Alice Boyd.

H. It seems to us that the proposal has great merit; we certainly endorse it.

I. We would like to proceed with these plans, and provided you support our effort I could complete the work by June 15.

J. Lately we have noted an alarming trend, one which concerns all of us a great deal, toward tardy reports.

Review

A. . . . maintains—and this is important—that . . .

B. . . . believed—and I want to stress this point!—

C. . . . history—with no missing entries—and three . . .

D. . . . by March 31—they will . . .

E. . . . provides—it is really impressive!

F. . . . and—above all!—simplicity of application.

G. . . . Campbell and—number one in my opinion—Alice Boyd.

H. . . . merit—we certainly endorse it!

I. . . . plans, and—provided you support our effort—I could. . .

J. . . . trend—one which concerns all of us a great deal—toward . . .

✳ Activity 47

Subordinate the definitions and explanatory comments by proper use of parentheses within these sentences:

A. The tables will be cleared as you say you wish, by 1:30 p.m. so the speaker will not be distracted by the waiters and waitresses.

B. These forms must be prepared in triplicate. See Company Regulations Chapter 34, Paragraph 35. They are then submitted to the Comptroller.

C. Let's handle this as confidential data, at least for the present, and await the competition's reaction when they next request federal subsidy.

D. There is no reason to think that pending legal action by the members of the union we can take any official action to solve the problem.

E. There have been numerous complaints. See the files on Holder and Co., Exodus Tours and General Travel. We must look into our tardy shipment of the ticket stock and take corrective action if we can do so.

F. The Management Appraisal program, hereinafter referred to as MAP, will become effective early next year.

G. We can define jargon, slang and technical terms, by enclosing it in parentheses.

H. We hope to complete the interviews, thirty in all, no later than May 5.

I. *Manage Magazine* to which we subscribed last year contains an excellent explanation of job enrichment.

J. In this case SLA, South Latvian Airways, claims no responsibility for our employee's lost luggage.

K. The displacement in Region II, Ohio, Michigan, and Indiana, is balanced by increased activity in Region III.

Review

A. . . . (as you say you wish) . . .

B. . . . triplicate (See Company Regulations, Chapter 34, Paragraph 35) then submitted . . .

C. . . . (at least for the present) . . .

D. . . . (pending legal action by members of the union) . . . Or at least use commas to distinguish that "pending" element from the rest of the sentence.

E. . . . (See the files on Holder and Co., Exodus Tours and General Travel.) . . .

F. . . . program (MAP) will become . . .

G. . . . jargon (slang and technical terms) by . . .

H. . . . (thirty in all) . . .

I. . . . (to which we subscribed last year) . . .

J. . . . (South Latvian Airways) . . .

K. . . . Region II (Ohio, Michigan, and Indiana) is balanced . . .

✳ Activity 48

Make all the changes you wish to convert this to a friendly letter:

Dear Mr. Handler:

Reference is made to your recent pleasant visit to this office. Later analysis indicates that the undersigned needs additional information in order to implement the agreed-upon actions.

Specifically, the measurements are needed to establish proper distance between the screen and the last row of viewers. It is my belief that you referred to a formula of 1W through 6W. Attention is requested for specifics of this formula.

Additional information is requested about square footage recommended for each participant in conference, theatre, and banquet arrangements. Regret is expressed at my unexplained loss of this data which I am certain you left in this writer's office.

Your fine cooperation is appreciated in this matter.

If there is any further way the writer can be of assistance to you please do not hesitate to contact us.

Yours most cordially,

J. K. Lambert

J. K. Lambert
Manager of Facilities Planning

✱ Activity 49

Write a friendly version of this letter, using just as many techniques as you can—after you have tried to put yourself into the reader's position.

TO: All Members of the Employee Development Committee:

There has been a considerable period of time since the Tuition Refund Committee was formed at our President's request and it is incumbent upon all members of the subject committee to report what progress has been made as of this date. All members of the larger committee are being addressed to underline the importance of this request.

It is the position of the Subcommittee on Tuition Refunds that the function of any tuition refund program is to make education and appropriate self-improvement activities available to our employees. Subject employees need not receive discounted fees or reimbursement from this organization to enjoy such benefits.

Arrangements have accordingly been made with two local community colleges, Stark Rock and Steamboat Hollow, to secure Continuing Education Units, often referred to simply as CEU's, for our standard in-plant programs labeled Business Communication and Supervisory Practices. The former is valued at 3.4 CEU's and the latter at 3.2 CEU's. The rewards for self-improvement are thus perceived as not always adhering to tuition refunds.

However, a policy statement is being formulated since there have been a few occasions where supervisors have not encouraged self-improvement because of low or nonexistent job relevance. The official statement is still in a cut-and-paste stage but I am able to take the liberty to tell you that it will call for a 50% refund to totally related education and 25% of semi-relevant self-help efforts, provided said education is secured from an approved local community or state owned educational institution.

Your comments at your earliest convenience are solicited.

CHAPTER 5

EFFECTIVE
BUSINESS REPORTS

IN A NUTSHELL

Three fundamentals of good business writing are solid organization, clarity, and friendliness. When readers sense a logical pattern, grasping each idea as they follow your reader-centered style, they are more likely to respond as you hope they will.

But the question arises: does your writing need to change with the form you are using? Do memos sound different from letters? Are letters written in a different way, with a different style, from reports?

In this chapter, we will concentrate on reports.

A report differs from a memo or a letter in the amount of data we must share. Reports are longer—although the data included in the final report may be considerably fewer than the total data we uncover and examine in the process of completing the report.

A report also differs from most memos and letters in the scope of the audience. There are frequently two kinds of readers for our reports: key readers who use the report as the basis for decisions, and secondary readers who read the report for information or as a document to follow when management accepts the position and recommendations outlined in the report.

If only business reports could always be as short and as definite as the "report" we hear when we shoot a pistol! Readers and writers alike would have fewer grey hairs . . . fewer ulcers. Provided of course that the reports hit their target. The target of a business report is a decision. The function of a useful business report is to help the decision-making process. To be sure, some reports merely document what has already happened. But organizations with a preponderance of documentary reports are looking backward too much and planning too little! Good reports lead to decisions—and action!

To fill this important role, report writers try to follow a four-step process. We can remember the steps by the acronym DRAW:

D — Determine the purpose of the report, and the scope of the research.

R — Research the data needed to develop that purpose.

A — Analyze the data to determine your Position and your Areas of Discussion.

W — Write the report.

As that plan reveals, the actual writing is only the final activity. It may consume less time and effort than the other three steps. Since this program is a business writing program, we will want to see how our behavior at each of the first three steps impacts upon our writing.

First, let's consider some special writing techniques by which organization and style contribute to effective business reports.

The first element is an Opening Statement. This important element comes at the very beginning of the final report—but it can be composed only after we have completed our research and analysis.

An Opening Statement contains two elements: a Position Statement and a list of the Areas of Discussion.

The Position Statement tells your reader what you think about the topic—or what you think the reader should do about the subject. It may be a general statement of the action your key readers should take. For example: assume that the topic is the Corporate Automotive Fleet. Your research convinces you that the organization should convert to station wagons. That is your Position Statement.

A well-written Position Statement is a complete sentence. As a rule of thumb, try to state it in as few words as possible. (Some experts urge that the Position Statement be no longer than a dozen words "which a high school student could understand.") The Position Statement will contain your generalization about the *entire* subject. It may be a general recommendation or a statement of conditions. It is important that it give your key reader "the big picture" in a nutshell. Unless you have sifted the data so you can state the impact effectively in a simple sentence, you are not sufficiently organized to write a really good report.

(That doesn't mean that you always must know what to do to solve a problem. For example, the Position Statement might be: "After examining the absenteeism problem, we believe there are three optional solutions." Or take another example from an investigative report: "Our analysis of the fire has failed to uncover the basic cause.")

The second part of the Opening Statement is the list of the Areas of Discussion. This is nothing more than the titles of the major sections of your report. For example, if the Position is "We should convert the fleet to station wagons," the Areas of Discussion might be "for economy, cross-utilization, and comfort."

Or another example: If you are recommending a new Marketing Analysis Department, your Areas of Discussion might be: (1) to keep us competitive, (2) to investigate future directions, and (3) to utilize available employee talents.

Example (3) might appear after your investigation of new plant sites. The criteria for acceptance might be: Availability, Cost, Appreciation Potential and Accessibility. These criteria might very well be your Areas of Discussion. If so, they appear as a list—the second element in your Opening Statement.

Next, let's consider that other special factor in organizing a report: your readers. The audience for a report is usually larger than it is for a letter. Therefore, as a writer you'll want to analyze your readers before you state your Position and as you select and sequence your data.

As we have already noted, our reader-audience consists of two groups: the key readers and the secondary readers.

Let's find out who these readers are. Your key reader is the person—or more likely, that small group of people—who will make a decision after they read your report. They are the people who should say "Yes" to your Position and "I see" and "I agree" or "That proves it!" to your data. Once you have determined who your key readers are, your Position Statement is much easier. You can also more quickly decide what to include, what to exclude, and from whose viewpoint to express your ideas.

Secondary readers are people who will read your report to get information or to carry out actions on the basis of the information you provide. They will not influence the decision. Your report must do that. Secondary readers will take action only after key readers have accepted your Position and told these secondary readers to do so. Other secondary readers will read the report only to find out what happened or what might happen. They should not exert any influence on your thinking about what position to take, how to organize, or how to express the data.

Material included for your secondary reader should meet these criteria:

* Will it cloud the decision-making process for my key readers?
* Is it essential in order for secondary readers to "do" what the report recommends?

Let's study that placement a bit more. It means that the main thread of thought should be immediately clear to all our readers—but particularly to key readers. Data needed by secondary readers should not be placed where it will interfere with the key readers' understanding or agreement.

When key readers need prime ideas or evidence, they should find it in the Body of the report. Our most incisive logic and our most conclusive evidence should be there in the Body. When secondary readers need details, background, or related facts and comment, they should find it in footnotes or appendices.

The Body is for key readers; footnotes and appendices are for secondary readers . . . or those rare paranoid key readers who aren't satisfied with the normal amount of proof.

Your duty to a reader is to place your exhibits so they enhance rather than hinder understanding. Thus footnotes appear at the bottom of the page; charts and graphs should accompany (but never interrupt) the paragraphs they explain. Thus background exhibits are placed in an appendix; graphic presentations of key concepts appear in the Body.

That takes us from the subject of key readers and secondary readers to the task of organizing the Body of our report.

Organizing the Body is rather easy once the Areas of Discussion are identified. Each Area of Discussion listed in the Opening Statement becomes a separate section in the Body of your Report.

But how do you settle on the Areas of Discussion? By intelligent pre-planning and by alert analysis of the data as you collect them. Quite often you can make intelligent "guesses" by just thinking about the subject. If you must talk about sales performance in five regions, it's possible there will be one Area of Discussion for each region. On the other hand, as the facts emerge, your analysis may show that the regions are doing equally well—and that the really important indices are increase in sales, market penetration, and productivity-per-call. In that case, these three factors might become your Areas of Discussion.

In other words, your data lead you to conclusions. These conclusions fall into related "clusters" or categories. Each major category is an Area of Discussion.

Which Area of Discussion should you put first in the Body of your report—and for consistency, mention first in your Opening Statement?

Studies tell us that readers remember best what they read first and last. So to stress your most important section, you naturally put it first. Many writers like to put the next-most-important section last, so the final impression will be a strong one. In this scheme, we "sandwich" the least important sections in the middle.

If our total purpose is to persuade key readers, we may opt for a pattern which places the most acceptable ideas first, and continues in this vein until the least acceptable idea at the end. This is especially useful when we expect key readers to oppose or be surprised by our Position or by our recommendations. These same criteria (importance and acceptability) can help us sequence subpoints, evidence proving a point, or items in a list.

Once you have sequenced your Areas of Discussion, you're ready to organize each Area. Your first task? To share the conclusions you draw from the data. These become "opening statements" of your Area of Discussion and of the smaller subsections within each Area. They also become topic sentences for your paragraphs.

Each paragraph starts with a conclusion! But these "conclusions" are inferences drawn from the data; they are topic sentences telling your reader what the paragraph will prove. In these cases, "conclusion" doesn't mean "the end."

How do you sequence the paragraphs? Let the sequence reflect your analysis of your key readers' interests and acceptance. Within each paragraph arrange your ideas on the same basis. Present your evidence to prove points so readers will quickly say "I agree," or "I understand." When you get to trivial data, quit.

Omit inconsequential ideas or evidence. If it won't produce insight or agreement in your key readers, it belongs in an appendix or a wastebasket.

Here's a tip: as you are gathering data, make three piles or folders. Put your most conclusive evidence in the pile marked "Top Priority." You're pretty sure you will use this material. Then make a "Questionable" file to contain data you'll use only if better evidence doesn't come along. Finally, make a "Low Probability" file of data that's duplicated, obsolete, from questionable sources, or only loosely related to your probable conclusions. You can always come back to this material, or change data from one file to another. But in the meantime, because of your tentative evaluation, you'll save yourself all kinds of paper shuffling!

When you are in doubt, as you analyze and as you begin to write, keep the communications channels open with the people who requested the report. This usually means with your boss. The research and analysis stages are the time to clarify signals about scope and approaches—not after you've begun your first draft. The pre-writing phases are the time to discover constraints and requirements . . . the time to negotiate differences about touchy points. If you wait until you draft your final report, you risk some unhappy surprises. (You may also encourage nit-picking editorial changes which do little to enhance your report and a lot to develop your ulcers!)

When you have organized the Body of your report, you face the issue of a Summary. Readers want recommendations and major conclusions as soon as possible, so the only reason for summarizing them is to repeat them in one place for reference purposes—and maybe for just a little emphasis. But if you have developed the Body logically and psychologically after a clear, persuasive Opening Statement, you don't need to summarize.

There are really only four times when you need a Summary to a well-organized report:

1. When the report is very long,
2. When the report is very complex,
3. When the position is controversial, or
4. When the position is apt to be very unpopular.

More important than summaries are transitions. These may be as simple as punctuation showing the relationship of parts of sentences. Transitions may also be words or phrases showing the relationship between sentences. They may be entire sentences showing the connection between paragraphs. Transitions may also be entire paragraphs showing the transition from one section to another.

Now that we have considered special methods in organizing a report, let's talk about the prose style of business reports. (How's that as an example of a paragraph that exists just to provide a transition?)

Well, obviously the style must be clear. How about "friendly"? Assuredly we want our reports to avoid unfriendliness. But beyond that there are things we can do to reader-center our reports.

Clarity comes from effective use of words, sentences, and punctuation. These tools work in a report in exactly the same way they work in a letter, a memo, or a manual. Just as a stool needs three legs to stand, writing needs these three elements to be completely clear and to sound friendly.

Sentences tend to be as clear and friendly as they are short and varied. Above all they need unity and continuity.

Words are as clear and friendly as they are concrete, positive, and reader-centered. That means they must be familiar—or must be made so. "Signpost" words help each reader find the way from one idea to another. Readers would rather deal with short words; too many long words make for difficult reading.

Quite often, words are not as dramatic in presenting the data for a report as graphic forms of communication. Graphics are effective ways to share key statistics, noteworthy trends or startling contrasts. Bar charts, pie charts, trend lines—all these can help your reader get key ideas better than words can—provided the data has something significant to say!

Graphics depicting significant concepts should appear in the Body of your report. They should be accompanied by a very brief comment about their significant point—and that comment should appear immediately before or after the chart or graph. This proximity is important. If you ask your reader to turn pages to find the graph, you will cost emphasis—not gain it!

Finally, there is punctuation. It adds a great deal to the clarity and variety of your report writing. Careful use of these many punctuation marks adds clarity and color to your reports.

But friendly writing is always more than mere technique. Friendly writing involves "writing from the reader's point of view."

"Writing from the reader's point of view!" That's really what we have been considering throughout our analysis of writing the business report. Our organizational strategy and our prose style should conspire to permit our readers to say "Yes!" to our position and all the supporting ideas —and to reach that agreement with maximum pleasure in their reading experience.

IN GREATER DETAIL

How reports differ from other forms of business writing

What makes a report significantly different from other forms of business writing?

Only two differences really impact upon our behaviors as writers: the scope and the audience. The scope of the business report tends to be wider than that of memos or letters. The audience is greater. This greater readership consists of two groups: key readers who will make decisions as a result of the report, and secondary readers who read just for information. These secondary readers may be asked to carry out action plans recommended in the report, or they may want the information just to answer their curiosities.

When we're writing letters, we shouldn't start to write until we have our purpose clearly in mind, and that purpose should be formulated as a response we want from our reader. When we sit down to write a report we should be similarly ready to write. This means we are ready to take a solid Position. But that happens only after a great deal of work.

We have probably spent a good deal of energy and resourcefulness just finding out how the organization will use the report, the constraints and requirements of the project. After that we engaged in a considerable amount of research and analysis before we had any conclusions to share. Then there was double-checking effort, testing those conclusions for their validity. And finally there was synthesis: putting the conclusions together to form a solid single Position. Not until that was done were we ready to write.

And when we do write we must meet the needs of both types of reader. Thus the way we organize and the way we express ourselves will be adjusted somewhat to the medium: the business report.

One important point! The mere fact that we must analyze a great deal of data in order to write a report doesn't mean that the report itself must be long. Sometimes the shortest reports do a perfect job of sharing vast amounts of data. For example: the classic report from World War II. It read "Sighted sub. Sank same." For other examples, consider newspaper headlines. They are pure reports, miniaturizing complex events: YANKEES WIN PENNANT; LINDBERGH REACHES FARIS; MANSON FOUND GUILTY.

Unfortunately, not all business writing can be so short. Our readers need explanations; they want proof. Thus we supply ideas and evidence, examples and illustrations and anecdotes.

But key readers want different types and amounts of detail than do secondary readers. They want assurance that any detail is critically relevant to the basic Position. Secondary readers may want less detail if they are idly curious; but vastly more if they are skeptical, or if they must carry out the recommendations as a result of key readers' acceptance of the Position taken by the report.

Key readers have a different perspective about the subject, and a different motive for reading the report. This will make a difference in the things we emphasize, the words we choose and the way we build our sentences. It will even make a difference in what we include and what we omit. What do good report writers do when there is a conflict between the needs of key readers and secondary readers?

To answer that, let's look more closely at the reason reports get written in the first place.

A useful report is an instrument to aid the decision-making process for the management of an organization. A report comes about because the management has said, consciously or unconsciously, one or more of these things:

"We have a problem here. We don't know what to do about it. Someone should investigate and *report*."

"We may have a problem here—now or in the future. We haven't enough facts to know for sure. Someone should investigate and *report* the answer to us."

"We have (or recently had) a problem, and we don't know what caused it. Someone should look into it and *report* on causes and cures."

"We have a problem keeping our perspective. Someone should check into the operation (or part of it) to see how it's going and how it can be improved, and then *report* back to us.

"We have (or had) a problem and we don't know the cause; someone should investigate and *report*."

"We have a need to know how things are going in all or part of this organization. Someone should audit and *report*."

The last two deserve special comment. To find out what is wrong, or who is to blame, produces purely investigative reports. When organizations devote heavy energy or funds to find out "What went wrong?" or "What is wrong?" or "Who's to blame?" they are looking backward, not forward. Such backward-looking reports are a sign of organizational decay, or organizational paranoia, or of poor planning. Dynamic reports solve existing problems in ways which avoid repetition of those problems, or they propose action to avert future problems before those problems ever materialize.

Activity 50, on page 226, gives you a chance to distinguish between decision-making and "What happened?" reports, as does Activity 51, on page 227.

THE TARGET OF AN EFFECTIVE BUSINESS REPORT IS A DECISION.

The report executes its function in one of two ways:

1. It recommends a course of action to key decision-makers, when the reporting group is not empowered to make the decision, or

2. It announces a decision which will be implemented. For this type to be complete, the reports must include (a) a full explanation of the decision, and (b) complete instructions for carrying out the recommended actions.

Before any reporter can begin intelligent research into an assigned subject, problem, or issue, the reporter must know the purpose. It is therefore imperative to find out whether management wants action plans, generalizations, or just statements of who the culprit is! What could be more embarrassing than to submit a report showing what caused the accident—only to have management ask, "But what do you recommend so we'll avoid it in the future?" What would be more crushing than to complete a report outlining the sales history of the organization and then hear the Vice President say, "But I only wanted to know how the competitor's new product is hurting us in the Southeast Territory!"

The review process

This implies that it is important to have a great deal of open, two-way communication between reporter and requester before the research starts. You had better believe it! As the next chart indicates, such an investment in questions-and-answers can pay big dividends during the research, analysis, writing and follow-up. We might call this the DRAW chart, because it shows that we DRAW up a report in four phases:

D — Determining the purpose
R — Research
A — Analysis
W — Writing

The Report in Progress

RESPONSIBILITIES OF THE REQUESTER	RESPONSIBILITIES OF THE REPORTER	RESPONSIBIL-ITIES OF THIRD PARTIES
(These may or may not be the key readers; they usually include the boss(es) of the reporters.)		

DETERMINE THE PURPOSE

1. Makes request.	**1.** Accepts request.	
2. Defines scope.	**2.** Clarifies scope.	
3. Defines constraints. (as "no-no's" or positions that have been predetermined).	**3.** Accepts constraints or explains that the purpose cannot be achieved if they continue.	
4. Identifies available resources.	**4.** Secures credentials to access data sources.	
5. Gives friendly counsel about sources, approaches and possible areas of discussion.	**5.** Suggests fresh approaches or additional data sources.	
6. Clarifies purpose: *what key readers expect*. (If they have made up their minds	**6.** Insists upon accurate statement of scope and purpose. (May need to make decision about accepting	

RESPONSIBILITIES OF THE REQUESTER	RESPONSIBILITIES OF THE REPORTER	RESPONSIBIL-ITIES OF THIRD PARTIES

about the position, this should be explained at the outset; possibly confron- ◄ ► tation could dissolve the bias or save the effort of a report.)	assignments with "loaded" Position.) **7.** Clarifies precisely who the key readers will be. **8.** May draw up scratch outline based on probabilities (but never certainties) of major research areas. **9.** Prepares tentative instrument to use in research: questions for interviews or surveys; "probe points" when examining statistics, actual operations, or real objects.	

Research

1. Provides counsel when ◄── asked. **2.** Notifies chief reporter of ◄── any changes in scope, purpose, or key readership.	**1.** Gathers data, checking for accuracy and completeness. **2.** Refines instruments for data-gathering. **3.** Locates and probes additional sources. **4.** Evaluates suggested changes in scope, purpose, or key readers. **5.** May suggest added scope or new approach. **6.** Classifies data for: emerging Areas of Discussion, emerging conclusions, and values: high, low, and "?"	
3. Intercedes if needed to ◄── unblock data-gathering.	**7.** Reports to Requester any significant blockages to data-gathering processes.	

Analysis

	1. Continues Step 6 of the research phase, watching especially for: emerging Areas of Discussion, over-all Position.	

RESPONSIBILITIES OF THE REQUESTER	RESPONSIBILITIES OF THE REPORTER	RESPONSIBIL-ITIES OF THIRD PARTIES
	2. Condenses categories to final Areas of Discussion.	
	3. Validates conclusions by testing or securing more evidence.	
	4. Re-evaluates data, holding the most valuable (cogent, pertinent, or pervasive) in the "High—will use!" file.	
	5. Draws up position statement when it is determined.	
	6. Establishes final outline and reviews with requester(s).	
1. Make final comments on ← → proposed outline and position. May request changes.	**7.** May accept suggested changes and implement them; may need to negotiate suggested changes with requesters.	

WRITING

	1. Writes first draft. (Probably revises first draft for clarity, continuity, style).	
	2. Requests review of draft by friend who doesn't know ← → the subject or the situation!	Cites flaws and blocks to comprehension.
	3. Revises on basis of third-party comments.	
1. May review smooth draft and request a few minor ← → changes.	**4.** Optional step: Reviews smooth draft with Boss/Requester.	
	5. Makes suggested changes.	
	6. Supervises preparation/printing.	
	7. Submits report through approved channels.	

Note the great number of two-way exchanges between the reporter and the boss/requester during the first two phases. And note also the limited number of such exchanges during the final activities. There may indeed be none at all after the outline and before the first draft. In the most efficient organizations, those which produce the best reports and the best report writers, that is exactly how it happens.

Here's why. There are several good ways to express any idea. Therefore an organization must decide how many revisions it can really afford in its search for an elusive "perfection." This is especially important when the organization has acquired the habit of review by several levels of management, some of which were not party to the original request. Such reviews add incredibly to the cost of written communication: they multiply the economic price, and they compound the psychic costs.

One basic issue is this: does the reputed extra "polish" really appear? If it does, does it really pay for itself in better, faster results? . . . in a better image? Quite often—a lot oftener than editors would like to admit—the answer is "No." Editing managers often ask the equivalent of what Moliere had his idiot *Bourgeois Gentleman* exclaim: "Make this more powerful. Don't change any of the words, but make it more powerful!"

There is a second basic issue involved in all this review: what it does to the original writer. Editorial changes can have one of two effects on writers: they can train you for better writing practices, or they can tear the heart out of you. To achieve the former, desirable result, the boss/editors must be competent writers themselves. They must be able to explain the technical reasons why their versions are more appropriate than the original. In other words, the edited version must be *technically* more appropriate to the purpose and to target readers. Boss-editors who cannot give such technical explanations should not make incisions in the prose they review. If they aren't making demonstrable improvements, they are incompetent and harmful. When the writing was delegated, there must have been an assumption about the competence of the report writers to whom it was delegated. If that assumption was wrong, then training and coaching from competent editors is the only defensible management program.

This doesn't mean bosses can never help achieve effective, efficient business report writing: It does imply that the assistance they can give lies in:

1. Giving precise direction about purpose, scope, and key readership when the report is delegated and assigned;

2. Providing consistent two-way communication as problems arise or as directions change;

3. Communicating writing standards and parameters, if any exist; and

4. Making a minimum number of editorial changes in polished drafts, changing only when they can provide a technical reason for the change.

What constitutes a "technical reason"?

If the editor can say: "By indenting this list you will get the action words stated first in *every* recommendation, right there at the left margin of the list. In addition, the list calls attention to each recommendation; none of them gets 'lost' in the printing of that long paragraph," *that* is a technical explanation.

It is a technical explanation if the editor says: "Let's put this into the active voice. That way we get the word 'supervisor' right up there at the start of the sentence. That's good, because the supervisors are the ones who really make the program work." If the boss/editor says, "It sounds better that way," that is *not* a technical explanation!

Not all reviewing is done by the immediate superior. In some systems as many as five levels of management scrutinize reports. Each level makes some change. After all, if the document were routed to you, you'd probably feel yourself derelict if you didn't alter something. That's exactly how it happens. So it is small wonder that such organizations have the poorest reports and the most miserable report writers. When organizations spend so much time reviewing subordinates' writing, they train subordinates to write it any old way: it's going to get changed anyhow! They also create incredible myths about "how you're supposed to write around here." Example: "The commissioner before the last commissioner loathed the word 'upward,' so we never say 'upward' in our reports."

The rationale for all this reviewing varies, but the common themes are:

"We want to make sure it is absolutely correct."

"We have a good deal of pride of authorship and the big wheels at the top like to put their own personality into it."

The first reason is questionable: how can executives who didn't give the signals or do the research vouch for the relevance or accuracy of the data? The second reason is inefficient to the point of absurdity: if executives adore pet phrases or constructions, then these should be part of the behavior taught in the organization's writing training, or recommended in the Correspondence Manual.

What can conscientious writers do when innumerable or irrational changes are made to their writing?

Well, the first decision is to make sure they *want* to do something. Writers who are haunted or hurt by incisions into their prose should take action—or remain quiet! More than one disenchanted employee has been known to use the boss's changes as a "cat to be kicked" whenever anything at all goes wrong. Whenever such people get fed up and want to let off steam about any work-related problem, they moan and groan about how their boss changes their writing. It seems as if they would rather suffer the indignity of the editorial ignoramus than take action against the practice. It also seems that these martyrs would be miserable if the boss quit editing!

But those who *do* want to do something, there are several worthwhile actions. One or more of these strategies can help to eliminate the problem, or make it easier to live with.

First, and most promising, is for you, the writer, to analyze the changes. Is there any pattern? Does the boss/editor substitute longer words for your short ones, or vice-versa? Do the changes produce short sentences for long? Do paragraphs become longer, or more numerous? Do certain words and phrases appear repeatedly? When a pattern emerges, follow that pattern. Even if the changes strike you as unwise, the boss is the boss—and thus has responsibility for the written communication of the unit. If the changes consistently represent an intolerable habit, there is always the possibility of talking it over with the boss. You may be able to cause some upward education in a frank talk where you explain why you think the changes weaken the report.

Conversation is also mandatory if you want to act but can find no pattern in the boss's changes. Maybe the best approach is to say something like this: "I am aware that you need to make a great many changes in my writing. I have analyzed the changes you do make, and can't seem to find the pattern. So I am asking for help. What are the *technical* things you are looking for?" Be sure to stress that word "technical." The boss may not be able to answer—may even feel a bit trapped by your question. But the odds are that there will be fewer changes in the future. Especially if you follow up on the vague answers you might get. When the boss says, "I'd like it to be more direct," you look innocent-eyed and say, "Good! What structures do you like to use to achieve directness?"

If these seem to put the boss/editor on the spot too much, then compile a list of technical questions yourself, and ask the boss for an opinion. Ask:

- Do you generally prefer short sentences or long sentences?
- Do you prefer long paragraphs, or putting sub-subtopics into separate, short paragraphs?
- When do you want me to use a short word instead of a long word with the same meaning?
- What particular "gobbledygook" is most offensive to you?

- Do you feel that a short-short sentence now and then makes the report easier to read?
- Is it okay to use contractions in letters or reports that go out over your signature?
- May I have your permission to indent and list when it will make the paragraph easier for our reader to follow?

In such a conversation, the boss/editor has a chance to state preferred styles and standards. Once again, bosses so interviewed tend to make fewer future changes. In any event, they will probably look at you with a new respect. They never knew there was all that much to writing! All they knew was that they had a blue pencil and the authority. Since they had never been trained in how to write or how to edit, they made changes just to justify their editorial existence. By your conversation, you just might relieve the boss of considerable anxiety.

Another troublesome kind of editing occurs when the boss changes the draft so it becomes inconsistent with an existing policy or style manual. About all one can do in this case is have a gentle, interrogative confrontation: "Boss, I'm curious about this change. I'm wondering what reason you have for making it an exception."

If none of these approaches helps you solve your own particular problem with editors, there may be value in agitating for a style manual. How can you do that? Well, the possible methods involve use of an existing Suggestion Program, enlisting the support of other downtrodden writers, direct confrontation with the boss/editor, appeals to managers in high places or making a formal proposal at a staff or department meeting.

Another strategy for unhappy victims of ponderous review systems is agitating to eliminate levels of review. This can be a systematic campaign, actually trying to get policy changes. It needs to call management's attention to the savings which accrue when levels of review are eliminated. If you are now reviewing the writing of any subordinates, you might start the process by truly delegating—by ceasing to do the reviews yourself. Ask yourself: Is your review really helpful? Really necessary? Perhaps your staff is quite capable of the trust you showed when you asked them to do the writing in the first place! If you continue to review, when you do change their version, do you give a technical reason for the change?

There is one other method to use in controlling capricious boss/editors. The one resource of which you can always deprive them is time. Now this is serious advice: if you are beset by inept editing, then *meet but never beat your deadline!* Why tempt fate? Why tempt a boss who must

edit but who does not know how? Why give enough time to permit those changes which make your life miserable but which make the writing not one bit better? They often make it worse.

A final strategy against whimsical editors is to submit nothing in less than perfect condition. Make sure the typing is impeccable, that the report looks pristine. Dress up the cover and the titles and make certain there are no strikeovers or smudges. Rough drafts are clear invitations to make change; smudges or careless preparation invite alteration. And above all there is that basic policy: write it so well the first time that when the editor sees it, any change would be clearly inappropriate.

If you couple this "excellence of the product" with depriving the editor of time to make changes, you can sometimes exert a powerful, positive control.

This means that when you submit your report to the boss/editor/requester, you have organized the data well, documented each idea with convincing evidence, and expressed the ideas with your key readers in mind at all times.

The people who really matter are the key readers—not the editors. Key readers should say "Yes" to your Position and "I see" to your explanations. They should start saying "Yes" right at the beginning. Thus the ultimate testimony to your logic and to your business report is the key reader who says, "Let's do as this report suggests," without ever having read all the report!

How can you bring about that happy result?

Let's look first at some organizational strategies which help key readers.

Organizing techniques

Of prime importance in a well-written business report is the Opening Statement. Your Opening Statement creates the reader's first impression, and it should accomplish two things for both your key readers and your secondary readers: they should—

1. Learn the fundamental Position of the entire report, and

2. Discover what Areas of Discussion will support that Position.

What, exactly, do we mean by "Position" and "Areas of Discussion"? The Position is the big picture of the whole report; it is a generalization to which all other conclusions are subordinate. It is the most sweeping statement—but of course the rest of the report gives concrete evidence that it isn't a hasty, unsupported generalization. The position of the French Revolutionists was "Liberty! Equality! Fraternity!" A churchgoer's religious position is "Love thy neighbor as thyself." A report might take the position: "There are three serious problems with our EEO Compliance programs." The rest of the report would establish those problems. It would also develop their seriousness, and hopefully would suggest solutions. A short report might take the position: "Ms. Nadine Vernon is ready for promotion"; another: "Agent Charles DeVry should be released."

Positions can be neutral: "All Gaul is divided into three parts." "We are unable to discover the cause of the fire in the Wooster Assembly Plant " "We believe there are four workable courses of action for expansion of our Asian Market." "This report analyzes the causes of employee unrest in the South Wabash retail stores." Readers of reports taking those positions would know that every detail in the report developed the subject—and that the report would not try to persuade them to a particular viewpoint or action.

Let's look at it this way: key readers are usually busy executives. Writers don't want key readers searching through the report to get the big picture, or wandering through a lot of background just to get up to the present. It is, after all, the future which really interests dynamic key readers. If the report is to be an instrument to the decision-making process, then the Position must be immediately available to key readers.

In this sense, the final report is a direct reversal of the process by which the report was created. The schematic presentation shown here should explain how the process (top) relates to the product (bottom). The finished reports tends to be a selective mirror-image of the work which goes into its production. Those professional judgments which the writer achieves after all the research are exactly the things key readers want at the very beginning. The overall professional judgment is the Position of the business report.

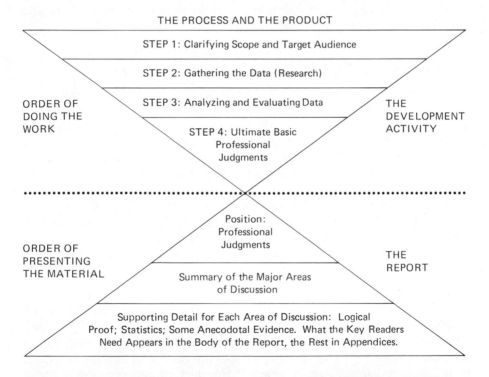

THE PROCESS AND THE PRODUCT

STEP 1: Clarifying Scope and Target Audience

STEP 2: Gathering the Data (Research)

STEP 3: Analyzing and Evaluating Data

STEP 4: Ultimate Basic Professional Judgments

ORDER OF DOING THE WORK

THE DEVELOPMENT ACTIVITY

Position: Professional Judgments

Summary of the Major Areas of Discussion

ORDER OF PRESENTING THE MATERIAL

THE REPORT

Supporting Detail for Each Area of Discussion: Logical Proof; Statistics; Some Anecodotal Evidence. What the Key Readers Need Appears in the Body of the Report, the Rest in Appendices.

Now we know about Positions; what are Areas of Discussion? Well, every report is divided into major subsections. These sections are called Areas of Discussion. A report on a fire might be divided into these Areas: Extent of Damage, Causes, Preventative Actions for the Future. A report on the impact of new legislation might be divided into three sections: Impact on Sales Policies, Impact on Employee Policies, and Required Safety Engineering for the Future. Reports on our universe have been divided into Animal, Vegetable and Mineral—or Earth, Air, Fire and Water. These major divisions are the Areas of Discussion.

The Position is the ultimate professional judgment developed by the report; the Areas of Discussion tell the readers what logical divisions to expect while reading.

Activity 52, on page 228, offers you some practice in identifying both Position Statements and Areas of Discussion.

Together, the Position and a list of the Areas of Discussion make up the Opening Statement. The Opening Statement should be just that—the *opening*. Remember, the readers need to get the big picture and a glimpse of the structure at the earliest possible moment. When readers know what the Position is they can channel their concentration; when they know the Areas of Discussion they can (1) set expectations for themselves as readers, (2) immediately refer to that Area of Discussion which rates highest in their personal priority system, and (3) discover the reporter's priority system by noticing the sequence in which the Areas appear. This section is often called an "Abstract."

That's how effective report writers use the Opening Statement to set reader expectation. The same principle works in a kind of "cascading" effect if there are Opening Statements for each Area of Discussion. This next example uses rhetorical questions as well as the "cascade effect" to share the total structure with readers.

Our Future Products

"Our future growth depends almost totally on new products. We reach this conclusion by examining three basic questions:

1. Why are new products so important to our future?

2. What new products are most promising?

3. How should these new products be introduced?"

The first Area of Discussion begins with a repetition of the question:

"Why are new products so important to our future? There are actually four major reasons:

1. The market has evaporated for many of our previous "hot" items.

2. Our competitors have made heavy inroads into our best markets.

3. The population of our chief marketing area has shifted from lower income to middle income brackets.

4. Our image has grown tarnished: we are perceived as old-fashioned, rural, and reactionary."

As the second Area of Discussion starts, there is a Sub-opening Statement reading:

"What new products are most promising? Calculators, recreational radios, and miniaturized tape recorders merit our special attention. They are in heavy demand right now; their appeal promises to grow; and we already have promising items in experimental stages."

The final "cascade" appears at the start of the final Area of Discussion:

"How should the new products be introduced? We recommend a four-step process:

1. Accelerated experimentation and testing.

2. Concurrent advertising planning (as experimentation continues).

3. Multi-media 'blitzes' in magazines, local newspapers, local radio and television.

4. Thorough product-knowledge training for all employees and franchise managers."

Activity 53, on page 229, will give you some experience in composing an Opening Statement for a brief report.

How do you, the writer, discover these Areas of Discussion for your report? Well, the discovery happens in several ways. Occasionally Areas are inherent in the project, emerging during the initial-assignment conversation. For instance, in that example about the fire, it's quite apparent at the outset that the Area of Discussion just about has to include extent of the damage, causes, and preventive steps for the future. If the purpose is to decide "Yes" or "No" on a given proposal, there's a probability that the Areas of Discussion will be "Pro" and "Con" and "Conclusions." Another frequent inherent set of Areas of Discussion is "Scope of the Problem," "Causes" and "Solutions." Many audit reports inevitably have sections on Criteria, Conditions, Cause, Effect and Recommendations. (If these are not the major Areas of Discussion in the audit report, they almost always appear as the divisions within each Finding.) If the customary headings observed in your organization happen to coincide with the data, you're in luck. You know what types of data to look for—and need only be alert to important data which doesn't seem to fit into any of the inherent categories.

We have really found two sources: Areas of Discussion which are inherent in the subject, and Areas of Discussion which the organization has ordained as tradition.

In most reports, the Areas of Discussion don't really emerge until the data are in and pretty well analyzed. But they usually do emerge as the analysis continues. You may discover that you are getting a great deal of data about employee attitudes, so that may be one big Area of Discussion. Or in another case you discover that there is strong difference of opinion about a given issue.

In that case, either the issue itself or a Pro/Con analysis of it may become an Area of Discussion in your report. Or perhaps as you do the research it becomes increasingly apparent that the decision will depend upon certain key criteria—maybe economics, legality, and ethics. These may very well become your Areas of Discussion.

Remember: A report probably involves discovering and examining a great deal more data than you process when writing a letter. How do you handle all that volume? Let the potential use of the data tell you how to handle each datum. (We know that's the correct usage, but it sure does feel awkward! No wonder you don't see it in print very often!)

The first thing smart report writers do is put one datum only (or extremely similar data) on a single sheet of paper. If you have even relatively related data on one page, you're sure to be unable to find one of those facts just when you need it the worst. It will be hidden beside or beneath another datum and you'll get furious in your search. That's why so many report writers use index cards, like students doing research or term papers. So we have our first tip:

> TIP 1. ONE DATUM PER PAPER.

The next practice also helps increase your efficiency. Make a tentative evaluation of each fact as you acquire it. If it seems to be "right on target," put it in a "Top Priority" file or folder. If it doesn't promise to be very helpful, put it in a "Questionable" file. If you think it has little chance of being used, put it in the "Low Priority" file. But *don't throw it away!* Those probable low-value items may take on new lustre as you get more data, as you do more analysis and trends begin to emerge. If it never appreciates in value, it may be a useful item for some secondary reader because you held on to it and because you finally printed it in an appendix or addendum.

> TIP 2. THROW NOTHING AWAY!
>
> TIP 3. FILE DATA ON THE BASIS OF THEIR PROBABLE USEFULNESS WHEN YOU BEGIN TO WRITE.

On what basis would you file a datum in the "Low Priority" collection?

Well, one big reason is that it may duplicate other items. After all, when people have said that the fire started in the drying room, you really don't need another comment to that effect. Another reason might be that the data have grown obsolete. For example: you have the employment totals for the first quarter; then they come in for the second quarter. You might downgrade those first-quarter figures to the Low Priority file. Later analysis may alter this decision: you note that the first quarter was the lowest in the past decade; this may merit comment. It may trigger new research or a different conclusion. The point is that when you assign facts to one or another priority, you are making a highly flexible decision. It's revocable. You can always re-appraise and retrieve. But in the mean-time—and this is the important point—your active analysis is limited to those data which are probably most important. You free yourself from unbelievable amounts of paper shuffling.

As the analysis continues, conclusions emerge. If enough people say that there is considerable boredom on the assembly line, you may have enough data to draw a conclusion. If conclusions from other parts of the shop show similar boredom and disinterest in assigned tasks, you might even have a recommendation: Investigate a Job-Enrichment Program. Possibly there is an Area of Discussion in this lack-of-job-satisfaction data.

In other words: data lead to conclusions, and conclusions lead to Areas of Discussion, and Areas of Discussion lead to the Position.

When it comes time to write, what do you do with all those data?

By the time you are ready to write, those little bits of paper from your "Top Priority" file should be gathered into separate clusters. Each cluster is stapled together, or rubber-banded together, or equal to a major section—probably to an Area of Discussion—of your report. If there are too many clusters, you need to do some consolidating in the form of an outline. This requires the final "professional judgment analysis" on your part. Hopefully you won't have too many Areas of Discussion—or too few. If there are more than five or six major Areas, your readers will have trouble remembering them; if there are fewer than three, your report is apt to "fall apart in the middle."

At any rate, at the stage when your Position and Areas of Discussion begin to grow firm in your mind, your notes are probably incoherent to anyone but you. Perhaps this is the time to convert those little pieces of paper into an outline. A topical outline—not a fancy, polished-sentence outline. The outline which most people must have before they can write or dictate includes words and phrases. There may be a few clauses—but not many. The outline is apt to look like this:

CAUSES

— Old equipment
    1934! (Cryogenic Adapter)
    Average age: 23.6 years
    75% of "in place" over 14 years
— Procedures
    Vague (add example: Ch. 45 maybe?)
    Missing (Cryogenic Adapter)
    Hard to read (25.7 fogcount; Ch. 42—quote par. 26)
    Inaccurate readings on meters right on machine faces:
    Flowthrough on Pulser, Plant 6
    Pressure tanks throughout all plants
— Carelessness
    Quote from President Fox
    Accident-rate (organization-wide only!)
      High shop (unnamed) ????
      Median shop
      Best shop, for positive reinforcement (?)

CURES

— Systematic Replacement
    $1,000,000 per year for five years
    Start w/electronic gear
— Standards Manual
    Revise
    Expand
    Pages to replace instructions on the machines

When everything you want to tell your key readers is in place in an outline, you are ready to write or dictate. (True, you may have jotted down little bits here and there on those data cards. The inspiration of the moment can come during research and analysis, and shouldn't be wasted. These "great ways to say it" sentences will speed your first drafting. But your systematic first draft comes only after you have a clear plan—a "clothesline" on which to hang every idea and every shred of evidence.)

There may be exceptions to this timing; you may have an outline which identifies what you still need in the way of supporting detail. Note in the example that the writer is still awaiting a statement on "carelessness" from President Fox; that there are still paragraphs to select as examples of the vagueness of printed regulations. But the writer knows where to locate these supporting details, and how they will fit into the final report. In the meantime, the writer's mind isn't preoccupied with minor details; rather it is synthesizing the total pattern of the report.

When is your outline complete? When it provides for sufficient ideas to develop each Area of Discussion, and enough Areas of Discussion to support the Position. You will have proved your point when key readers can say "I agree," or "I understand." That holds true for each point in your outline. If your key readers say "Yes" to each point along the way, they will just have to say "Yes" to the Position. This means that your final validation of your outline is the "acid testing" of the relevance of each detail. If it contributes toward a key reader's acceptance of the Position, it belongs. If it doesn't contribute, it belongs in something other than the Body of your report.

So you have begun to write. When do you quit? When you have explained or proved each point in your outline. Now remember, those ideas are only the ideas which contribute directly to your Position, and that you explain and prove with only the most convincing logic and the most cogent evidence. But your research has produced all that good stuff! Why not pile it on so there can be no doubt?

Because to "pile it on" is to risk failure. Have you ever noticed how children, caught in a naughty act, give so many excuses that there can be no doubt of their guilt? Well, as a report writer you've done nothing naughty; but if you have assembled good arguments and excellent evidence, don't weaken what they can do for you by accompanying them with questionable data.

Remembering that, we can also draw some conclusions about how to sequence our evidence, our conclusions, and even our Areas of Discussion. Since we want key readers to say "I agree" or "I understand" as often as possible, we ought to consider at least these sequences:

	ON THE BASIS OF READER ACCEPTABILITY	ON THE BASIS OF READER ESTIMATE OF IMPORTANCE
THE DIRECT APPROACH	**1.** Most acceptable item **2.** Next acceptable items **3.** Least acceptable item	**1.** Most important item **2.** Next-most-important items **3.** Least important item
THE "SANDWICH" APPROACH	**1.** Most acceptable item **2.** Least acceptable item **3.** Items with intermediate acceptability	**1.** Most important item **2.** Least important item **3.** Items of intermediate importance

Just a couple of words of caution about those sequences:

1. The acceptability and importance are the writer's estimate of the *key reader's value systems*—not those of the writer.

2. The "least acceptable" or "least important" doesn't mean inclusion of the trivial! Nor does it mean omission of the necessary or the ethical. What it does mean is that you quit writing when the idea or the evidence will no longer add new meanings or greater credibility. What it does mean is that if ideas or data would preserve the honesty and integrity of the report, you include them—even if they will prove unpopular with key readers.

Altogether different principles of sequencing are available. In *Principles of Technical Writing* (pp. 104-105) Hays suggests these:

- Chronological order
- Space-Geographical order
- Topical order
- Formal order (set orders dictated by a particular organization's culture)
- Inductive and Deductive orders.

Activity 54, on page 230, gives you some practice in sequencing Areas of Discussion and data. Activity 55, on page 232, allows you to make decisions about sequencing data within an Area of Discussion.

In a report, as in any other form of business writing, your readers should be able to follow the main thread of thought as they read. This means that you provide effective transitions between Areas of Discussion and subsections. Such transitions follow up on the expectations you established when you listed the Areas of Discussion in the Opening Statement.

But remember. Your key readers and your secondary readers have different motives for reading. The key readers want help in making a decision. Secondary readers will (1) carry out the recommendations if key readers "buy them," or (2) just want to satisfy their curiosities. Your organization and presentation should always be made to help the key readers. This is a basic principle of effective business reports:

> ORGANIZATION AND PRESENTATION SHOULD ASSIST KEY READERS IN THE DECISION-MAKING PROCESS.

Secondary readers may need to work harder as a result of this, but that is as it should be. The needs of secondary readers should never interfere with the usefulness of a report to its key readers. Anyhow, the inconvenience to secondary readers usually boils down to just a few minor things:

- They may find too little detail in the Body of the report; they may need to check the footnotes or appendices.
- They may need to read technical explanations, background or arguments which they already know. These are vital to securing the desired response of key readers, so they *do* belong in the Body of your report.

That's not much of a price to pay, and no report writer need apologize for these inconveniences to secondary readers if they are making the "Agree and Understand" response simple and pleasant for key readers.

Knowing where to put each type of element thus becomes a major skill for report writers. The chart on the next page should help.

In the upper right-hand corner of that chart, one detail requires special comment: that Summaries, if any, appear throughout rather than at the end of most reports. Summaries *within* a report can provide thoughtful transitions. A final summary at the end of a complete report seldom does the readers much good. A report is a *written* document; readers can go back and check if they need to. But if we have done a good job of organizing, and if we have provided effective transitions, they won't need to go back. Nor will we need a summary; we will have tied the ends together through the logic of our plan and through the clarity of our transitions.

Activity 56, on page 234, gives you the chance to apply some judgments about which kind of materials should appear in which elements of a typical business report. The items which you will analyze do not include anything for a final Summary. Even if a Summary existed, it would merely repeat the Opening Statement.

When we communicate orally, the message may be clouded by time or dimmed in the memory. A summary is useful to our listeners in ways which are not useful to readers. Indeed, summaries on the printed page can be offensive if they imply that the reader has too little wit to get the message on the first reading . . . or may have "cheated" by skipping. Only on rare occasions do business reports profit from summaries. Those occasions might be:

- When the Position is very controversial;
- When the Position is going to be very unpopular with key readers;
- When the report is very long;
- When the structure of the report is very complex. "Complex" would

mean many levels of subordination with a great deal of cross-referencing. Cross-referencing is usually unnecessary if the writer has found true, mutually exclusive Areas of Discussion.

So much for structure. What about writing style in the business report?

Where do They go?

GENERALIZATIONS Professional judgments Conclusions	SHOULD APPEAR IN: Opening Statements Opening Statements of Areas of Discussion and subsections Summary transitions at ends of Areas of Discussion or subsections Summaries of reports (seldom needed) Topic sentences of paragraphs
EVIDENCE Analytical statements Quotations Critical statistics Examples Graphs and tables of key statistics and processes Definition of unfamiliar terms for key readers	SHOULD APPEAR IN: The Body (Now and then a remarkably cogent item may appear in an Opening Statement as a way to capture attention or enlist great feeling.)
Definition of unfamiliar terms for secondary readers	Footnotes
Technical explanations for secondary readers References and sources Background and history Supplementary statements Detailed or long-range trends Duplicated data Detailed, long-range statistics Detailed working drawings	Appendices
TRANSITIONS Sentences and paragraphs Titles Words used as transitions Punctuation for transitions	SHOULD APPEAR IN: Body Body and appendices Everywhere Everywhere

Style

If there is any perceptible difference in the writing style of a report (as opposed to letters or memos) it is that reports may be less conversational. This doesn't mean that reports use a formal style. They need not be formal at all, but they do achieve their friendliness without the conversational stylistic details used in letters and memos.

Otherwise, report writers build their sentences so readers can identify the Subject-Verb-Object pattern as quickly as possible. They select the shortest possible concrete words. They punctuate to provide clarity rather than to provide informality.

Graphic presentations

Another stylistic difference appears in the greater use of graphic forms in reports. Writers can often share more data, and share it more effectively,

SELECTING GRAPHIC FORMS

IF YOU WANT TO COMMUNICATE	THEN TRY	EXAMPLE	TIPS
Contrast	Bar charts		Use symbolic bars: people, cars, planes, machines, products. Make sure the data are remarkably different, otherwise the graph won't tell your story.
Ratios Shares Proportions	"Pie" chart		These need not be "pies." Again you can symbolize: cars, people, dollars, building, products — all these can be divided to show each element's share of the total.
Trends	Line charts		Limit any one chart to a maximum of three lines. Use colors to add drama to the different trends.
Statistical mass	Tables	*Managers* *Men* 4 6 8 8 9 *Women* 0 1 2 5 ⑧ *55 Yr+* *Men* 3 4 6 6 6 *Women* 0 0 0 4 5	Vary font types. Leave plenty of room between columns. Encircle or draw arrows to key data.

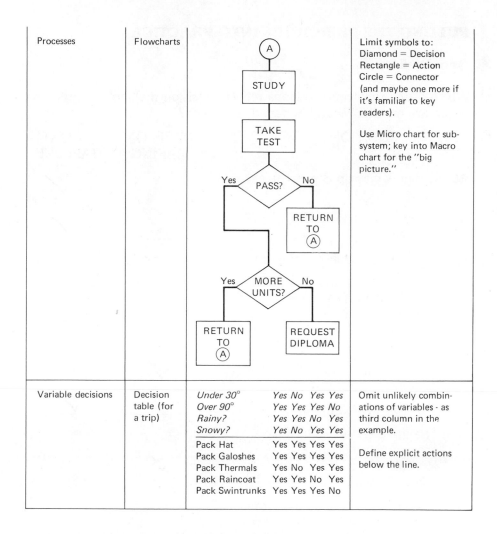

Processes	Flowcharts		Limit symbols to: Diamond = Decision Rectangle = Action Circle = Connector (and maybe one more if it's familiar to key readers). Use Micro chart for sub- system; key into Macro chart for the "big picture."
Variable decisions	Decision table (for a trip)	*Under 30°* Yes No Yes Yes *Over 90°* Yes Yes Yes No *Rainy?* Yes Yes No Yes *Snowy?* Yes No Yes Yes Pack Hat Yes Yes Yes Yes Pack Galoshes Yes Yes Yes Yes Pack Thermals Yes No Yes Yes Pack Raincoat Yes Yes No Yes Pack Swimtrunks Yes Yes Yes No	Omit unlikely combin- ations of variables - as third column in the example. Define explicit actions below the line.

by visual presentation. They tend to decide about which graphic approach to take according to the reader response they have in mind.

Activity 58, on page 237, gives you guided analysis of an actual report
from your own organizations.

Activities 59 and 60, on pages 238 and 239, are your opportunity to
measure your own progress as a result of your study of business writing.
In addition, the Chris Dawson In-Basket forms a kind of sixth chapter,
and enables you to apply every technique studied in the program except
the skills of report writing outlined in this chapter.

Well, this has been a long chapter, and in some ways a complex chapter.
But let's practice what the chapter preaches. We can find no overpowering reason for having a summary—so we're omitting it.

PUTTING THE PRINCIPLES INTO PRACTICE

✳ Activity 50

Which of the following Positions reflect "decision-making" reports, and which are merely "What-happened" Positions?

POSITION	DECISION MAKING	WHAT HAPPENED
A. Business was up 8 percent last year.		✓
B. Business was down 8 percent last year.		✓
C. We should increase our radio advertising.	✓	
D. The Shipping Department caused the problem by not adhering to standard procedures.		✓
E. The Shipping Department should install three new control measures.	✓	
F. The Sales Department		✓
G. The three causes of turnover are vague selection policies, low salary, and limited employee benefits.	✓	✓
H. This report considers the scope of the turnover problem, traces its causes, and recommends corrective action.	✓	✓
I. We recommend that the agency convert the automotive fleet to station wagons.	✓	

Review

Examples C, E, H, and I promise to help the decision-making process. Positions A, B, D, and G seem only to consider causes or conditions; they show no signs of aiding the decision-making process—at least as they now stand.

Example F is merely a title; it cannot be regarded as a Position at all.

✱ Activity 51

Select the Position Statements from the examples, indicating which are directly helpful to the decision-making process.

A. The price of tomatoes.

B. Seven percent of the people interviewed favored the bond issue.

C. We should issue bonds to cover the cost of the new sewage system.

D. Of the three proposals, we favor cancelling the contract with Acme.

E. The price of tomatoes has increased 41 percent in the last 8 months; we should therefore boycott this product.

F. New trends in industrial films are alarming, expensive, and interesting.

G. We should computerize these accounts in three phases.

H. This report outlines reasons for installing new payroll procedures.

I. Here is a list of 14 demands made by the union.

J. Here is a list of 14 demands made by the union. We recommend granting numbers 3, 5, 8, 11, and 13.

K. Due to his tardiness, violation of safety regulations, and poor performance, Herman Hendricks should be released.

L. Considering manpower availability, building costs, and transportation, we recommend West Seattle as the site of the new warehouse.

M. The disadvantages of the South Tacoma Site

N. Economic Trends which Affect Our Organization

O. Having considered Seattle, Tacoma, and Portland, we find no compelling reason to recommend any single site as the location for the new warehouse.

P. We need to take positive action to fight inflation.

Q. The Management Principles class was helpful in some ways, but a waste of time in others.

Review

Positions are presented in all except A, M, and N.

Positions C, D, E, G, H, J, K, L, O, P, and Q would probably help decision-makers.

✳ Activity 52

Here are some Opening Statements. Underline the Position Statements, and put numbers to indicate each Area of Discussion.

A. Your company made significant strides last year in new product research, market analysis, personnel development, and cost controls.

B. Mr. Armour's candidacy is enhanced by his education, experience, and moral character.

C. We recommend developing our own computer programmers because there are so few available on the open market, because we can develop an in-house training capacity, and because this approach would help morale throughout the organization.

D. After answering the questions of available sources, cost, time-lapse, and quality, we urge use of an outside agency for future advertising.

E. Her superior production, good attitude, and long years of service entitle Ms. Georgina DeWitt to become "Employee of the Year."

F. Key factors in the ethical future of our organization will be our sales strategy, product integrity, and EEO compliance.

Review

POSITION	AREAS OF DISCUSSION
A. Your company has made significant strides last year	1. new product research 2. market analysis 3. personnel development 4. cost controls
B. Mr. Armour's candidacy is enhanced	1. education 2. experience 3. moral character
C. We recommend developing our own computer programmers	1. so few available on open market 2. can develop in-house training capacity 3. would help morale

D. We urge use of an outside
agency

1. available sources
2. cost
3. time-lapse
4. quality

E. Ms. Georgina DeWitt is entitled
to become "Employee of the
Year"

1. superior production
2. good attitude
3. long years of service

F. Our organization's ethical future
will involve (as key factors)

1. sales strategy
2. product integrity
3. EEO compliance

✳ Activity 53

Write an Opening Statement for this report. (There's room at the top.)

The illumination problem at the training center may be summarized in just three words: total lack of flexibility. The problem stems from the glass walls. Window-type walls make it impossible to darken classrooms. Trainers are unable to make effective audio-visual presentations. All switches are the standard ON/OFF variety; partial dimming is not available. There is just one switch per classroom, so instructors cannot control lights from their teaching positions.

Storage space is also a major problem. The closest storage closet is more than 200 feet from any classroom. To avoid long trips, instructors store equipment and training aids in the rear of classrooms. This becomes a very distracting litter; trainees look at it instead of the presentations. It leads to yet another distraction when the rest of the staff comes to collect materials left in the rear of the classrooms.

The basic heating/cooling system is inadequate. It was planned for a building about one-third this size. In a single day the temperature can climb or fall as much as 40 degrees Celsius. The unit is inadequate for its normal work, much less for a building with glass walls, which respond quickly to outside temperature. That can vary from minus 29 degrees to 43 degrees Celsius. (WRITE YOUR OPENING STATEMENT BEFORE READING FURTHER.)

Review

One possible Opening Statement would be:

There are three problems with the training center: illumination, storage space, and the heating/cooling system.

✳ Activity 54

Here is the first draft of an Opening Statement:

Because of land availability, traffic patterns, and population growth, OKLAOIL should build a new service station at the corner of Main and Spruce Streets.

When you get ready to revise that first draft, you feel that there is over-whelming evidence about traffic patterns, and that the availability issue is of least importance. Indicate on your draft the proper sequence for each Area of Discussion.

Printed below is the data needed for the Land Availability Area of Dis-cussion. First, select the "sub-position" for that Area of Discussion. Second, arrange the data into a coherent paragraph. Add transitions as you need. You can do your work on both this and the opposite page.

- The lot is about 80′ x 125′
- The cost is $43,750.00.
- The corner location gives maximum access.
- The budget originally allowed $45,000 for land.
- Other buyers are keenly interested in this lot.
- A speedy offer would be wise.
- The land is available now.
- The price of the lot is within budget.
- R. J. Smyth, Inc., holds clear title at the present.
- The shanties now there could be razed for $350.
- Greater-Gas inspected the property last week.
- The value should appreciate 100 percent in 20 years.

Review

Traffic patterns would be 1; population growth 2; availability 3. We are dealing with this third Area of Discussion. The Position is probably a duo-statement: "The land is available now, and we should make a speedy offer." The other elements can fit into several good patterns. Check to see that you provided some form of transition between the subsections. The last item in the list may not belong on this paragraph: "appreciation" is not truly directly related to "availability."

✳ Activity 55

Now let's organize the section about traffic patterns in that report about the site of the filling station.

First, select the topic sentence from the list of data below. Then find the logical subsections and arrange the data in a good psychological order. There is room on the page for an outline, and for your first draft of the paragraph itself.

A. Present traffic is steady, but not jammed.

B. Traffic patterns justify the purchase of this property.

C. Future traffic estimates are optimistic.

D. About 5700 cars a day pass eastbound on Main; about 5550 westbound.

E. Southbound Spruce traffic averages 9750 daily cars.

F. Northbound Spruce traffic averages 9675 autos daily.

G. A 10-percent increase is forecast for next year's total traffic.

H. The AAA predicts 12,500 northbound vehicles next year.

I. This year's traffic is up 6.5 percent over last years, both directions on Main.

J. A left-turn lane will be installed next month, allowing northbound Spruce traffic direct access to the station.

K. By the year after next, both Main and Spruce will be six lanes.

L. Add data and transitions as you feel you need to to round out this Area of Discussion.

Review

Of course the Topic Sentence (Sub-Position) is that "Traffic patterns justify this purchase." The data seem to fall into two subsections: Present Traffic and Future Traffic. Did you find those two subsections? Did you sequence them so the contrast helped you persuade readers? Did you provide a transition between these two subsections?

✳ Activity 56

Here is additional data gathered in your research for OKLAOIL about where to locate a new service station. The Opening Statement will read:

Because of traffic patterns, population growth, and land availability, OKLAOIL should build a new service station at the corner of Main and Spruce Streets.

Assume that you are now making decisions about the final draft. Where do these items belong? Check whether each belongs in

		THE BODY	AN APPENDIX
A.	We originally considered five sites.	_____	_____
B.	Land at Main and Spruce is $45 higher per acre than at any other location.	_____	_____
C.	There were five members on the study team.	_____	_____
D.	Employment may be a problem at Main and Spruce.	_____	_____
E.	Population at Main and Spruce is growing 10 percent faster than the city as a whole.	_____	_____
F.	Land at Main and Spruce is about $1875 per acre.	_____	_____
G.	Land values at Main and Spruce have appreciated about 80 percent in the past 10 years.	_____	_____
H.	Population of this city exceeds statewide growth curves by 6.7 percent.	_____	_____
I.	Land at Spring and Crane sells for $975 an acre.	_____	_____
J.	The population of the city is increasing about 8.7 percent annually.	_____	_____
K.	The complete appraisals of all five sites by an outside appraiser.	_____	_____

L. These appraisals cost our firm a total of $750.   _____   _____

M. The appraisal of the DeVon at 17th Street was the most expensive due to title searches.   _____   _____

N. The appraising agency was Wendt-Marsh-Culp.   _____   _____

O. This new station is part of a 10-year expansion program.   _____   _____

P. Members of the study team were freed from 30 percent of their normal duties.   _____   _____

Q. The wording of the disclaimer which accompanied appraisers' inquiries to current landowners.   _____   _____

R. R. J. Smythe holds the title to the Main and Spruce property.   _____   _____

S. R. J. Smythe also holds title to the property we considered at Grand and Henderson.   _____   _____

T. Wendt-Marsh-Culp are located at 34 Division St.   _____   _____

U. Land at Devon and 17th Street has appreciated 10 percent in the last 10 years.   _____   _____

V. Population at Devon and 17th Street has actually decreased in the past 10 years.   _____   _____

W. Pollution counts for all five sites.   _____   _____

X. Land at Spring and Crane has appreciated about 40 percent during the past ten years.   _____   _____

Y. The owner of the Bingham Street property said informally that he would never sell to an oil company.   _____   _____

Z.   A transition between population
data and land availability data.   _____   _____

Review

We believe that the Body would contain A, B, D, E, F, G, N, R, and Z.

Under certain circumstances, you might put these in the Body:

C — To give recognition
I — For contrast or justification
O — To "position" your reader or your findings
U, V, and X for contrast.

All other items probably belong in the appendix, with the possible exceptions of H and J. They don't seem relevant to the report at all; the decision has been made to build a station; the only issue is *where* to build it.

Item Y *might* be included if you were anxious to add color. Its relevance
to the logic of your report is questionable.

✸ Activity 57

Which of these Opening Statements would lead to a report requiring a
summary? If you check YES, give the key reason for the summary.

A. We believe everyone should support Motherhood, because to do so
is noble, traditional, and popular.

   YES   NO   REASON_____

B. There are three basic reasons why Acme should found a Research
Division immediately: competition, public relations and appeal to
prospective employees.

   YES   NO   REASON_____

C. For each of the 11 candidates, we considered experience, education, and personality before selecting Ms. Martha Howard as Presi-
dent-nominee.

   YES   NO   REASON_____

D. Of the five alternative solutions to our current economic crisis, we
recommend reducing executive salaries by 35 percent.

   YES   NO   REASON_____

E. Our study of employee relations recommends a total of 17 different
changes in policy, procedures, and training. Of the 17 recom-

mendations, 11 impact upon two or more general areas, and upon more than one organizational element.

YES NO REASON_____

F. Due to consistent absenteeism and substandard performance, Mr. Gene Logan should be suspended for 60 days.

YES NO REASON_____

G. Due to your consistent absenteeism and poor performance on the job, you are suspended for a period of 60 days effective March 1 of this year.

YES NO REASON_____

Review

In our opinion, A, B, C, and F require no summaries. (F is apparently directed to management, so the Position is not necessarily unpopular. G is apparently directed to the suspended employee, and would be very unpopular.) We would suspect that a summary might be useful in reports D and G due to unpopular positions, and in E because of the complex, interrelated structure.

✱ Activity 58

Secure a recent report by your organization, or the annual report of another organization. Analyze it:

- What does the Opening Statement say?
- Does the Opening Statement establish a clear Position?
- Does the report develop Areas of Discussion mentioned in the Opening Statement?
- Does the sequence of the major sections reveal the priorities of the organization? The priorities of the reporter?
- In what specific ways does the reporter show concern for the key readers?
- As a secondary reader, do you find what you need in the Body or in footnotes or appendices?
- Are graphic presentations appropriate?
- Are graphic presentations effective?
- Locate at least three effective transitions.
- To what use does the reporter put titles? (Do they serve as transitions?)

✳ Activity 59

Here is your chance to measure your own progress in business writing.

Look again at the letter you wrote in response to Activity 1. Measure your progress by answering these analytical questions.

A. Encircle the Purpose Sentence.

B. Is it located in the best possible place—probably first?   _____

C. What are the supporting ideas or subsections?

D. Are they clearly identified with topic sentences—or a list in the first paragraph?   _____

E. Does each paragraph have unity, with no irrelevant details?   _____

F. Compute the average length (in words) of each sentence.   _____

G. Count the words in the shortest sentence.   _____

H. Count the number of words with three or more syllables.   _____

I. Is it more than 15 percent of the total words?   _____

J. Count the number of personal pronouns and proper nouns.   _____

K. How many *types* of punctuation do you use?   _____

NOTE: If you have more than 5 percent of your words in the "personal" category (Item J) and seven types of punctuation, you're doing fine!

L. Did you use any questions to get involvement?   _____

M. Did you miss any opportunities for an indented list?   _____

N. Encircle all the "signpost" words and phrases. How many?   _____

NOTE: If there are at least as many signposts as paragraphs, you're probably sharing your structure pretty well.

O. Did you define any technical jargon which your reader might find unfamiliar?   _____

P. Is your last paragraph really functional?   _____

Q. If you used any apology or thanks, did you do it first, and for something specific?   _____

✻ Activity 60

Now that you have reviewed the letter you wrote at the beginning of this training program, how about making a few important changes . . . so it represents the very best you can do!

BIBLIOGRAPHY

Bernstein, Theodore M., *The Careful Writer,* New York: Atheneum, 1965.

Flesch, Rudolf, *The Art of Readable Writing*, New York: Collier Books, 1949.

Fowler, H. W., *Modern English Usage*, Second Edition, New York and Oxford: Oxford University Press, 1965.

Gunning, Robert, *The Technique of Clear Writing*, New York: McGraw-Hill, 1952.

Hays, Robert, *Principles of Technical Writing,* Reading, Mass.: Addison-Wesley, 1965.

Laird, Dugan, and Hayes, Joseph R. *Level-Headed Letters*, New York: Hayden, 1964.

Nicholson, Margaret, *A Dictionary of American English Usage*, New York: Oxford University Press, 1957. (Republished in New York by The New American Library of World Literature, Inc. as a Signet Book.)

O'Hayre, John, *Gobbledygook Has Got To Go*, Washington, D.C.: U.S. Government Printing Office, Undated.

CHAPTER 6

THE CHRIS DAWSON "IN-BASKET": A SIMULATION

In this simulation, you assume the role of an administrator with several items in your IN-Basket. You have a limited time in which to act on them. You should try to process just as many as possible. If your instructor has set time limits too short for you to do all the items, handle those which will complete the largest volume of work while allowing you to apply what you have learned in this course in writing skills. The important thing is to write well, and to finish just as much work as you possibly can.

When your instructor calls for you to stop, there may be a general review of your accomplishments. If no such group discussion is scheduled, your instructor may collect your work and return it later with comments about your achievements—and suggestions for improvement. Of course, if you are completing a self-study program, there will be no instructor and no discussion. You can provide feedback for youself by using the checklist starting on page 261.

Now on to the simulation!

Your name is Chris Dawson. You work for Electro-Engineering, a middle-sized manufacturing and sales organization with plants throughout the nation. You are Manager of Administrative Services for the

Costa Plant, and one of three managers reporting to Al Barnes, Plant Superintendent.

The organization chart will explain how you fit into the total structure, name your peers and subordinates, and explain a bit about who holds which responsibilities.

Today is July 6, and you are in the office on this Sunday afternoon because you want to clean out your IN-Basket before you catch a plane to Portland. It's an important meeting, so it may take most of the next week. Last Friday you were unable to handle the correspondence, so *you are determined to do every bit you possibly can today!* Your plane won't wait for you, but you should try to achieve just as much results-centered writing as possible. Assume that you know the answers needed to handle this correspondence. (You can have a lot of fun "manu-facturing" rather than researching data!) Take just a minute or two to understand your organization:

ELECTRO — ENGINEERING: COSTA PLANT

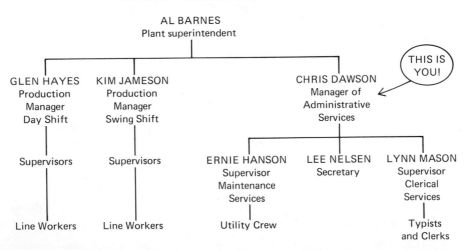

Just a quick glance will tell you that Glen and Kim are your peers; that Ernie, Lee, and Lynn report to you.

To set up the IN-Basket situation:

1. Remove pages 243 through 259 from your book.

2. Get seven to ten pages of paper on which to do your writing.

3. Remember the effective business writing techniques you've learned.

Remember! Your name is Chris Dawson. You have recently completed a course in Effective Business Writing. This is your chance to put that new skill to work.

ELECTROMEMO

Confidential

TO: Chris Dawson

FROM: Al Barnes

SUBJECT: Lynn Mason

DATE: Friday the 4th

After thinking over your problem with Lynn Mason, as we discussed in my office earlier today, I have come to the conclusion that your idea to write a disciplinary letter is the best approach to take.

I appreciate your request that I review subject letter and will be happy to do so. Of course, as you know, I'll not be here when you get back from Portland, so I should like to see it Monday or Tuesday.

Knowing Lynn and how these things go, I suspect you will have to back up every charge with at least one example. Like fouling up on the photocopy order as an example of not following directions. And be sure to let Lynn know that the next time there will be more than just a letter!

Have fun! You have my sympathies!   *AB*

June 9
113 Brayqood
Dodge, Ark.

Electro-Engineering
123 Devers Avenue
Costa, California 94445

Gentlemen:

Your product is no good and your advertising is just
plane desceptive. I recently purchased a Electromate
radio Model S to my complete disappointment.

When I wrote your Chicago office they said the darn
thing was made at Costa so that is why I write you.

The volume control is a farce. Slips away when I have
it on loud and blasts me out of my skin when if goes off
in the morning after I have set it for "soft." There is
nothing more unpleasant than to be blasted when you want to
wake up to soft music.

Then in the ad I got from Carol Wrigley the little
carrying case was a nice bright red. I don't much appreciate the dull orange you sent instead. It's just ugly and
I am just disgusted.

And nowhere in your fancy ad did it say anything about
I must bear the cost of postage. One dollar and eighty
seven cents is what it cost me just to get it from the
postman. He brought it COD which I never expected having
sent my check for $29.98 as advertising in those coupons
from Carol Wrigley. And then it was packed so bad I
knocked the volume knob loose just trying to get the thing
open.

I wanted red and didn't get it and I wanted a radio that
worked. I'll bet you don't even answer this letter but I
am going to tell my neighbors that Electromates are not
worth the postage you have to pay but didn't expect to have
to!

Elven Suthers

Chris — Your move!
AB

ELECTROMEMO

TO: Chris Dawson   FROM: Ernie Hanson

SUBJECT: Writing Bulletins   DATE: June 30

Chris, I need some help.

You know I have to post the new procedures for all the cleaning
and maintenance crews. Well I get so many questions about what
I meant, and they do not follow the directions so ~~bad~~ ~~poor~~ I need help.

Is there a course I could take or a book I could read - or
just anything at all?

Ernie

567 Twelfth Avenue
 Craig, Arizona
June 17

Electro-Engineering
123 Devers Avenue
Costa, C alifornia 944445

 Attention: Mr. Albert Barnes
Plant Superintendent

Dear Mr. Barnes,

With this letter I should like to be considered as an
applicant for any challenging positions you may have open
in the near future.

 At the end of the recent semester I completed my formal
education at W.S.C.U. with a major in mathematics and a
minor in physics. Any of the professors there will be
happy to s peak in my behalf, they have assured me.

 I am especially anxious to locate in your part of the
State of California, and to find a position with a
reputation for quality and quantity such as yours.

Hoping to hear from you,

D. L. Kirk

D. L. Kirk

P.S. Do you promote from within?

Chris – this kid doesn't look very promising, but we want him to keep liking us. Please handle so you can find out what he's really like.

AB

ELECTRO - ENGINEERING

123 DEVERS AVENUE
COSTA, CA 94445

Ms. Roberta Stiles
157 Gloucester Drive
Meridian, Arizona 88888

Dear Ms. Stiles,

We are delighted to tell you that we will have an open
position in our typing pool starting Monday, August 6.

You may consider this letter a firm offer of employment
as a Clerk A on our regular payroll.

I'm enclosing the booklet YOU AND ELECTRO. It explains
salary schedules, working hours, employee benefits and
regulations. It's more of a reference than anything else,
since I am sure you covered these points with Lynn Mason
when you visited us last month.

Please call me collect to tell me your decision about our
job offer. Of course we hope to see you on the 6th!

Cordially,

Lee Nelsen
Secretary

LN;ln

Chris — I didn't mail this until you had a chance to make changes. Please show me what to do to make it a good letter.

Lee

ELECTROMEMO

TO: All Management Employees   **FROM**: Al Barnes

SUBJECT: Safety Posters   **DATE**: Thursday the 3rd

At last week's regular staff meeting, and in several personal contacts with various individuals, I've acquired the feeling that there is deep disagreement about the value of our Safety Poster Program (SPP.)

I am not at all sure than any more staff discussion would cause any of the addressees to change opinions, so I am asking each of you to let me know if we should continue or drop the program — in your opinion.

The majority will rule. Chris tells me we must re-order by the end of next week if we continue. Therefore all addresses will please let me have their vote no later than Tuesday next.

ELECTROMEMO

TO: Chris Dawson

FROM: Glen Hayes
Kim Jameson

SUBJECT: Help with Report to AB

DATE: July 2

Chris, this report is due Wednesday the 9th. You promised to write the opening statement for us - remember? We've left you room to do that at the top - and typed the rest up rough.

Our big need is to improve interviewing skills. This should include questioning techniques for new hires and for grievance hearings. Good listening habits apply too. So do counselling tehcniques to make others comfortable so they will tell what is really bothering them. If there's anything supervisors can do to prepare themselves for interviews or hearings that should be included too.

We could use Project Control training for ourselves and supervisors. None of us really knows PERT or how to set critical paths. Any visual charting ond monitoring method would be a big help.

Several supervisors have expressed a need for a basic college level economics course. They want down-to-earth study of supply and demand, inflation patterns and trending.

Nearly 45% of our local supervisors want a course in public speaking. The course conducted by Lorraine Hagen at the Costa Communiȼty college was specifically recommended. Let's see what it would cost to have Ms. Hagen teach her course at our plant on an off-shift basis.

End of Report

Chris, we sure appreciate you help in writing an opeȷning that will get this brief report off to a good start.

June 20

Chris Dawson
Electro-Engineering Company
123 Devers Aveneu
Costa, Calfironia   94445

Last year you gave a very good speech to the Costa County
Council of Officers in the Tomorrow's Business Leaders
movement. We would be very happy if you could do the
same thing for us again this year.

We will have our August meeting at The Pacific Plaza
Motel in Costa on the 17th at 7:00 p.m. We would want
you to be our guest for dinner and then give us your talk
on the subject "What Must Go on Behind the Scenes in a
Modern Business Organization."

We wish we could offer you more compensattion than just
dinner. But as you know we are a group of high school
agers who use the Tomorrow's Business Leaders program as
a way to prepare for positions in the future business
activity of this community. As such we have no funds
for speeches. But we want you with us. Thank you.

Cordially,

Dennis Kraemer

Dennis Kraemer
Student Education Chairman
3593 Belmore Drive
Costa, California   94454

ELECTROMEMO

TO: Chris Dawson   FROM: Al Barnes

SUBJECT: Letter to the President   DATE: July 1

Chris - I've gotta get that letter in to the President's office explaining why we need a style manual. Soon.

Would you draft a good argument - like you were talking about in our office that day a couple of months ago.

Since we are talking about a style manual, and since I'm not too well known for classy business correspondence, I hope you can make this a super duper effort.

A CHECKLIST FOR REVIEWING THE CHRIS DAWSON IN-BASKET

If you are an Instructor you can use this quick way of making comments to your students. You need only copy the number preceding relevant feedback comments onto your students' work. (They have the same list in their text and can read the entire comment when you return their work.)

There are several ways in which you can adapt these structured comments:

1. Withhold certain items from the IN-Basket. (The last item, the request for a letter justifying manuals is dispensable. This item is the least directive, and may take the most student time. Most of the basic writing techniques taught in the program can be applied in the earlier items of the IN-Basket.)

2. Refrain from copying the number of any comment with which you disagree.

3. Add comments of your own. You're heartily encouraged to do that as a way to put proper emphasis on principles you wish to stress.

If you are a student using this book for self-study, you can use each suggestion as a way to check on how well you apply the principles and techniques acquired in the training program.

Disciplinary letter to Lynn Mason:

1. This is really a short report. Thus your first paragraph should be an Opening Statement. The Position might read something like this: "This letter reviews your unsatisfactory job performance in three areas." Apparently "Failure to Follow Directions" is one of those Areas of Discussion.

2. Good Opening Statement. It has both a Position and a list of the Areas of Discussion.

3. Where is the Position?

4. Where is your list of Areas of Discussion?

5. In disciplinary letters we need to set specific expectations, or performance standards. The employee has a right to a clear statement of what is expected. Where are these?

6. Good! You've given Lynn a clear statement of what is expected in the future. This is important in disciplinary reports.

7. Did you really prove this point with examples? Giving precise cases is a good form of evidence in disciplinary letters—and not just because Al Barnes, your boss, urged you to do so! Charges must be documented, and examples of actual negligence make good documentary evidence.

8. Good! You kept each charge (or Area of Discussion) in a separate section or paragraph.

9. Be sure to keep each charge (or Area of Discussion) in a separate paragraph.

10. That's a good way to avoid threats—saying "Unless you improve your performance by (_____date_____), we will need to take more serious disciplinary action."

11. Could this be interpreted as a threat? See Comment 10 for ways to express this problem of "the next time."

Letter from Elvin Suthers

12. Good! It's important that this first paragraph show Mr. Suthers that Electro-Engineering cares.

13. Doesn't your first paragraph need to show Mr. Suthers that Electro-Engineering cares?

14. How about one of these "reader-centering" approaches?
    • A short apology?
    • An offer of reparations—as a replacement?
    • Thank him for calling attention to faulty product, pointing out immediately after that that you do care and are taking action.
    • Offering an immediate refund (plus postage!) if he will ship the radio to your attention.

15. Does this approach (or this wording) make the letter seem just a bit defensive?

16. Are you really taking a positive approach?

17. A good, positive approach. Congratulations!

18. Is this looking at it from the customer's viewpoint?

19. This is a good example of looking at the issue from the customer's viewpoint. Great!

20. You want this letter to be friendly. Are you using enough personal pronouns and proper nouns?

21. Good use of personal pronouns and proper nouns to give warmth.

22. Did you sequence the responses in the same order Mr. Suthers used in his letter to you?

23. Good! You used the same sequence Mr. Suthers did.

24. Why blame the advertising agency for misrepresenting the color? Just apologize and be done with it.

25. When making a replacement, refund or adjustment it's best to do so at the beginning . . . gets you off on a positive, active note.

26. Good—making the action come ahead of the explanation.

27. Will this really influence Mr. Suthers to think better of your product or your organization?

Ernie Hanson's request for help

28. How many of these resources did you offer?
    - You own counsel for each message?
    - Some "manufactured" night school program.
    - Others of your own invention?

29. Did you tell Ernie you were glad to know of his concern?

30. Did your first sentence "cover the subject" by letting Ernie know you want to help and that there are several sources of help?

D. L. Kirk's letter of application

31. Glad you didn't let any of Al Barnes's negativism show up in your reply.

32. Did you possibly let some of Al Barnes's negativism show up here?

33. Does just sending a regular application form "keep him liking us," as Al Barnes wishes?

34. Good! You responded to his footnote.

35. What about the request in Kirk's footnote?

36. Don't you need to ask specific questions?

37. Glad you used the question format in getting these data.

38. Wouldn't the question format be more certain to secure exact data?

39. Do you want to encourage him so much?

40. Would this detail maintain his favorable impression of your company?

Lee Nelsen's request for review of a letter

41. Good. Glad you commended the friendly tone of this letter.

42. Why change anything? Lee has written an excellent letter, as you must know by now.

43. Congratulations on not changing anything!

44. Don't you think Lee deserves some praise for the good work?

Al Barnes's request for an opinion

45. Good. Excellent idea to answer right on the same document.

46. Glad that you remembered to change the direction with those arrows on the FROM and TO elements.

47. That circle around the "decision word" answers Al's request perfectly. Good work! Glad you circled "continue" or "drop."

48. Wouldn't a circle or an underlining or an arrow to the word of your choice save you from any writing at all?

49. Why not just send Al's memo back to him with your reply? This doesn't really require a second sheet of paper.

50. Did Al ask for a reason—or just for a vote?

Glen and Kim's request for an opening statement

51. A complete opening statement would probably run something like this:

Training needs in the production Department include Interviewing Skills, Project Control, Economics and Public Speaking.

OR

We have identified four training needs: Interviewing Skills, Project Control, Economics and Public Speaking.

52. Aha! Good Position Statement. Where are the Areas of Discussion?

53. Aha! You've listed the Areas of Discussion completely. Where is the Position Statement?

54. Can you express all this in fewer words?

55. Why change the sequence in which Glen and Ike list their Areas of Discussion?

56. You could just write your Opening Statement (suggested) on the memo they sent you.

57. Did they ask you for comments about the Body of their report? It's friendly to help them, but perhaps you should use some informal "entry"—as "Oh, by the way," or "Just a thought, but I noticed . . ."

Dennis Kraemer's request for you as a speaker

58. A good positive first sentence.

59. Are you making Dennis feel glad that he asked you?

60. Glad you kept this short and direct. No need to build it up so a so-called "polite length."

61. Is this really relevant to your purpose?

62. Is your style (sentences, words, and punctuation) as friendly as your message?

63. Details like this permit your style (sentences, words, and punctuation) to reflect your friendly message.

64. Is this the positive approach?

Al Barnes's request for your draft of a letter

65. Wouldn't this be a good chance to use indented lists for
  - the advantages?
  - the elements?

66. Did you put your strongest points first?

67. Does this really belong in this paragraph?

68. Good beginning.

69. Does this beginning really prepare the President for the purpose of the letter?

70. Glad you resisted the temptation to use some of those funny, stilted phrases that creep up in Al's own writing.

71. Sure, Al sometimes uses funny, stilted phrases. Do you think it's a good idea to do so when you're writing for his signature—on a letter to the President?

General comments

These comments will fit any of the units in the IN-Basket Exercise. They give you a chance to praise or redirect your students.

72. A nice touch!

73. I'm not sure what you mean by this.

74. Can you think of a totally different approach to take on this?

75. Nice approach.

76. Very creative! Nice.

77. A well-organized message.

78. Where's the topic sentence for this paragraph?

79. Good topic sentence!

80. Where is your statement of purpose?

81. Doesn't this first paragraph need something to make your reader receptive to your purpose?

82. Is your first sentence doing all it should for your reader?

83. Very clearly expressed.

84. I'm not sure what you mean here. Want to try again and show me your clearer version?

85. Nice friendly touch.

86. How can we make this sentence friendlier?

87. How can we make this sentence more positive?

88. Can we get rid of (or break up) some of these long sentences?

89. How can we get more variety into the sentence structure?

90. Can we find a shorter word?

91. What punctuation would make this idea clearer?

92. What punctuation might we use to make this idea friendlier?

93. Does this really belong in this paragraph?

94. Would a paragraph break here help clarify your structure?

95. Good use of transition words.

96. What transition word would help your reader at this point?

97. Transition missing?

98. Good transition sentence.

99. Good transition paragraph.

100. Good use of numerals or alphabetic symbols to share your structure.

These next general comments summarize the total performance on the IN-Basket exercise.

101. Congratulations on a job well done!

102. What you have written is very well done. How might you organize your time to accomplish more writing?

103. Did you handle the really important items?

104. You certainly managed your time so you handled the most important items. Congratulations.

105. You have expressed everything very clearly. Did you perhaps sacrifice some warmth and reader-centering along the way?

106. This is rather disappointing. Why don't you drop by so we can talk it over?